THE DAY I MET FATHER ISAAC
at the
SUPERMARKET

Lessons in How to Live
from the Jewish Tradition

RABBI JACK RIEMER

KTAV Publishing
New York

The Day I Met Father Isaac at the Supermarket:
Lessons in How to Live from the Jewish Tradition
by Jack Riemer
Copyright © 2018 Jack Riemer

Typeset by Ariel Walden
Printed in USA
First Edition
ISBN 978-1-60280-309-1
KTAV Publishing
527 Empire Boulevard
Brooklyn, NY 11225
Tel. 718-972-5449
www.Ktav.com

Library of Congress Cataloging-in-Publication Data
Names: Riemer, Jack, author.
Title: The day I met Father Isaac at the supermarket : lessons in how to live from
  the Jewish tradition / Rabbi Jack Riemer.
Description: First Edition | New York : KTAV Publishing, [2018] |
Identifiers: LCCN 2018024365 | ISBN 9781602803091 (pbk. : alk. paper)
Subjects: LCSH: Bible. Pentateuch — Sermons. | Jewish sermons, English.
Classification: LCC BS1225.54 .R54 2018 | DDC 296.4/7 — dc23 LC record
  available at https://lccn.loc.gov/2018024365

"*Each year* a new interpretation of the Torah comes into being. In every generation a new insight into the Torah descends from the heavens, suited to that generation. And the task of the teacher is to perceive in the Torah that which is needed by that generation."

The HIDDUSHEI HaRIM
(Rabbi Yitzchak Meir of Ger 1797–1866)

Contents

Introduction

If what you write is good, no introduction is necessary; and if what you write is not good, no introduction will help.

But I do feel the need to introduce this garland of my writings with just these few words:

First, I need to say thank you to my parents, of blessed memory, who first taught me that the Torah was the meaning and the measure of our days. And I need to say thank you to my teachers, who taught me that the words of the Torah take on new meaning in every generation, not because they change, but because we do.

Second, I need to say thank you to Sue, who has lived with these pages, and who has made them better, with her keen eye, her sharp pen, and her wise and understanding heart, and who has made me better by her love.

Third, I need to say a word of blessing to Yosef, Vitina, and Adena, and to Nathan, Lisa, and Naomi with hope that they will find within these pages some wisdom that will help guide them on their paths in life.

Fourth, I need to say a word of thanks to Robert and Judy, Steve and Sterling, Richard, Grace and Pete for having shared their mother's love with me.

Fifth, let me say a heartfelt word of gratitude to Steve, who has cared for my computer and for me, and who has kept us both from having a breakdown, with his great skill and his remarkable patience.

Sixth, let me say a word of thanks to the many people whose stories and whose insights are found in this collection. Some of you I can thank by name because I know who you are, and some of you I can only acknowledge with these general words because I no longer remember when or where I learned from you. You should know, dear reader, that only the *Ribono shel olam* creates '*yesh me-ayin*' — that only the Master of the universe creates out of nothing. Every writer, every poet, every storyteller, and surely every teacher absorbs wisdom from others, and then incorporates this wisdom into whatever he writes.

Sometimes he remembers where he learned these insights and is able to thank those who have taught them to him, and sometimes these insights have become so much a part of him that he forgets where he first learned them. And so, let me thank not only those whose names I remember, but those whose names I have forgotten. May those whom I cannot thank by name forgive me, and may they find a measure of pleasure in knowing that their words affected me, and through me, that they have reached those whom I have taught.

Seventh, let me thank those who have listened to me over the years. Without you, these words would have never come into being, or they would have disappeared as soon as they were uttered. I am grateful – more than I can begin to say – to those of you who have told me that these words have made a difference in your lives. I thank you for having listened to me, and I promise to listen to you in exchange if you ever ask me to.

It is my hope that these words have not yet completed their journey, and that there are some people out there who will pick up this book and read it, and that they will find some of its insights helpful in their lives, for this is the greatest reward that any teacher can ever hope for.

To the sacred memory of my dear friends Birdie and Chicky Grossman, who supported every worthy cause, including this book, with their generosity. Birdie was Chicky's best friend and his loving partner for many, many years, and Chicky was a real renaissance man: a pilot, a collector of classic cars, a sculptor, a painter, and a study companion to me. May their souls be bound up in the bond of life, and may their memories be a source of blessing to their children, their grandchildren, and their great grandchildren, and to all who have benefited from their generosity.

And now: enough. Let these words speak for themselves.

Sincerely yours,
Jack Riemer

A Sermon Addressed to the Rich People
in this Congregation

THIS SERMON IS ADDRESSED to the rich people in this congregation, and to those who hope to someday become rich.

So if you are in this category, hear me well. And if you are not, then you don't have to listen to this sermon.

The insight that I want to share this morning with those of you who are rich and with those of you who hope to someday become rich, comes from a brief and simple comment that Rashi, the great commentator, makes on a passage in today's Torah reading.

But first, let me set his comment into its context.

Abraham and Sarah go down to Egypt because there is a famine in the land of Canaan. In Egypt, they get into trouble, for reasons that I do not want to go into today. And as a result, they are sent out of Egypt by Pharaoh. The Torah says that Pharaoh sent them out with great wealth.

The Torah puts it this way: "*V'Avraham kaved m'od bimikneh, bikesef ubizahav*" – Abraham left Egypt loaded down with cattle, with silver, and with gold.

Imagine the scene: He arrived in Egypt as a refugee from famine. He probably came into Egypt with very little, if anything, in his possession. And he leaves with a great fortune.

And then the Torah says: "*Vayeilech limasa'av minegev v'ad Bet El, ad hamakom asher haya sham ohalo batchilah*" – He journeyed in stages from the Negev to Beth El, to the place where his tent had been originally.

On this passage, Rashi makes the comment: "On the way back home, Abraham stayed at the same lodging places that he had stayed in on his way down to Egypt."

What does that mean?

And why do we need to know that?

It means that, even though Abraham went down to Egypt with little and came back wealthy, nevertheless, he stayed at the same hotels on the way back as he did on the way down. If he stayed at a Motel Six on the way down to Egypt, he stayed at the same Motel Six on the way home.

Why?

Rashi does not say, but my guess is that it means that Abraham was not spoiled by the wealth he acquired in Egypt. He was the same person when he came back as he was when he left, even though he was now incredibly wealthy. And for this, he deserves our respect and our admiration.

I know lots of people, and you probably do too, who have been spoiled by success, who have been corrupted by their wealth. When they were poor, they were nice people. They had time to talk to anyone and everyone. But once they acquired wealth, they became arrogant and unfit to live with. Once they acquired wealth, they needed to flaunt their new status to everyone. And so they had to have only the best clothes, and they had to go to only the fanciest places, and they had to stay only at the swankiest hotels.

Do you know any people like that? I suspect that you do.

The point of Rashi's comment is not that Abraham was frugal. It was that he tried to live the same way now that he had money, as he had lived when he had no money. The point of Rashi's comment is that Abraham did not let his newly acquired wealth go to his head, and make him a different kind of person than he had been before.

There is a lovely Jewish folktale about the shofar that expresses this same truth. The story is that a certain poor man was chosen to be king over a great empire. The poor man accepted the honor reluctantly, and only on one condition. He insisted that one day a year, he be allowed to spend by himself. The people of the community loved this poor man and so they accepted his condition, even though they did not understand it.

All during the year, the king lived in a splendid palace. All during the year, he had a host of servants at his beck and call. He had only to snap his fingers and one of them came running to do his will. All during the year, this king dressed in royal robes. But one day a year he disappeared – and no one knew where he went or why.

Finally, one of the courtiers became curious: Where could the king possibly go one day a year? And so he determined to find out where the king went. He hid in the palace and waited all night to see where the king would go.

Early in the morning, the king slipped out of the palace – incognito. He went out, not dressed in royal robes, but in the overalls and the plain shirt that he used to wear. The king walked through the woods, and the courtier followed behind him, going from tree to tree, making sure that the king did not see him. After some time, the king arrived in the town that he had come from. He went into the shack that he had lived in until he became king, and he stayed inside that shack for the whole day.

The courtier was puzzled. Why would the king do this? So he crept as close as he could to the shack and peeked inside. And this is what he saw:

The king walked up and down in the simple shack in which he used to live. And as he did, he kept saying to himself: "Remember that this is where you came from. Remember that this is how you used to live. And make sure that your new status does not fool you, and that it does not make you think that you are different from the rest of the people in your kingdom."

The people who told this folktale applied it to the Jewish people. In their times of glory and success, they might be tempted to think of themselves as special. They might be tempted to think of themselves as better than all the other people in the world. And so, once a year, they sound the shofar. It reminds them of who they used to be. It reminds them that once they were slaves in Egypt, and that God took them out of there with a Mighty Hand and an Outstretched Arm. It reminds them that, when they traveled through the wilderness, they were attacked many times, and that they had to sound the shofar each time in order to gather their troops to fight the enemy. It reminds them that they were not always rich and powerful. Just as the king in the story spent a whole day reminding himself of this truth, so the People of Israel remind themselves of this truth of who they were and where they came from once a year when they sound the shofar on Rosh Hashanah.

How many wealthy people do you know who have been able to meet the spiritual test that comes with success? I know some who have, and I know many who have not. I know some wealthy people who are so full of themselves, so impressed with themselves, so arrogant and so opinionated about themselves, that they offend everyone who comes close to them. Perhaps you know such people too.

But not all rich people are like that. Many wealthy people are good and modest and kind people in spite of their success.

Let me tell you about just one:

For some years now, I have been invited each year to give a memorial lecture in Baltimore. The sponsor is a very wealthy and generous couple. They are major donors to many Jewish and general causes. I have seen pictures of these people standing with the pope and with other dignitaries. But you would never know it from the way they behave at this memorial lecture.

The memorial lecture is always held in a small synagogue, not one of the most prestigious places in town. It is sponsored by the Bnai Brith Lodge to which the father of this philanthropist belonged. And the lecture is always preceded by a dinner. It is a fairly informal dinner. There are no waiters in tuxedos. There are no menus and no maître d's. The people who belong to the Bnai Brith Chapter serve the meal themselves.

And what always impresses me is that this man and his wife, the sponsors of this event, always help to serve the dinner. They go in and out of the kitchen, carrying trays of chicken and glasses of tea and plates of cake, just like everyone else. They go from table to table, bringing the food with a smile, and no one would know from seeing them – in their aprons – that they were people of great wealth. And whenever I see them do this, I realize that they may be people of considerable means – but more important – they are people who have great ends! Their goals at this annual event are to honor their parents' memories by associating their names with the study of the Torah, and to make the members of this Bnai Brith Chapter to which they belonged feel comfortable and appreciated.

I don't know whether my friends who sponsor this annual event and who help serve the meal at it know the commentary of Rashi on this week's *sedra*. They may – but either way, whether they do or not, these two people fulfill what Rashi teaches. And therefore they can serve as a model for all of us.

And so, let me make two wishes for you today. The first is a fairly easy one to achieve. The second is a little bit harder.

My first wish for you today is: may you become wealthy. May you be like Abraham, who started out a refugee in a time of famine and who ended up *"kaved bimikneh, bikesef ubizahav"* – "loaded down with cattle, with silver and with gold." May you end up loaded down with many stock certificates and with much real estate and with many certificates of deposit and bonds as well.

And my second wish for you today is: may you not be spoiled by your success. Just as Abraham stayed at the same lodging places on his way back from Egypt to Canaan as he did on the way down from Canaan to Egypt, so may you remain the same kind of human being when you have wealth as you were before you had wealth.

May you have both blessings, for they are both precious and valuable to have. And only when you have both these blessings – only when you have many possessions, and only when you are not possessed by your possessions, are you truly worthy of being called a descendent of Abraham and Sarah.

"Zalman, Now We Have You Back!"

VAYERA

I WANT TO SHARE a story with you today. I want to share it with you today for two reasons. One is because it casts light on a passage in today's Torah reading. And the other is because I think that it contains a lesson that all of us should take to heart.

The eulogy was given by a rabbi named Shelley Michael Waldenberg, whom I do not know. He is the rabbi emeritus of a congregation in Lafayette, California. But listen to the story that he tells about the eulogy that he once gave. He begins:

Growing up, there were days when my sister and I felt that we were living in a madhouse. When our father was in a good mood, he was funny and kind, intelligent and learned; and the next moment – for no apparent reason – he would scream at us, or remain sullen for hours. We wanted to run away. When we grew up, these memories of childhood haunted us. We did our best to forget them. Until Dad died in December of 1983. That changed everything.

My sister Ziona and I brought Dad's remains with us on board our flight from New York to Israel. When we landed, his coffin was carried by the *chevra kadisha* to the hearse, behind which was parked a long procession of cars, filled with our relatives.

Uncle Moshe, Dad's youngest brother, escorted us to the car behind the hearse, piled in with us, and the cortege headed for the hills of Judea and the Har Hamenuchot Cemetery which overlooks Jerusalem.

There was no opportunity to change into more formal attire, and so I felt uneasy in my beige corduroy jacket and my jeans. A few miles from Jerusalem, the caravan pulled over unexpectedly. Several women, the wives and friends of my father's three brothers and his sister, began milling around and peering into our car. One of them pointed in my direction, at my army jacket in particular, and called out to the others in Yiddish: "Look! He is so poor, *nebach*. He has patches on his elbows! *Vey iz mir!*"

"It's time to cut *kriah*," Moshe whispered to us as he hustled us out of the car and led us to the back of the hearse. A man in Chassidic garb approached me. At his direction, I recited the blessing: *baruch dayan emet* (blessed be the Judge of truth) and tore the lapel of my jacket near my heart.

But that did not satisfy him, and so he grabbed the torn cloth and ripped it all the way down to my waist, exposing my undershirt.

"Oh my God, I'm not wearing *tzitzit*," I realized as he cut the garment. "What will they think of me now?"

I had not worn *tzitzit* since I graduated from yeshiva high school in New York back in the 1950s. My sister's *kriah* went a little bit easier. It was conducted by a kind and gentle woman.

Back in our sedan, Moshe said that I would not be permitted to enter the cemetery and participate in the internment service. He said it was *minhag Yerushalayim*, a ritual that was exclusively practiced in Jerusalem, by which a son is not permitted to be in the cemetery during his father's burial.

"I'm going!" I said, "Whether they want me there or not."

Sometime later, we walked through the gates of the cemetery and made our way to the graveside. I could see my uncle, Rabbi Eliezer Waldenberg, chatting with his son, Rabbi Simcha Waldenberg. The moment they saw us, Rabbi Eliezer gestured toward us with an outstretched arm, and called out, "Let them stay." No one challenged his welcoming me despite the prohibition about my presence.

After all, Rabbi Eliezer Waldenberg was a *dayan*, a judge on the *Bet Din Elyon*, the Supreme Rabbinical Court in Jerusalem, and he was revered worldwide for his volumes of *halachah*: "Tzitz Eliezer." He was a kind and gentle soul whom everyone loved and respected. And so, thanks to him, my sister and I were allowed to stay.

As we approached the grave, several young men of the *chevra kadisha*, dressed in caftans, emerged from a van. They lifted Dad's body out of the hearse and placed it on the ground, wrapped as it was in *tachrichim* and in his *tallit*, short of one *tzitz*. Then hand in hand, they began circling Dad, weaving back and forth, chanting psalms, and sprinkling pebbles all over his body. Suddenly they turned, approached me, and sprinkled pebbles on my head and into my shoes.

"See how we treat our own in Jerusalem?" Moshe whispered to me proudly.

I was dumbfounded. What on earth were they doing? Then they raised Dad's body up over their heads, passing it from one to the other, and then they lowered it into the grave.

There was no coffin. It was literally dust to dust.

Rabbi Eliezer Waldenberg stepped forward to deliver the *hesped*, the eulogy. He spoke lovingly of his brother, Zalman Chayyim, but only as he remembered him through the age of eighteen, when Dad left for the United States. Nearly all of Eliezer's sentiments related to Dad's Talmudic acumen back then, little else. And then he took a deep breath, and cried out: "Zalman, now we have you back!"

I was dismayed. Not a word about Dad's entire life following his departure for the States. Not a word about my mother, Shulamis, who was buried only a few feet away. Nothing about his struggles, his character, his accomplishments. It was no eulogy, but a talk more in line with the literal meaning of the Hebrew term *hesped* which is: "a reckoning."

Why the glaring omissions? Anyone standing there could have told you why. For a sabra, for a Jew born in the land of Israel, to deliberately leave Israel, as Dad did, to leave the land to which our people have longed to return for more than two thousand years was considered nothing less than heresy in the world of Charedi Jerusalem. How many times had I heard some Charedi rabbi quote Rabbi Akiva's dictum in the Talmud: "Do not move to a foreign land, lest you become an idolater."

That my father, the oldest and the most learned of Yankef Gedaliah's children, the one who studied with the greatest rabbinic luminaries of the time at Rav Kuk's yeshiva, would deliberately run away from Eretz Yisrael was considered nothing less than a betrayal.

And on top of that, Dad's becoming a Conservative rabbi was the ultimate heresy.

Standing there at his graveside, I began to grasp for the first time the pain and the shame, the unremitting pain and the never-ending shame, that Dad's family in Jerusalem made him pay all his life for having left. Even the love and the respect that was lavished upon Dad all those years in the States by our immediate family, by his friends, and by his congregants was never enough, never authentic enough, to satisfy Dad's family in Israel, and to satisfy Dad.

Not knowing whether or not I would be invited to speak, the moment Rabbi Eliezer finished, I stepped forward, and began. I spoke about Dad's abiding love for his family in Eretz Yisrael, and about how much courage it must have taken for him to leave his birthplace and go to a strange land. I talked about how he built a family in the United States and about how he made a living as a rabbi and as a *shochet*, and about how he earned undergraduate degrees and graduate degrees at both NYU and the Jewish Theological Seminary. I ended by talking about his *mentshlichkeit*, his integrity, his life-saving humor, and his sweet and gentle soul.

When I finished, there was silence. I looked around. They were not touched or impressed. I could feel it. I could see it on their frozen faces. It was as if I had been talking to myself.

I paused and took a deep breath, as verses from the Torah began swirling around in my head like sharks. I was furious. I continued: "In the Torah it is written: how were Abraham and his nephew, Lot, different in the way they treated strangers? What does it say in the Torah? 'Two messengers came to Sodom, and Lot sat at the gate of Sodom, and Lot saw them, *vayakom* – and he rose up to meet them.'"

Notice that Lot kept his distance, and let the strangers come to him. But of Abraham it is written that when he saw the strangers approaching, what did he do? The Torah says: "He lifted up his eyes and looked, and lo, three men stood over against him; and when he saw them: '*vayaratz likratam*' — he RAN to meet them from the tent door, and he bowed down to them."

And then I applied these two verses to the people who were standing there around me. I said to them: "When my father came here to visit you, year after year, for the past sixty years – with the exception of the war years – like Abraham he ran to you and embraced you, and loved you unconditionally. And what did you do? Whenever my father approached you, like Lot, you stood your ground, and you never, never once reached out to welcome him. And you should know that by doing that, you broke his heart."

I cannot recall anything else that I said. I just stood there shaking, my eyes surveying the throng of people. I felt that moment that my fate among them hereafter would be much akin to what Dad suffered all those years. I would only have their indifference and their contempt, as he did. In fact, as a Reform rabbi, my name was probably anathema to them already.

When I finished speaking, I stood there feeling alone, and lost, and out of place.

And then, without warning, Rabbi Eliezer came bounding up towards me, his arms outstretched as he ran, and he embraced me.

And we wept.

End of story.

I hope that you are as moved by this story and by this eulogy as I am, not only because it explains the difference between the behavior of Lot and the behavior of our father, Abraham, in the Torah portion that we have read today. But because it is a powerful story about how the chasm that often exists within a family can sometimes be overcome. Here was Rabbi Eliezer Waldenberg, one of the greatest sages and scholars of the Charedi community of Jerusalem, coming forward with tears in his eyes to hug his nephew, a Reform Rabbi from America, and to ask forgiveness from him for what he had done to his father.

That must not have been an easy thing to do, but Rabbi Eliezer Waldenberg did it that day, and when he did, the words of his own eulogy came true: "Zalman, now we have you back!" And when he said those words, his nephew, the Reform Rabbi from America, understood, for perhaps the first time in his life, why his father had so often suffered from depression, and how his own childhood had been so often marred by his father's burden. And he had a sense that the long unnecessary battle that had gone on for so many years within his family, the battle that had cost his father so much – was over at last.

Why do I tell you this story today?

I do so, because I believe that Rabbi Eliezer Waldenberg of Jerusalem and his brother, the Conservative Rabbi in America, are not the only ones who have spent years of their lives separated from each other – not only geographically but emotionally and spiritually as well. I suspect that there may be some people in this room who have lived for years on the opposite sides of an invisible wall that has separated them from their siblings or from their parents or from their children, just as these two men lived for so long. And if you are one of these people, then I beg you to listen to what I am now going to say.

All of us are old too soon and smart too late. And therefore, I am sure that there are many of us who have lived for years not speaking to members of our family. It may have been because of a dispute over money. It may have been because of a dispute over a *shidduch*. Or it may have been over something that we no longer even remember or understand. But many of us have lived for years only politely acknowledging the existence of parents or children or siblings, because they did or did not do something that we think that they should have done or not done. And we and they have both paid the price for this stupidity. We and they have both lived lonely, empty lives, because we have allowed an invisible wall to stand between us and those whom we should have loved. And for many of us, it was only when we stood together with them at the graveyard, it was only when we said farewell for the very last time, that we realized that we should have been more like Abraham and less like his nephew, Lot.

Rabbi Eliezer Waldenberg will be remembered in Jewish history as a giant in Torah learning. He will be remembered for the many volumes of the Tzitz Eliezer that he wrote. But who can say? Perhaps in God's book he will be remembered, not only for these books that he has left us, but for the example of a brother who could cry, and who could embrace a nephew who came from another world, and who could say in truth: "Zalman, now we have you back!"

May his example guide us and teach us to do the same. And to do so now, now, now before it is too late.

Guess Who I Met in the Parking Lot of the Supermarket?

CHAYEI SARAH

DO YOU KNOW WHO I MET this week?

You will never guess – not in a million years – not even in two million years.

I was sitting in my study yesterday, working on my sermon for this Shabbat. I had been working on my sermon for this Shabbat all night, because if you are going to speak here in THIS synagogue – which has so many intellectuals in it, and which has so many cultured people in it – you want to be prepared. I usually start working on my sermon for the next week on Saturday night, and I work on it all day Sunday and all day Monday and all day Tuesday – and by Tuesday night I usually have it done. And then all I have to do on Wednesday, Thursday and Friday is go over it and revise it a little bit and practice it. But for some reason – I don't know why – this week's sermon was just not working. It was already Thursday and I was still stuck on it. And so I worked on the sermon all day Thursday and all night Thursday trying to get the sermon right. And I was still working on my sermon Friday morning, when my wife came into my study and said to me: "Darling, would you please go to Publix, and pick up some things that we need for Shabbat?"

Do you know what I do whenever my wife asks me to go to the store and pick up some things that we need for Shabbat?

I go to the store and pick up some things that we need for Shabbat.

And guess who I met when I got there?

You'll never guess.

I bumped into Father Isaac in the parking lot of the supermarket. Honest!

I had parked my car, and turned off the motor, and I closed my eyes for just a minute before going in, and when I opened them up again, there he was! Father Isaac was standing right there – in the middle of the Publix parking lot!

I hadn't seen him in a long time. In fact, I had not seen him since the second day of Rosh Hashanah, when he was in the Torah reading, and so I was delighted to see him again.

I said: "*Shalom aleichem*, how are you?" And he said: "*Baruch Hashem*, not bad for an old man."

And then he said to me: "What's new?"

And I didn't know what to say when he asked me that question. How do you tell a person who has not been around for several thousand years what's new? Should I tell him that there is now such a thing as television? Or that there is now such a thing as airplanes? Or that there is now such a thing as telephones? Or that there is now such a thing as computers? Should I tell him that you can now fly to Europe in less than six hours, when in his time there not only were no such things as airplanes – there was not even such a thing as Europe?

Should I tell him that we can now send an e-mail from here to China, and get an answer back in less than a minute?

If I do, will he believe me? Or will he think that I am just making these things up and that they couldn't really be true?

I thought about all the things that have happened in the world since his time, and I couldn't decide which one to tell him about first. Should I tell him that people are still killing each other in wars or fighting with each other over property? Should I tell him that people are still fighting about who the city of Hebron belongs to today, just as they did in the time of the Torah? If I told him that, he would probably say to me: that's not new. People were doing all those things back in my time.

And so after thinking about it for a while, I decided to tell him about a pastoral case that I am dealing with instead.

A young man came to see me this week in order to ask for my advice about a woman that he was dating. I wasn't sure what advice

I should give him and so I told the young man to let me think about it and to come back next week and I will tell him what I think then. And so I thought that maybe I should ask Father Isaac what he thought I should tell this young man. So I told him the story.

The young man had told me that he has been dating this woman for a long time now, and that he still couldn't make up his mind: should he marry her or not? And so he said that he was thinking of putting himself and his lady friend to a test. He said that he was going to ask her to go off with him to a lovely resort on the seashore for a weekend.

"If we click, I'll be able to tell," he said. And then he asked me what I thought of his plan.

I must tell you that I wasn't sure how to answer him.

On the one hand, I couldn't think of any source in Jewish law that would permit him to do what he was planning to do. How could I tell him that he can go away with a girl for a whole weekend – without a chaperone? It's obviously forbidden.

I ask you: what would you say if your grown up son came to you and asked your permission to go away to a hotel for a weekend with the girl that he is dating?

What would you say?

How many of you would give him your permission?

Would those of you who would give your son permission to do this, please raise your hands.

And would those of you who would say no please raise your hands.

Some of you would probably say: good luck, and some of you would probably be so surprised that your son asked you for permission to do anything that you would not know what to say.

I was tempted to tell this young man what the law says.

But on the other hand, I was sure that if I told him that it is forbidden in Jewish law, he would think that I was absolutely out of touch with the way the world is today. And so I was up all night, trying to decide what to tell him.

And so, when I happened to meet Father Isaac in the parking lot at Publix, I decided to ask him what advice he would give to this young man who wanted to take his girlfriend away for a weekend at a resort by the seashore to see whether they clicked or not.

And do you know what he told me?

He said to me: "Would you please tell him in my name that I think HE IS AN IDIOT!

Tell him that I said: There is no worse way to determine if two people 'click' – whatever that means – then by going off together to some secluded resort on the seashore.

What will happen is that they will hold hands and walk on the beach, her body flashing in the sunlight, her hair bouncing on her shoulders. And his mind will go: 'click, click, click, click, clickety click.'

And then they will have dinner by candlelight on a terrace over-looking the water. They will have fine wine – one drink, maybe two, who knows? – Maybe even three. And she will smile at him seductively and tell him how good the food he has chosen is. And his mind will go 'click, click, click, clickety click' even faster.

And then, after they take a stroll on the beach, they will retire for the evening, I assume that they will retire to separate rooms but who knows? Maybe not. And either way, all during the night this young man's mind will be going click, click, click, clickety click, so fast that he won't be able to sleep a wink.

And then, the next morning, after a leisurely breakfast in bed, with strawberries dipped in champagne, they will sit out on the balcony, dressed in their robes, and while they do, his mind will be going click, click, click, clickety click.

Of course they will click. What kind of a test is that?" said Father Isaac.

"In that kind of a setup any woman who didn't set him clicking would have to be senile, deaf, dumb, ugly – and have bad breath besides."

And then Father Isaac said to me: "Tell your young man that if he really wants to find out whether he will click with this woman for the rest of his life or not, I'll give him a test that will be much better. It is a test that I learned once from my neighbor up here in heaven, Mike Royko, who is a very smart man. We were having drinks together one afternoon at a bar that is located halfway between the Jewish and the Catholic sections of heaven and we started discussing a case just like this one that had come to him back in the days when he was writing for a newspaper in Chicago. And so the answer that I am going to give you comes from him as well as from me.

Mike told me to tell this guy that his advice would be to spend a couple of days with her, not at a resort on the beach, but at his house. And instead of going into the Jacuzzi with her, I should tell him to go to the local supermarket with her to buy groceries. And tell him that I said that he should try changing his mind as to which brand of tuna he wants to buy at least four or five times and see how she reacts. And then, when he gets the grocery cart to the car, tell him to see if she unloads the heavy bags herself, as my Becky would have done, or whether she thinks that he ought to help her with the job.

And then, tell him that I said that he should try throwing his underwear on the floor, and putting his shirt on the windowsill, and tell him that I said that he should leave the top of the toothpaste off every day, and that he should throw his pants over a chair, and see how many minutes it takes for her to pick them up.

And then, tell him that I said that he should borrow or rent some small children for a couple of days. Tell him to put them in the car and go for a drive on a hot day. And tell him to pretend that the air conditioning is broken – and he will see what kind of a traveler she is. And I said: My Becky traveled all the way from Haran to Canaan – which is a journey of seventeen days – in the heat – and she never complained even once! See if your friend's girlfriend does as well as she did or not.

Tell her that you are going bowling with the guys, and say that you won't be gone very long. And then, stagger in at around two in the morning with some of your buddies and sit in the kitchen drinking beer and telling jokes. Ask her to make some sandwiches for the guys and see how gracious and hospitable she is. Watch to see if she does it cheerfully – or grudgingly. My Becky would have whipped up a feast for them in no time, believe me.

Then let her invite some of her close friends over for an evening. In the course of the conversation, let them know that you think that they are all nerds and jerks. See if she appreciates your honesty or not.

I said: "If I tell this young man to do that, she will never speak to him again."

"That's the whole point," said Father Isaac. "If he does what I am telling you, he will find out what she is really like – not what she is like at a resort on the beach. Does he want to spend the rest of his life with someone who can run with him on the beach but who will be of no use to him when he has a cold, or who expects him to carry in the groceries, God forbid, or who expects him to carry his share of the household responsibilities?

Tell him from me that if he wants to find out whether they click or not, my way is a much better way to find out than his is. And tell him: believe me I know. Because my Becky and I have been married a long time now, and we have had our good days and our bad days, like every married couple does, but we have made it, so I know."

And with that Father Isaac disappeared, right there in the parking lot of Publix, and left me sitting in my car there all by myself.

At first, I didn't know what to do. Should I tell this young man the advice that Father Isaac gave me to give him or not? I was sure that if I did, he would not listen to me. He would say: "What does Father Isaac, who lived so long ago, who lived before no-fault divorce, and before men and women lived together before marriage the way they do now – what does he know about how to find out if you are really compatible or not?" He will say, "Thank you for the advice but no thank you." And he will go off to the resort and see if they click just the same.

I remembered the advice that I once got from my teacher, Rabbi Harry Halpern. He used to say that whenever people came to him for advice, he would ask them what advice they wanted to hear – because that was the only advice that they were going to listen to anyway.

And then I realized that this whole encounter in the parking lot of the supermarket was a fantasy! I had been up all night the night before, trying to decide what to tell this young man who had come to me for advice, and trying to figure out what to tell you in today's sermon, and so I was sleepy. In fact, I was so sleepy that I had fallen asleep right there in my car in the parking lot of the supermarket, and I had imagined the whole thing!

So I bought the groceries that my wife had sent me for, and then I went home and took a nap. And when I woke up, I opened the

Torah to look at today's Torah reading. And guess what I found?

Right there – right in front of my face – was the story of how the servant of Abraham tested the girl he met at the well in order to see if she was the right one for Isaac or not!

How did he test her?

He didn't take her away to a hotel for a weekend. They didn't do that in those days.

Instead, what did he do? He asked her to give him some water to drink from the well.

And what did she do in response?

She not only gave him water to drink. She gave water to the ten camels in his caravan as well!

And if you think that is easy to do, then you don't know much about camels.

Dr. Nahum Sarna, who was a great Bible scholar, went to the zoo when he was writing his commentary on this *sedra*, and he asked the zookeepers: "If a camel travels from Canaan to Haran, which is a journey of seventeen days, how much water does it need when it gets there?"

And do you know what they told him?

They said that a camel that travels that far, a camel that journeys from Canaan to Haran, uses up AT LEAST twenty-five gallons of water – if not more.

Which means that if Rebecca had a pitcher that held half a gallon of water – which you must admit is a pretty heavy pitcher to have to carry on your shoulder – if Rebecca had a pitcher that held half a gallon of water, then she had to go down the steps of the well, fill up her pitcher of water, climb back up again, and give water to his camels, at least fifty times. . . until they had enough to drink!!

Let me tell you, THAT is a test!!!!

And anybody who does that – UNASKED – he only asked for water for himself, he never said: give water to my camels too. . . any woman who does that is really generous, and really hospitable, and really energetic, and really fit to be the daughter-in-law of Abraham who was famous for his hospitality to strangers.

Rebecca passed the test – with flying colors!

Though I can just imagine how much aspirin or how much Aleve she must have had to take that night, for her sore back, and for her aching feet after the hard work that she put in that day.

And look with me at one more detail of the story. The Torah says that Isaac married Rebecca, and then it says that he took her into his tent, and THEN it says that he loved her!

There was no dating before; there was no 'clicking' before; there was no nothing before!

Evidently, Isaac understood that real love is the result of a lifetime of living together. Evidently he understood that real love is the result of a lifetime of sharing together, of working together, of building together, of failing together, and of starting over again together. And that any love that you have before is just puppy love, superficial love, not real love. Isaac and Rebecca clicked together – if I may use that strange expression, which really belongs more in the realm of photography than it does in the realm of love – Isaac and Rebecca clicked together after they had gone through the pain of dealing with infertility for many years until she finally became pregnant, and after they had gone through the pain of giving birth to twins who were totally different in personality and who were rivals from the day they were born, and after they had gone through the heartache of Esau's intermarrying and of Jacob's leaving home. Sure they had some communication problems along the way, but they hung on and they held on and they worked things out. And so maybe Isaac knew more about clicking and about how to make a good marriage than I thought he did.

And so maybe I ought to tell the young man who is coming to see me tomorrow what Isaac says he should do if he wants to find out if this is the right woman for him or not. Maybe I ought to tell him that relationships do not usually click by themselves – YOU have to do the clicking – and sometimes you need to do the clicking over and over again for a lifetime – but if you do, your marriage will be a blessing.

(With thanks to Mike Royko, the columnist of the *Chicago Sun* and the *Chicago Tribune*, who once had a similar encounter with a young man who was considering going away for a weekend with a prospective wife, and who gave this man very similar advice to the advice that Isaac told me.)

A Florida Midrash

BEFORE I BEGIN, let me ask you a personal question:
How many of you are widows or widowers or have parents who are widows or widowers?

If you do, then I ask you to listen carefully to the Midrash that I want to share with you today.

I am going to share with you what may sound like a far-fetched Midrash when you first hear it. And then I am going to tell you why this Midrash speaks to me, and to all those rabbis who serve in Florida with special meaning, and why I believe that this Midrash should speak to those of you who are widows or widowers or who have parents who are widows or widowers as well.

Are you ready?

The Torah says that when Rebecca comes across the desert and meets her bridegroom, Isaac, "he was coming back from Be'er-Lahai-Ro'i." What was he doing there? And why is that detail worth mentioning in the Torah? The Torah does not spend valuable space telling us everywhere that the patriarchs went. If Jacob went to the drug store, or if Abraham went to the movies, the Torah does not bother to tell us. So why does the Torah make a point of telling us that on the day when Isaac met his bride for the first time, he was coming from Be'er-Lahai-Ro'i?

Be'er-Lahai-Ro'i is mentioned once before in the Torah. Who remembers where?

Do you remember Hagar? She was the maid of Sarah, and Sarah gave her to Abraham so that he could have a child with her, since she was having great difficulty in becoming pregnant herself. And like many surrogate marriages in our time, it did not work out so well. As soon as Hagar became pregnant, Sarah became jealous, and began to mistreat her. And so in chapter 16, we learn that Hagar ran away from the house, because she could no longer endure the mistreatment that she received at the hands of Sarah. She ran away to a place called Be'er-Lahai-Ro'i, and it was there that an angel appeared to her and comforted her, and promised her that God would protect her and bless her.

Why would Isaac go now to this place where Hagar once was?

Says the Midrash: Isaac went there to bring Hagar back to his father, Abraham, so that he might marry her, now that Sarah was no longer alive.

I must tell you that this Midrash is not the *pshat*. It is not the literal meaning of the passage. I am sure of that for several reasons. One is that the new wife whom Abraham marries after the death of Sarah is called Keturah, not Hagar. Second, Hagar was at Be'er-Lahai-Ro'i only the first time she ran away; the second time she went back to Egypt where she came from. So we cannot take this Midrash literally. And yet I find it to be a fascinating Midrash on several counts.

First, consider the irony of this Midrash. The bulk of this sedra is devoted to Abraham's efforts to find a wife for Isaac – and at the very same time that Abraham is busy choosing a wife for Isaac, Isaac is busy trying to find a wife for Abraham!

I imagine that both Abraham and Isaac, both the father and the son, must have been devastated by the loss of Sarah. Isaac must have loved her, because she was the doting, pampering parent who took such loving care of him. She even sent Hagar and her child, Ishmael, away for his sake. So I can only imagine how much Isaac must have been devastated when his mother died. The Torah says that only after he married Rebecca and took her into his mother's tent was he comforted for the loss of Sarah.

And Abraham must have been devastated too. The Torah says that Abraham wept for her, something that is never mentioned anywhere else. We don't hear that Adam wept for Eve or that Noah wept for Mrs. Noah. If they did, it is not recorded. This is the first time in the Torah that we hear of a husband weeping over the loss of his wife. He must have been a broken man in his time of bereavement, and this is why Isaac cares about him, and wants to help find a new wife for his father.

And yet, at least according to this Midrash, he not only helps his father remarry, but helps bring him back together with the woman whom his mother, Sarah, hated and whom she had driven out of the house!

How can this be? How can Isaac, who loved his mother so much, betray her this way? How can he be involved in bringing back the woman that she drove out?

My guess is that, much as he loved his mother, he cared about his father too. He saw his father in inconsolable grief, and he worried about him. He understood that his father could not go on this way, weeping and grieving for his wife; that if he did, it would make his last days on earth bitter, that it would destroy him. And so he put the needs of the living over the memory of the dead. And he did what he could to reconcile Abraham and Hagar and bring them together again, so that his father could have a new life. And perhaps it was out of delicacy, out of sensitivity to the feelings of Sarah, that the Torah calls the new wife Keturah instead of Hagar, so as not to embarrass Sarah. At least that is what Rabbi Samson Raphael Hirsch seems to suggest in his commentary on this passage. Isaac did not want to betray his mother and yet he wanted to help his father. And so he brought Hagar back to Abraham, and persuaded his father to marry again.

Why do I call this a Florida Midrash?

Because Isaac's situation is one that I see often here in Florida. I see widows and widowers in large numbers here in this community. I am sure you know many of them, as I do. Often, they are broken people, depressed and disheartened, morose and melancholy, withdrawn into themselves, living in the past, barely able to function, living lives of never-ending grief. And sometimes I meet some of them who would like to rebuild their lives if they could, but cannot find someone with whom to do it. I know one woman who said to me sarcastically: "It's hard to find a good man nowadays. And when you do, you find that they are looking either for a purse or a nurse."

But sometimes, some of these people are able, after some time, to find a mate, a person who comes into their lives and gives them a reason and a partner for living.

And when they do, some of these people come to me and ask me to perform their wedding service. And when they ask me, I tell them that I would be honored to do so, but I must interview them first and that I must ask them a number of questions that will help me prepare the wedding service. So they come to the house, and we talk. And one of the questions that I always ask them is: "Do you each have children? And if so, will they be at the wedding?"

And when I ask that question – will your children be at the wedding? – there is sometimes a long silence. And I know what that silence means. It means that the children are upset that Papa or Mama are remarrying. They feel that this is not the right one for their parent to be marrying, or they feel that it is too soon, or they feel that it is a betrayal of the first marriage. And so they are not coming to the wedding ceremony.

And sometimes I get a frantic phone call from up North. It is the children calling to ask for my help. They tell me that Papa is marrying a floozie, someone who is only interested in his money, and they ask me to please help them break up the shidduch. I don't promise to do that, but I do agree to meet with the couple and see if they are right or not. And when I do, I often find that she is not a floozie at all; she is a fine, upstanding woman, often with money of her own. And Papa and she want to get married, simply because they care about each other and because they want to rebuild their lives together. And when I call and report this to the children, they hang up indignantly, and I can hear what they must be thinking: "Of all the rabbis in Florida – our *mazel* – we had to get this idiot!"

And whenever I have these experiences, whenever I hear from children who are ready to do anything and everything they can in order to stop their parent from remarrying and from having a new life, because they feel that it is a betrayal of the one who is gone, I think of what Isaac did in this Midrash. At the very same time that his father was busy trying to arrange a *shidduch* for him, he was busy trying to arrange a *shidduch* for his father – not because he loved the memory of his mother less, but because he cared about the well-being of his father more, and he knew that his mother would have wanted him to care about that too!

How different these children I deal with are from Isaac, and how much they could learn from him about what a child's real responsibilities to a parent are. There is a time and a place for grief. To lose a partner after many, many years of marriage is an amputation – nothing less than that. But for children to want their parents to live in perpetual grief is not a tribute to the memory of the one who is gone. It is a perversion of what the one who is gone would want. Isaac understood that. Would that some of the people whom I deal with understood that too!

There is need for tact and delicacy in such cases. I understand that. Perhaps that is what the Torah is hinting, according to this Midrash, when it refers to this woman as Keturah, and not as Hagar, so as not to embarrass the memory of Sarah. Perhaps the second wedding ought to be low-key and not extravagant, because both partners bring some measure of grief along with them to the chuppah. A friend of mine once said that whenever a widow and a widower remarry, there are four people under the chuppah: him, her, his first wife, and her first husband. But a second marriage can be a *mitzvah*. It can be a declaration of faith that life is worth living, and children owe their parents the respect to understand that.

Let me tell you about one of the nicest marriages that I have ever attended. It was a remarriage of a widow and a widower. And every one of us who was there was feeling the same thing. We were thinking of the mates who were gone, although none of us said a word out loud about what we were thinking. And then came the moment when the bride and groom placed the rings on each other's fingers. And as they did, they each made a simple declaration. They each said: "Just as I loved my first spouse – with all my heart and soul, so I will love you in the same way." And when they said those words, every person in the room breathed a sigh of relief. Here was a couple who were wise enough not to deny the past, not to pretend that the past was over, but to acknowledge the past, with its good and with its pain, and to resolve to go on living in the present while honoring the past. I was deeply moved by what this couple did that day under the *chuppah* and I think that they should be an example to all those who have the courage and the resiliency that it takes to love and lose and love again.

And I was also moved by the support and the love that this couple received that day from their children. The son and the son-in-law of one of them were rabbis, and they co-officiated at the wedding. And all of the children came – one from as far away as Israel! And by their presence, they gave assent and encouragement to what their parents were doing. And there was not a crumb of guilt in the room, not one! Instead there was only joy and love and appreciation for the fact that it is a *mitzvah* to live, and to love, and to begin over again after the defeats that life deals out.

Isaac was the first son who had this kind of wisdom, who went to the effort of finding a *shidduch* for his bereaved father, at the very same time that his father was busy finding a *shidduch* for him. And as a result of that good deed, they were both healed. Isaac was able to recover from the loss of his mother and build a life with his bride. And so was Abraham. The Torah says that Abraham had children with Keturah, and that they lived together for many years.

And so I want to suggest to you today that they should be the role models for all the bereaved parents and all the bereaved children in our midst. They teach us that remarriage is not a betrayal of the first marriage; it is an affirmation of how good the first marriage must have been that the survivors are willing and able to live and to love again. I find it fascinating that it was *davke* Isaac, the one who was most attached to his mother of all the patriarchs, who, at least according to this Midrash, was the one who persuaded his father to remarry after she was gone. Abraham was able to leave his mother behind and go off to a new world when God summoned him. Jacob was able to go to Haran when he had to, and never see his mother again. Isaac was the only one of the patriarchs who never left the land, who never left his home, all his life. And yet, even he, the one who mourned his mother the most, was comforted over his loss when he married Rebecca. And he is the one who helps his father remarry after the loss of Sarah, and who persuades his father that to remarry is not a betrayal of Sarah but a tribute to her life.

If there is anyone here today who is bereaved and bereft and who lives with a broken heart that does not heal, I ask you to learn a lesson today from the example of Abraham and Keturah. And if there is anyone here today who is angry that their parent has picked up the broken pieces of his or her life and has decided to go on living and loving, I ask you to learn from Isaac in this Midrash. Isaac was the first to face this challenge that faces so many of us in our time, now that life expectancy has gotten so much longer. If we are tested as Isaac was, may we respond with the same wisdom and the same compassion and the same maturity and the same respect for parents that Isaac demonstrated.

I Have a Proposal to Make Today

I HAVE A PROPOSAL to make today.

It is a proposal that I believe is one of the most important, perhaps THE most important proposal that I have ever made to this congregation. I believe that this proposal, if it is accepted, and if it is carried out seriously, has the power to transform this congregation and, more important than that, I believe that this proposal has the power to transform the lives of many of our families.

So will you please hear me well today.

Before I tell you what my proposal is, I want to study with you the story that we have been reading from the Torah for these last two weeks: the story of the marriage of Isaac and Rebecca.

Let me begin by saying that I envy Abraham. This was a man who knew how to marry off a child. When it came time for Isaac to get married, Abraham chose a *shadchan*, a man named Eliezer, and he sent him off to the land that Abraham had come from, to the land where his relatives still lived, and he said to him: "Bring me back a wife from there for my son, Isaac."

Eliezer went, and he chose a fine woman, a woman named Rebecca. She was kind and hospitable, judging by the way she welcomed Eliezer when she met him at the well. She was energetic and generous, judging by the way she gave him water, and then gave water to his camels.

She was decisive, judging by the way she was ready to leave on one day's notice. How many women do you know who can pack for a trip on one day's notice?

And she was pious and modest, judging by the way she put on her veil, when she met her groom for the first time.

Now that's the way for a father to choose a wife for his child! Right? None of this romantic stuff that our kids seem to believe in nowadays. None of this ridiculous idea that you hear about nowadays that children have the right and the ability to choose their own mates. None of this silly idea that our children should date for a while before they marry. A father should choose a mate for his child – right? Right!

THIS is the way to arrange a successful marriage!

Right?

Wrong.

Wrong, because, if you study today's *sedra* you will see that this marriage that Abraham arranged for his son was not really such a great success as we thought it was.

It started out fairly well. Isaac was in great grief for the loss of his mother, and the arrival of Rebecca gave him a measure of comfort. But then, as the marriage went on, and the first bloom wore off, problems developed, and the marriage began to show some strains.

First of all, Rebecca and Isaac had trouble having children. I don't know whether it was his fault or hers, whether his sperm count was low, or whether she was infertile but, for whatever reason, it took them twenty years before she was finally able to conceive.

That can be a serious strain on a marriage.

And then finally, finally, after years of waiting, after trying every fertility clinic in the country, after trying every herb and every medicine they could find, Rebecca becomes pregnant.

And *auf tseloches,* she has twins! Twins can be a strain on a marriage.

And what is worse, from the moment they are born, these two children compete with each other. One is an athlete, a hunter, a redheaded good-looking, physical kind of a person. And the other is a pale, thin, scholarly, studious kind of a person. One loves to be outdoors and enjoys hunting. The other loves to stay home and cook in the kitchen. One was a Papa's boy, and the other was a Mama's boy. From the very beginning, Isaac favored Esau – perhaps because he had the qualities that Isaac himself did not have. And from the beginning, Rebecca favored Jacob – perhaps because she sensed that he had the brains and the spirit that were necessary to carry on the covenant. From the beginning, Papa sided with Esau, and pampered him, and spoiled him, and took care of him. And from the beginning Mama sided with Jacob, and defended him and pampered him, and spoiled him, and protected him, and took care of him.

And what was worse: these two parents never talked to each other about what was going on. They never communicated. And that eventually led to the great catastrophe – in which Isaac sent Esau off to hunt for venison, and promised to give him the blessing if he did, and Rebecca overheard this conversation, and so she ran and got Jacob, disguised him as Esau, gave him some food to bring to his father, and managed to get him the blessing instead of his brother.

As a result of this incident, Esau became angry, and vowed to kill Jacob. And so Rebecca had to send Jacob away, for his safety. And she never got to see him again. He was gone for twenty years, and when he came back, neither she nor Isaac was still alive.

What a tragic marriage this was – the marriage of two people who were both good people, but who had no idea how to communicate with each other – not about how to raise children and not about anything else.

I ask you: If you were going to write your will and if you were going to divide your assets between your children, wouldn't you talk it over with your wife?

And yet Rebecca only finds out what Isaac is going to do by eavesdropping?

And I ask you: If you overheard your husband planning to divide his assets in a way that you believed was absolutely wrong, wouldn't you say something to him? Wouldn't you go in and say: "Ike" or "Isaac" or whatever she called him: "Listen to me, I think that you are making a mistake!" But Rebecca says nothing to him. Instead, she maneuvers to disguise Jacob to look like Esau, and she tries to get him the blessing by trickery.

I ask you: why didn't she talk to her husband instead?

Evidently, neither one of them was very good at communicating with the other.

I don't know why. Perhaps she was shy, because she came from another country. Perhaps she spoke with an accent. Who knows?

Perhaps he didn't consult her or ask her advice because he came from a world in which men did whatever they wanted to do without asking the advice or the permission of their wives. Who knows?

What is clear is that this husband and this wife were not very good at communicating with each other, and that the result of that inability was disastrous.

Why do I tell you this story today?

Because I believe that Rebecca and Isaac are not the only ones who entered marriage totally unprepared. And because I believe that the results of this lack of preparation are just as disastrous in our time as they were in their time.

We now have a situation in this country in which at least one out of every three marriages – perhaps more – ends in divorce. And we have the same situation in the Jewish community that we have in the general community. At least one out of three marriages – and perhaps more – ends in divorce. And every divorce is more than just a statistic. It is a "loch in harts" – a hole in the heart of the husband and the wife, and their parents and their children. Every divorce is a painful amputation. "A good divorce'" – ask anyone who has ever gone through one – is an oxymoron.

Forgive me for joking about this serious matter, but do you know the story about the man who meets his friend whom he has not seen in a long time? He says to him: "How is your daughter, the one who is married to a C.P.A.?

The man says: "Oh, they divorced some time ago."

The friend says: "Oh, really. I am sorry to hear that."

The man says: "Oh, don't be. After she divorced him, she married a lawyer."

The friend says: "Oh really. Mazel tov!"

The man says: "Thank you, but then they got divorced too."

The friend says: "Oh, I am sorry to hear that."

The man says: "Oh, don't be. A year later, she married a doctor."

The friend says: "A CPA? A lawyer? A doctor? *Fun ein kint azoi fill naches!*"

The truth is that it is not really so much *naches* – not if it is your daughter.

There must be something wrong with our system of making marriages if so many end up in divorce. What would you say if a company manufactured light bulbs, and customers reported back that one out of three light bulbs that they bought didn't work? You would say that there must be something wrong at the factory, that there must be no quality control, if such a thing can happen. Well, that is what is happening to Jewish marriages today. One out of three don't work.

There are many explanations available, and some of them may be right.

We Jews are the most urbanized group in America. And the divorce rate is highest among those who live in cities.

We Jews are the most mobile group in America. We move from job to job, from city to city, even from country to country constantly. And mobility is considered one of the causes of divorce.

Jewish women are among the most educated women in the country. Many of them have careers and professions. And the divorce rate is highest among people in this category.

But the real question is not why is this happening but what are we going to do about it?

What are we as a Jewish community going to do about it? And what are we as a synagogue going to do about it?

Are we going to sit on the sidelines and bemoan the situation? Or can we be a part of the solution and not just spectators who sit on the sidelines and complain?

I believe that the synagogue ought not to be a place where we play Trivial Pursuits! I believe that the synagogue should be involved in dealing with the real issues that confront our people. Otherwise, they will look upon us as irrelevant, and they will go elsewhere in search of help and guidance, and have nothing to do with us.

And therefore, this is my proposal:

From now on, I propose that the rabbi of this synagogue, together with the rabbis of all the other synagogues in this community will agree not to perform a wedding for any couple – until and unless they agree to go through a course in how to make marriage work! I propose that the rabbis of this community agree not to perform a wedding for any couple until and unless they agree to take a course in how to be married, how to communicate, how to deal with each other and how to deal with their in-laws, how to parent and how to determine when and whether to parent, and how to fight fair when you have a disagreement.

I propose that the synagogues co-sponsor such a course with the Jewish Family Service of our community and that we make this course mandatory for all those who come to us to be married.

I make this proposal because I believe that the chief cause of divorce in our time is not only the sociological factors that I mentioned before – not only education and mobility and career conflicts – but the woeful lack of preparation with which our young people get married.

You cannot get a driver's license in this country unless you first pass two tests: a written one and a driving one. But you can get a marriage license in this country without taking any test at all!

All you need to do is pay the fee. You used to have to take a blood test before you could get married, but now, even that has been eliminated in many states. The reason that the blood test has been eliminated by many states is that they do not want to be liable in case there is a mistake and they end up permitting someone to get married who has AIDS and does not know it.

And therefore, we have couples who get married in our community who spend much more time and much more energy worrying over the décor of the tables, and the choice of the orchestra, and the menu of the caterer than they do over learning how to be a husband, or how to be a wife, or how to make a good marriage. And that is a scandal!

So let me say it clearly:

Any rabbi and any synagogue and any parent who allows such a marriage to take place, who worry more about the color of the flowers and over who gets to march down the aisle and in what order, and over the details of the menu or the color of the gowns that the bridesmaids will wear than they do over whether this couple is really mature enough and prepared enough to marry – that rabbi, and that synagogue and these parents are guilty of terrible negligence!

And therefore, it is time for rabbis and for synagogues to take a stand on this issue. We need to say loud and clear that WE ARE NOT JUST CATERING HOUSES, and that we do not exist in order to provide a fancy facility in which young people can get married. There are hotels that exist for that purpose. We are a synagogue, and we exist in order that young people can get married in a Jewish and in a proper way, and with sufficient preparation so that there is reason to hope that their marriages will succeed.

And therefore, this is my proposal.

I believe that the Catholic Church already does this. I believe that you cannot have a Catholic wedding until and unless you have gone through a course in how to be married. I believe that many rabbis already do this. There are rabbis who take pre-marital counseling seriously, and do it well. But I believe that the time has come for the whole Jewish community to say that we will not be involved in any wedding that takes place without proper and sufficient spiritual preparation.

If we do this, we will transform the synagogue into a serious place, into a place that has standards, and that means what it says when it claims to be a holy place. If we do this, we will transform the Jewish community into a place that stands for something, and that shows that it means what it says by what it does. And if we do this, we may be able to save some of the marriages of our children from ending up in pain and sorrow and distress.

Let us learn from what happened to the marriage of our ancestors, Isaac and Rebecca, and let us do better than they did.

And may God help us in this task. May God bless us in this new venture, and may He help us find the wisdom that we need in order to make our marriages as good and as sacred and as life-enriching as they should be.

Stuff

I WANT TO SUGGEST a new way of reading an old story today. It is the story of what happened when Jacob met his brother, Esau, after twenty years of separation.

What does Jacob do before they meet?

The Torah says: "*Vayikach min haba b'yado*." Jacob took from whatever happened to be handy, and he sent it as a present to Esau.

Listen to what he sent:

> 200 she-goats,
> 20 he-goats,
> 200 cows,
> 20 rams,
> 30 camels,
> 40 cows,
> 10 bulls,
> 20 female asses,
> And 10 male asses.

If you do the math, that comes to 550 animals!

Why does he send so many animals as a gift to Esau?

The usual explanation is that he sent them in order to placate Esau, in order to win his favor, because he was afraid that Esau was going to kill him, as he once threatened that he would. That is possible. That could be the reason.

Or: some commentators say that he sent him this lavish gift out of guilt. He sent these presents in order to atone for having taken the birthright and the blessing from him. That too could be the reason.

If so, this lavish gift that Jacob gave his brother turns out to be unnecessary, because Esau is no longer angry at him. When they meet, they hug, they kiss, they weep, and they make up, and all their old enmity is forgotten. And then Esau says: "What is the meaning of all these presents that you have given me?" And Jacob answers: *limtso chen b'eynei adoni* – "I have brought you these things in order that I may find favor in your sight, O my master."

To which Esau answers with a statement that has always impressed me. He says: *Yesh li rav* which means: "I already have plenty" – I don't need anything more. And so let what is yours be yours.

But Jacob does not accept that answer. Instead, he works on Esau, and works on him, until he persuades him to keep the gift that he has brought.

That's the story, as we usually read it.

But let me offer you a suggestion for your consideration today of a different way to read this story.

I am not sure that I am right, but it could be – it could be – that Jacob, who tricked Esau out of his blessing one time, and who then tricked him out of his birthright a second time, succeeds in tricking him a third time in this story.

How does he trick him this time?

I don't know about you, but if I were invited to somebody's house and it was not for a formal dinner, and if it was not for a whole weekend, if it was just for an informal get-together, I don't think that I would bring five hundred and fifty animals as a house gift.

Would you?

And if somebody brought you a gift of 550 animals as a house gift, what would you do?

Would you smile, and say: "Oh thank you, you shouldn't have bothered?" Or would you say: "How lovely. This is just what I needed!" Or would you mutter to yourself under your breath: "What am I going to do with five hundred and fifty animals? And where am I going to put them? Even if I move both of my cars out of the garage, where am I going to put five hundred and fifty animals? And what kind of an idiot brings me a gift like this?"

Notice that the text says that Jacob took these animals from whatever happened to be handy, which means that he had lots and lots more. And notice that Esau tries to refuse them, by saying: "I too am a rich man. I have plenty, and so I don't really need these animals, really I don't."

But Jacob is a persuasive person, and so he is able to talk Esau into taking all these animals as a gift, and then, after they have had a good reunion, the two of them part once again, and Jacob rides off with his family and his possessions, leaving Esau to worry about what is he going to do with, and how is he going to care for, five hundred and fifty animals.

Whenever I read this story, I think of the story that is told about Abba Eban and Chaim Weitzman. The story is that Weitzman went on a state visit to one of the countries in Africa, and while he was there, the leader of that country wanted to give him an elephant as a gift. Weitzman did not know what to do: Should he refuse the gift? If so, he might offend the leader of this important country. Should he accept it? If so, what was he going to do with it, and how was he going to get an elephant on the plane for the trip back to Israel?

Weitzman turned to Abba Eban for advice, and Eban is supposed to have said to him: "Mr. President, my advice is: Beware of gifts that eat."

My suggestion – and I told you that this is only a suggestion – I can't prove it – my suggestion is: that the reason that Jacob gave all these animals to Esau, and the reason he persuaded him to take them all was that Jacob was trying to get rid of some of his excess baggage. He was trying to get rid of all this excess baggage that was literally weighing him down, and that he did not know what to do with, and so he said to himself: "I'll give it to Esau, and let it be his problem, and not mine."

I could be wrong, but if my theory is right – then Jacob is the patron saint – even though I know that we Jews don't have patron saints – if we did, Jacob is the patron saint, and the role model and the guide to us all, because we live in an age when all of us are simply inundated with excess stuff. And therefore, whether I am right or whether I am wrong about Jacob, I ask you to listen to what I have to say to you today, because I think that I am surely right about what is happening in our time.

Houses are built much bigger nowadays than they were a century ago – not because we have more children now – we don't. In fact the average family has fewer children now than it did a century ago. The average house is built bigger today, not because we have more children, but because we have more stuff. The average house a century ago had one or two closets. The average house that is built today has five or six or even seven closets, and every one of them is filled to the gills with stuff.

Are any of you old enough to remember the radio program about "Fibber Magee and Molly"?

On every program there was one scene where somebody would open a closet door without permission, and loads and loads of stuff would come tumbling out. And the audience would roar with laughter. Today, you can open any door in any house in suburbia and loads of stuff would come tumbling out – and no one would laugh.

The truth is that we no longer own our stuff. Our stuff owns us.

Somebody said to me the other day: "I was thinking of moving to another house. It would have been closer to where I work. It would have been in a better school district. And so for a while, I was tempted. But then I said: Nah. How would I move all my stuff? And so I changed my mind." That is what I mean when I say that we don't own our stuff. Our stuff owns us.

Rabbi Jamie Korngold tells the story that her husband once asked her what she wanted for her birthday. She thought about it and she said: "I would like to have less for my birthday." He said: "That's nice, but how do I buy you less? Should I go to the store and ask if they have less for sale?"

She insisted that she wanted less, and so do you know what they did? They hired a babysitter to take care of their kids, and they spent the whole day going through the house, room by room, seeing what they had, and deciding what they did not need. They gave away old dishes that they had not used in years. They stuffed bags full of clothing that no longer fit, and they threw away *tsatchkes* that they no longer liked.

And when they were through, they looked at their uncluttered shelves, and at their uncrammed closets – and it felt so good.

And that is the way that I suspect Father Jacob must have felt when he rode away with his family and his servants, and his flocks and his cows and his camels, and left the ones that he did not need behind – for Esau to worry about. I can't prove it, but I wonder if the purpose of this lavish gift of five hundred and fifty animals that he gave was his way of getting rid of extra stuff that had become a burden to him instead of a pleasure.

Buying stuff that we don't need with money that we don't have has become one of the great addictions of our society. We talk about the obesity of our bodies, and I don't mean to deny that obesity of the body is a real health hazard, but maybe we should also talk about the obesity of our houses, which are so stuffed from basement to attic with things that we do not use, and that we do not need.

I have a friend who tells me that he once went hitchhiking through Europe for four weeks, and the only things that he took with him were what could fit into his backpack.

And he said: "I felt so free. I felt so liberated. . . . That is until all the stuff that I had bought along the way and mailed home began to arrive – and I had no idea where to put it."

Let me finish with one of my favorite stories. It comes from the Chofetz Chaim, who was one of the great Torah scholars and one of the great saints of the last century. The story is that a wealthy American tourist once came to visit the Chofetz Chaim. He walked in and he saw a table and some chairs, a bookcase with some books, a desk in one corner of the room, and a closet in the other corner. And that was all.

The tourist was surprised.

So he said to the Chofetz Chaim: "Where are your possessions?"

The Chofetz Chaim answered: "Where are YOUR possessions?"

The tourist said: "What do you mean: Where are my possessions? I am a visitor here."

To which the Chofetz Chaim answered;

"So am I."

When we learn that truth, when we really learn that truth, when we realize and comprehend that we are only strangers and sojourners on this earth, when we realize that we are all here only for a brief time, then we will be able to get rid of much of the stuff that we think we need, some of the stuff that weighs us down, and when we are able to do that, we will be able to live healthier and happier lives.

A Story in Three Stages

VAYEITZEI

I WANT TO TELL YOU a story in three parts today. The first part appears in today's *sedra*. The second part was somehow lost in an attic in the tenth century and was only rediscovered many centuries later. And the third part occurred two generations ago.

If you put these three stories together, you will get some idea of how the Torah continues to live through the generations, and of how it speaks to different people at different times in different ways.

Let me begin with the *sedra*. The Torah tells of how Laban had two daughters, one named Leah and one named Rachel. And it says that Leah had weak eyes, but that Rachel was very, very beautiful. And it says that Jacob loved Rachel, but that he did not love Leah.

And then you know what happened. Jacob agreed to work for Laban for seven years in exchange for Rachel. But at the wedding ceremony, the bride wore a thick veil, and so Jacob could not see who was underneath the veil. And when Jacob awoke in the morning – behold it was Leah whom he had married by mistake!

When he went to complain to Laban, what does Laban say? He says: "We don't do that kind of thing around here – to marry off the youngest before the oldest." What does he mean by these words? He is saying: "We don't do here what you did there. You disguised yourself and pretended that you were your older brother, Esau, in order to get the Divine Blessing from your father. So who are you to complain if I disguised my older daughter as the younger in order to get her a husband? What goes around comes around. I only did to you what you did to your father."

And so Jacob has to work seven more years in order to get the woman whom he truly loves, in order to get Rachel.

I must tell you that every time I read this story, I wonder: who should I feel sorriest for? Rachel – who had to stand by and watch her sister take her place? Jacob – who was tricked into marrying the wrong woman, and who had to work seven more years in order to get Rachel?

I feel sorry for both of them, but I feel sorriest for Leah; really I do. Can you imagine how she must have felt getting her husband through trickery, and knowing that, ever afterwards, whenever he looked at her, he would remember the deception through which he got her?

You can feel the pain of Leah in the way she names her children. She has a son named Reuven, and she says: "Now my husband will see me." She has a son named Shimon, and she says: "Now my husband will hear me." She has a son named Levi, and she says: "Now my husband will be with me." And each time, her efforts fail. Leah keeps turning out children for Jacob, one after another after another, and yet Jacob loves Rachel, and not her. Your heart has to go out to Leah – for she is the unloved one.

She does everything that she can to win her husband's love, but to no avail. And therefore, I feel for Leah. Don't you?

In my imagination, I picture the rivalry between Leah and her sister ending when Rachel dies while giving birth to a second child. From then on, I picture Leah as the loving stepmother who raises her sister's two small children, and who tries her best to bring them up the way their mother would have wanted her to.

I picture Leah as the model for all the second wives we know who take on the task of raising the children of their husbands' first wives, and do their best to raise them well.

That is the first stage of the story: the way it is told in the Bible. It is the story of Rachel, the loved one, and of Leah, the unloved one.

Now come with me to the Middle Ages and meet a man named Yannai. Yannai was a very great Hebrew poet, who wrote poems for the synagogue service. Until recently, we knew almost nothing about Yannai. Some scholars thought that he lived in Italy in the tenth century. Other scholars thought that he lived in the land of Israel in the seventh century. But either way, we knew almost nothing about him, and we had hardly any examples of what he wrote. All we knew was that he wrote poems that were recited in the sacred services.

And then, at the end of the nineteenth century, Solomon Schechter, who at the time was Reader in Rabbinics at Cambridge University in England, and who was to go on to become the head of the Jewish Theological Seminary in New York, heard that there was a treasure trove of manuscripts in the *geniza* of a certain synagogue in Fustat, near Cairo, in Egypt. Schechter went there, and persuaded the officers of the synagogue to let him crawl into that attic, and lo and behold – he found thousands upon thousands of manuscripts there!

There were pieces of paper of all kinds. There were bills of sale and invoices left there by merchants who traveled the Mediterranean on business. There were questions on Jewish law addressed to Maimonides, and there were even answers to these questions, written in Maimonides's own handwriting! And there were scraps of parchment on which there were poems and prayers by many *paytanim* – including some by Yannai.

And so, for the last one hundred years, scholars at libraries in Cambridge, in New York, in Leningrad, in Jerusalem, and in other places have been going through these pieces of parchment, putting them together, deciphering their meaning, and learning from them what life was like for our people during the Middle Ages. And one of the discoveries that scholars have delved into was the piles of parchment that turned out to be a collection of poems written by Yannai. And so now, for the first time in many centuries, we know who this man was, and we know something of what he wrote.

One of the most interesting poems in the collection is a poem about Leah, a poem that is based on this week's Torah reading. You have to know that the custom in the Land of Israel was to read the Torah in a triennial cycle. That means that the Torah was divided, not into fifty-four sections, as we have it today, but into more than a hundred and fifty sections. The Torah reading was completed only once every three and a half years. And the poets would introduce each *sedra* with a poem about its theme.

Yannai wrote a poem about poor Leah, the unloved one. In his imagination, he pictured her as the symbol of the Jewish people, who are unloved by those among whom they lived. And he declares in this poem that: "not all those who are hated on earth are hated above."

Listen to what he says in the fourth part of this *kerova*:

> Our eyes are weak with longing for Your love,
> For we are loathed by a hateful foe:
> See how afflicted we are within,
> And how, without, we are abhorred –
> Like Leah, whose suffering You saw
> As You bore witness to her distress.
> She was hated at home,
> And despised abroad.
> Not each beloved, however, is loved,
> And all who are hated are not hated.
> Some are hated below, but loved on high.
> Those You despise are truly despised,
> Those whom You love are truly beloved.
> We are hated because we love You,
> You who are truly holy.

Do you understand what Yannai is saying in this poem?

He is speaking to Jews, who were suffering persecution. And he is saying to them: Don't despair! Don't give up hope!

Look upon yourselves as Leah of old, who was despised at first by her husband, and who was probably mocked by those around her for having obtained him through trickery.

She eventually won her husband's love, and she was the one who, together with her handmaiden, gave birth to half the twelve tribes of Israel. And in the same way, know O Jewish people, that, like Leah of old, you too may be hated by those around you, but you have the compassion and the love of God. Not all those who are hated below are hated above! And know and understand that the reason you are hated below is because you are loved on high! The nations mistreat you because they are envious of you. They know that God loves you, and they know that, no matter what they may do to you, you remain precious to God.

Can you imagine what an encouraging message these words of Yannai must have been to those Jews who heard them before the Torah reading when the story of Leah was read during the Middle Ages?

That is Stage Two of the story. Yannai transformed the biblical story that we have read today, the story of Leah the Unloved One, and made it the basis for a new love song between God and Israel. For him, the Jewish people are the Leahs of the world: unloved, abhorred, mistreated by their neighbors, but only because they are loved by God. And just as Mother Leah eventually ended up winning the heart of her husband, so, says Yannai, have the Jewish people succeeded in winning the heart of their Father in Heaven, by their loyalty and their unswerving devotion. Yannai taught the Jewish people of the Middle Ages to see themselves as the new Leahs, and to understand the persecution that they endured as a sign that the nations were envious of them, because God loved them.

And then this song of Yannai's, together with all the rest of his compositions, disappeared. There were no printing presses, parchment was rare and expensive, there were few libraries, and so eventually almost everything Yannai wrote was lost – except in the Cairo *Geniza*. There it rested for who knows how many centuries until Solomon Schechter came along and went into that *geniza*, and then other scholars followed him, and unearthed Yannai's poems and prayers, cleaned them off, read them, and prepared a new scientific edition of them.

And now comes Stage Three of the story.

Come with me to Nazi Germany, and come with me to the year 1936:

You should know that there was a very great man in Germany in the years of the Weimar Republic. His name was Zalman Schocken. He was the inventor of the concept of the department store. He built beautiful stores all over Germany, stores in which a person could buy anything he wanted under one roof. Schocken made a fortune from these stores, but when the Nazis came, his stores were confiscated and he lost his fortune.

But Zalman Schocken was not only a great businessman. He was also a patron of the arts. Early in his career he invested in a number of young and promising writers who were completely unknown at the time. He agreed to support these writers for life so that they could write without having to worry about working for a living. In exchange, they gave him the world rights to everything that they would ever write. Among these young writers whose potential Zalman Schocken recognized were Martin Buber, Shmuel Yosef Agnon, who ended up winning the Nobel Prize in Literature, and Franz Kafka. And it was through his investments in these writers that Zalman Schocken regained his fortune.

One of Zalman Schocken's pet projects was to rediscover the long lost treasures of Hebrew literature of the Middle Ages. And so he created a Center for the Study of Medieval Hebrew Literature, which was located at first in Germany, and was eventually transferred to Palestine. He appointed a scholar named Hayim Brody to be in charge of this Institute, and Brody set to work on the poetry of Yannai. Year by year he studied the pieces of parchment that had been brought out of the Cairo *Geniza*, identified the ones that were written by Yannai, put them together, and made of them a treasury of the works of this almost forgotten Hebrew poet.

And then came Hitler, and the world of German Jewry came crashing down. People who had believed deeply in German culture now found themselves excluded from German culture. People who had believed above all in Knowledge now found themselves expelled from the schools and the universities. What should they do? How should they cope emotionally with what was going on in their lives? How could they maintain their identity when the Germans had taken the German half of it away from them?

At this point Martin Buber sent for Ernst Simon, who was his devoted disciple, and asked him to come back from Palestine to help him create a new kind of Adult Jewish Education. They tried to provide new books and new works of literature that would explain to this bewildered German Jewish community who they were, and what their heritage was.

So they commissioned Fritz Baer, the historian, to write a book on *Galut*. It was supposedly about the Jews of Spain and how they had learned to cope with their exile at the end of the fifteenth century, but the German Jews who read it understood that it was a mirror into their own spiritual situation.

Buber also took the still unfinished translation of the Bible that he and Franz Rosenzweig had been working on and extracted Second Isaiah, the book that deals with how God can be trusted to comfort the remnants of His people, and he published it in 1936. And the German Jews who read it understood that the words of this book spoke to their own lives, and not just to those who had lived in Babylon many centuries ago.

Buber and Simon went to Hayim Brody, and asked for a selection from the work of Yannai that he had been working on for so long. And Brody gave him this poem, the story of Leah the Unloved One who is hated below but loved above. They took this poem and decided that they wanted to publish it in the Schocken Almanac of 1936.

But there was one catch. By then, nothing could be published in Germany without the explicit approval of the censors. Somehow, Fritz Baer's study of how the Spanish Jews coped with their expulsion had gotten through the censors. Somehow, the translation of Second Isaiah with its claim that a remnant would survive had gotten through. But would this poem get through the censors?

With fear and trepidation, Simon took the poem to the censors. They looked at it and saw some poem about Leah in the Bible. Who cares about that? And so some official stamped his permission on the poem, and it got through. And that year every Jew in Germany who read that almanac, which turned out to be the last document published by Jews in Germany until after World War Two, every Jew in Germany who read that almanac read this poem and understood what it said to them:

> "Not all those who are hated below are hated above.
> And not all those who are loved below are loved above.
> Some are hated below and loved above.
> Those whom You despise are truly despised,

And those whom You love are truly loved.
We are hated because we love You,
You who are most holy."

This was Stage Three in the story of how the story of Leah the Unloved One in the Bible became the Jewish People who were unloved on earth because they were loved on high in the Middle Ages, and then became the story of the Jews of Germany who found self-respect and meaning for their lives and who were able to endure and survive the hatred that they had to endure, thanks to poems like this one, which got through the censors and gave hope and meaning to their lives.

Is it not strange how a story can travel down through the centuries, meaning one thing in one generation, and something else in another, speaking to women who became stepmothers and who gathered courage for this task from the model of Mother Leah in the Torah, and then speaking to the victims of persecution in the Middle Ages in a whole different way and tone, and then speaking again to the victims of persecution in our time, when it was drawn out of the attic in which it has been gathering dust for over a thousand years, and coming out to speak again when its message is needed once more?

Surely ours is a *Torat Hayim*, a living Torah, that speaks in every century and to every spiritual situation. May it continue to do so.

The Female Elijah

I WANT TO STUDY WITH YOU today one of the least important women in the Bible. She is so unimportant that I promise
you that you will never be asked to identify her on Jeopardy.
She is so unimportant that you could be a professional Bible
scholar and never notice her existence. And yet, I want to tell her
story today, and then I want to suggest that there is a lesson we can
learn from her that is much needed in our time. Her name is Serah
bat Sarah and I have learned about her thanks to two essays, one by
Dr. Marc Bregman and one by Professor Howard Schwartz.

Her story begins in today's *sedra*. The *sedra* contains a list of those
who came down to Egypt with Father Jacob. And when it gets to
Asher, it says that the sons of Asher were Ishvi, Innah, Ishvah and
Beriah – and their sister was Serah. I promise you that you will never
be asked, not even in a crossword puzzle, who Ishvi or Innah or
Ishvah were. They play no role whatsoever in the biblical story. But
what strikes my eye is this mention of Serah, their sister. If Asher is
of almost no importance, and if his sons are of no importance, then
surely their sister was of no importance. So why is she mentioned?
No other woman is found in this list. Surely, there must have been
other daughters, other sisters? Why then is Serah, the sister of the
sons of Asher, mentioned in this list? That is our first question.

Now look with me at chapter 26 of the book of Bamidbar, which
is a list of those who went OUT of Egypt, several hundred years
later. It is a fascinating list, is it not? It reminds me of the song about
how on the first day of Christmas my true love gave to me . . . . It is

a chapter that will surely not win any prizes for poetic writing. It is just a long list of names of people who are never heard of again, neither before or after. But look at verse 46. Serah is mentioned again! The same name that appeared amongst those who went DOWN to Egypt appears again amongst the names of those who went OUT of Egypt several centuries later. How do you explain that?

One way to explain this is: coincidence. We can say that there were two different women, who lived more than two hundred years apart, who happened to have the same name.

That is possible. There are lots of different women who are named Louise or Elaine or Shirley, or Miriam or Sarah or Helen or Hannah.

Or: we can say that this one was named for that one. Lots of children are named for their grandparents or for their great grandparents. Perhaps she was too.

But the Sages of the Midrash did not accept these two explanations. Instead, they say that the Serah who is on the list of those who went down into Egypt and the Serah who is mentioned in the list of those who went up out of Egypt are the same person. And that she lived for more than two centuries. Perhaps much more.

Which raises the question: why? How come this woman lived for more than two centuries when no one else that we know of has lived that long? Was it because she was on the Atkins diet? That couldn't be, because the Atkins diet was not invented until much later. Was it because she exercised regularly? I believe that exercise lengthens your life but not by the amount of time that you waste exercising. (You know the story of the husband and wife who get to heaven, and everything is just wonderful there. The man says to his wife: see, if you hadn't made us live on such a healthy diet, we could have gotten here ten years sooner!) So how come she lived longer than anyone we know before or since? Was it perhaps because she did some very good deed? And if so, what good deed was it?

And now, the Sages of the Midrash use this story of how Serah seems to have lived so long and they make it the key for unraveling another biblical mystery, namely: how did the brothers break the news to their father that Yosef was still alive, when they came back from Egypt. How did they tell him that the son for whom he had been mourning so inconsolably for so many years was still alive, without causing him to have a heart attack? And this is their answer:

They say that Jacob had a grandchild, Serah, the daughter of Asher, a little girl whom he adored. And she would often sit at his feet and sing songs to him. And so the brothers went to her, and they asked her to sing to her grandfather a sweet, gentle song. And they asked her to make the refrain of the song: "Yosef is still alive, Yosef is still alive."

So she did. She sang the song, and Father Jacob jumped up and said: Really? Is it true? Could it be? And just then the brothers came in and said: Yes it is. And Jacob was so overjoyed that he didn't ask any questions and he didn't request any explanations. It was enough for him that his long missing child was really alive. And he was so moved that he picked up his little grandchild, kissed her on the forehead and said to her: *zolst lank leben, mein kint* – may you live a long, long time, my child.

Jacob's wish came true. And this is how Serah bat Asher was amongst those who went down to Egypt, and amongst those who came out of Egypt two centuries later.

So now we know the answers to two mysteries: how come Serah bat Asher lived so long, and how the brothers broke the news to their father that Yosef was still alive, without giving him a heart attack. But the Sages were not finished yet. They have several more puzzles that they were able to solve with the help of Serah bat Asher.

The first is: how did the Israelites know to believe Moses when he came and said to them that God, the God of our ancestors, has sent me to you? How did they know he was telling the truth? There are lots of cranks who come and claim that they are from God. How did they know this one was for real?

The answer? Serah bat Asher. She was old enough that she still remembered the last words of Yosef. When Yosef was on his deathbed, he said to the Israelites: someday the God of our ancestors will redeem you – the words that he used were: *pakod yifkod etchem* – and when He does, promise me that you will take my bones out with you. So when Moses came and used that very same word: *Pakad*, she remembered the word, and she said: "That's it! He's using the password that Yosef left for us. I remember it as if it were yesterday."

And so, thanks to Serah bat Asher and her memory, they believed Moses.

Second puzzle: the Torah says that on the night before the Israelites left Egypt, everyone was busy. They were busy stuffing things into their suitcases and their trunks and sitting on them so that they would close. And they were busy making the rounds and saying goodbye to their neighbors. And the Torah says that while they were busy doing this, what was Moses doing? They say that Moses was busy looking for the grave of Yosef, because Yosef had made them promise that, if and when, they ever got out of there, that they would take his body with them.

BUT WHERE WAS the coffin of Yosef? How do you locate a grave after more than two hundred years? Today the cemeteries have computerized records, and so, if you go to the cemetery office and say: where is the grave of so and so? They can look it up and tell you. But in those days, they had no computerized records. So how could Moses find the grave of Yosef?

The answer? Serah bat Asher. She came to Moses and showed him where it was. She was there on the day he died, and she remembered exactly where he was buried.

So look what we have done so far. We have solved the mystery of how come the name of Serah bat Asher is found both in the list of those who went down to Egypt and the list of those who came up from Egypt. And then we have used the answer to that mystery in order to solve the mystery of how the brothers broke the news to Jacob that his son was still alive. And then we have used the answer to that mystery in order to solve the mystery of how come the Israelites believed Moses was authentic when he came to them with a message from the God of their ancestors. And then we have used the answer to that mystery in order to solve the mystery of how Moses was able to locate the grave of Yosef.

But we are not finished yet. If this woman lived for more than two centuries, then maybe she continued to live for many more centuries?

In fact, maybe she is the female equivalent of Elijah. According to Jewish legend, Elijah never died. He was taken up to heaven in a chariot, and ever since, he pops up many times, as the stranger in disguise who helps poor people in distress and then disappears again. Now why should there only be a male mysterious stranger and not a female mysterious stranger who pops up out of nowhere in every generation? That's not fair! That would be sexism.

And so the midrashic imagination conceived of a female equivalent to Elijah, who also lives forever, and who also pops up in every generation – namely, Serah bat Asher.

So listen to this passage from a late Midrash. It says that Rabbi Yochanan ben Zakai was once lecturing in the academy at Yavneh. And he was teaching the story of the crossing of the Red Sea. And he said that the sea split and formed a kind of a lattice work. And the tribes crossed over within the lattice work.

And all of a sudden, there was a voice from the back of the academy. And an old woman stood up and said: "You don't know what you're talking about! It wasn't like that at all. The sea split into twelve sections, and each tribe went through in its own section. And the sections were transparent so each tribe could see the other tribes as they walked through the sea."

Rabbi Yochanan ben Zakai said to her: "I beg your pardon, but who do you think you are, interrupting my class?"

And she answered: "I am Serah bat Asher. And I was there, and I remember." And with that, she got up and left the academy, leaving the students and the teacher surprised and bewildered. That is the legend as it is found in a late Midrash.

But we are still not through with her. There are two separate versions of the ultimate fate of Serah bat Asher within the tradition. One version, which comes from Iran, is that she met her death in the fire that took place in the synagogue of Ishfahan, in Persia, which is now Iran, which took place in the ninth century.

That synagogue was later rebuilt by the Jews of Iran, and it was named for her. And it is still the holiest Jewish site in Iran. Almost all the Jews of Iran left in 1948, and those that stayed, left some years later when the Shah was overthrown. They made their way either to Israel or to Los Angeles and to some other cities in America and around the world. They have built good communities wherever they have settled. But many of these Jews still yearn for the day when there will be peace, and they will be able to go back and visit the homes of their childhood, and when they will be able to pray once again in the synagogue of Serah bat Asher which is located there. *Halevai*!

The second legend is that Serah bat Asher never died, that, like Elijah, she was taken up into heaven alive, and that she is still there. And that every so often she comes back to earth and visits classrooms where, with her sharp tongue, she keeps the record straight and she corrects the mistakes that people make when they describe the way it was in days of old.

Which version do you believe – that she died in a fire in Persia in the ninth century or that she still lives and that she still pops up every so often when you least expect her?

Which version do you believe? I have no idea. But I must tell you of a personal experience that I had some time ago. I was giving this talk somewhere else. I always try my talks out somewhere else before I give them here, because I know how 'culchehd' and how 'swayve' and how 'deboner' this group is and so I want to make sure that I have my talks down pat before I give them here. I was giving this talk about Serah bat Asher somewhere else, and I got halfway through it when an old lady, who looked like a bag lady, stood up and said: "You're an idiot! And you don't know what you're talking about!" And with that, she picked up her bag and walked out.

I was very upset, and so I asked the people: "Who was that old lady?"

And they all said that they didn't know. They said that they had never seen her before.

All except one man, who said: "Don't be upset that she called you an idiot. She has no mind of her own; she just repeats whatever everybody else says."

So was it her?

Could it have been?

Was she there to make sure that I prepared this talk carefully and that I got all the quotes from the sources right? Or was she just some bag lady who happened to come in that night?

I don't know. I have no idea. But ever since, I have vowed to be careful and to make sure that I quote my sources correctly, and that I never try to wing it or to teach without sufficient preparation.

Because you never can tell when Serah bat Asher is liable to be in the audience. You never can tell.

So this is the legend of Serah bat Asher, which has traveled down through the centuries, and which is found in many different countries to which the Jews have traveled. This is the story of the female Elijah.

Now, let me make a suggestion. In recent years, the Jewish feminist movement has rediscovered Lilith and it has rediscovered Miriam and it has rediscovered Vashti. May I suggest that perhaps it is time for us to rediscover Serah bat Asher. Elijah never married, Serah bat Asher never married – maybe we could make a *shidduch* between the two of them? They could travel the world together doing good deeds, and they could share the wine together on seder night. It is an idea to consider, is it not?

And now, let me be serious. Let me suggest that there is a lesson that we can learn from Serah bat Asher, and that is not only to prepare carefully when you give a talk because you can never know who is liable to be in the audience. In addition to that, I believe that the lesson of Serah bat Asher is: not to discount and not to disparage the wisdom of old people. Old people have memories, and old people have experiences, which the young do not have. They know that ideas which the young think are revolutionary have been tried before and have not worked.

Let me suggest that the lesson that we can learn from Serah bat Asher is that we should respect the wisdom and the experience and the memory of old people.

Back in the sixties they had a slogan: never trust anyone over thirty. Do any of you still remember that slogan? They do not use that slogan anymore, and do you know why? Because those who were once under thirty are now over thirty. And so now they want to be trusted.

Let me say in all seriousness, and I say this, not out of envy or out of frustration, that the most dangerous thing that can happen to a culture is when it disregards the wisdom and the dignity of the aged. The old deserve better than that – and the young deserve better than that! Because if you disregard the old, you lose out on the wisdom and the experience and the perspective that they possess.

Do you know the reason why we have so many therapists and so many psychoanalysts today? Because, in the old days, everyone had a wise aunt, who lived down the street. And when you had a problem, you could go over to her house and talk to her about it. But now, nobody has a wise aunt who lives down the street anymore. Now, nobody lives in the same state or the same state of mind as their parents or their children. And so we have to pay good money to talk to doctors about those things that we used to talk over with our old aunts.

And that, to me, is the lesson we can learn from Serah bat Asher, that the old have longer memories and that the old have better perspectives and that the old have more experience than the young do, and that therefore we should not malign them or disparage them, but instead we should listen to them and learn from them.

Let this be the lesson that we learn today from Serah bat Asher, the oldest woman in the world, the female Elijah.

And if you should ever meet her, if she should ever be in the audience when you give a talk and make mistakes and she catches you and corrects you, give her my regards and tell her what I said about her today, won't you please.

A Sermon in Favor of Running!

VAYECHI

(This sermon is dedicated to my grandchildren, Nathan and Naomi –
as teshuva for all the times that I have teased them about running,
And with good wishes for success in all the races that they ever run,
including the race of life.
With much, much, much love – From Bubbie and Zeidi)

THOSE OF YOU WHO KNOW ME know that on many, many occasions I have given sermons against exercise and against running. You have heard me speak out against running and against exercise on many different grounds. You have heard me say that if you want to go twenty-six miles, you should drive or take a bus or a cab or call Uber. And you have heard me say that if you are going to run twenty-six miles, you should at least run in one direction so that you get somewhere, instead of running around in circles, and ending up where you started, as they do in the New York marathon. And you have heard me say on many occasions that exercise may prolong your life, but not by as much time as you waste exercising. And so hear me well today, because today I am going to give a sermon IN FAVOR of running.

Let me begin by asking you a question:

Jacob had twelve sons and one daughter: which one of them is your favorite?

Some of you will probably say Yosef. After all, the Torah devotes more pages to his life story than it does to any of the other children of Jacob. And it is a fascinating story – it is a story of a person who goes, not only from rags to riches, but from narcissism to nobility and generosity of spirit. And so it is tempting to consider Yosef the best of the children of Jacob.

And yet Yosef is not my choice.

Some of you might choose Judah. After all, he comes through in the pinch, and stands up to the Egyptian prime minister in order to save his brother, Benjamin. And he deserves much credit for that.

And yet, Judah is not my choice.

My favorite among the children of Jacob is Naftali.

Why?

The reason that I am fond of Naftali is that he and I have one characteristic in common.

Can you guess what it is that Naftali and I have in common?

Anyone?

In today's Torah reading, Father Jacob blesses his children, one by one. And in these blessings, he sometimes refers to one or more of their qualities, whether good or bad. And when he gets to Naftali, Jacob says: *Naftali ayala shluchah* – which the new Jewish Publication Society version translates as "Naftali is a deer let loose."

Jacob describes Naftali as a deer – which I guess means someone who is capable of running fast. And the Jewish tradition picks up on this line, and tells stories about what a fast runner Naftali was.

And this is why I identify with Naftali. Those of you who have ever driven with me know that I sometimes drive very close to the speed limit. In fact, the truth is that I confess that I have on very rare occasions even driven a tiny, tiny bit beyond the speed limit.

And there are those who say that I am not a very, very careful driver. In fact, I have a good friend who says that he *davens* more fervently in my car than he does in shul. And so you can understand why I identify with Naftali.

I like to think of him as "Naftali the Jogger," gracefully running up and down the hills of the city of Beth El where he grew up. And I picture him as the person who would have been Israel's representative at the Olympics, if there had been an Olympics in his time. I imagine him as a long distance runner, or as a jogger, or as doing the hundred yard dash or the marathon.

And so, if there are any people here today who love running or jogging, I invite you to identify with Naftali, and to think of him as your predecessor and your model.

I want to tell you three stories about Naftali today, three stories that are found in the Midrash. And the reason that I want to tell you these three stories is because I believe that they can teach us that there are times when it is a *mitzvah* to run, as he did.

The first story concerns the moment at the pit, the moment when the brothers beat up Yosef, and then threw him into the pit and left him there to die. The Midrash says that Naftali was too young and too inexperienced to stand up to his brothers. He tried to reason with them, but they would not listen to him. And so he ran as fast as he could to get Reuven, the oldest of the brothers, figuring that maybe the brothers would listen to him, and that maybe he could stop the brothers from harming Yosef.

He brought the news to Reuven of what was going on, and Reuven came as fast as he could to rescue Yosef. But when he got there, it was too late. The Torah says: "When Reuven got there, and saw that Yosef was no longer in the pit, when he saw that he had been sold to a caravan of Midianites who happened to pass by, he tore his clothes in grief. And he said: 'The boy is gone! Now what am I to do?'"

Naftali failed that day, but at least Naftali tried. I picture him running, as fast as he could, his legs pumping up and down, his heart beating, his cheeks red with anxiety and with exhaustion, trying to reach Reuven before it was too late.

But alas, sometimes even the speed of a long distance runner is not enough. By the time Naftali found Reuven, and told him what was happening, and urged him to come save the boy – it was too late.

What should we learn from Naftali? The first lesson that we should learn from him is that when a life is at stake, you must go as fast as you can in the effort to save it. The clock may be ticking. Deep down in your heart, you may know that it is too late, and that you won't get there in time. But you have to run as fast as you can anyway, in the hope that you will make it.

I think of the people who drive the ambulances that we sometimes see hurtling down the highway as fast as they can go – with their sirens on full blast, warning people to get out of the way, so that they can get there on time, and perhaps save a human life.

These ambulance drivers are the children of Naftali today. And if you should ever see them, or hear them, pull over to the side at once and let them go by. And, as you do, bless them for the sacred work that these people do. These people are devoted to saving human lives, and there is no greater *mitzvah* than that.

The second Midrash about the speed of Naftali is this one.

Miracle of miracles: the cruel Egyptian prime minister, the one who has been torturing the brothers for so long, the one who has kept Shimon as a prisoner, the one who has made them bring Benjamin down with them, the one who planted a divining cup in their luggage and then accused them of stealing it – the prime minister of Egypt turns out to be their long-lost brother, Yosef!

They hug and they embrace. They cry and they laugh. And then, Yosef sends them on their way. He tells them to hurry back home in order to tell their father that the son whom he loves the most is alive – not only alive, but well – not only well – but that he is the prime minister of Egypt! He gives them food and gifts to take along with them, and he sends them on their way.

And according to the Midrash, while the other brothers traveled at their own pace, Naftali ran. He ran all the way from Egypt back to Canaan, in order to bring the good news to Jacob that his son was still alive. Naftali becomes a long distance runner, strengthened by the eagerness to tell his father the incredible news. Jacob has been inconsolable all these years. He has refused to be comforted. And now Naftali has unbelievable news for him and so he runs to deliver it as fast as he can.

And what does that Midrash teach us? That, if you can bring joy to someone, you should not take your time doing it, as the other brothers did. You should run as fast as you can to bring the news that will thrill your recipient.

After all, Jacob was an old man by now.

Who knew how long he still had to live? Would it not have been a terrible tragedy to have such marvelous news to bring to him and to arrive a day too late? And even if Jacob were well, if you can shorten a person's grief by just one day, is it not important to do so?

The other brothers could take their time if they wanted to. Naftali couldn't wait. He has to get there and get there soon – in order to deliver this incredible good news. And so he ran.

And so should we. If you can bring joy to someone who needs it – whether it is by bringing that person good news or whether it is by bringing that person food or water or whatever it is that he needs to have – do it and do it fast!

Most of us mean well – but when it comes to *mitzvahs*, we tend to be too patient. We say: 'I'll do it, but not today,' or we say: 'It's cold outside,' or: 'It's hot outside,' or: 'There is a good movie on today' – so I'll do it tomorrow. And we forget that tomorrow may be too late.

And so the lesson we should learn from Naftali is that if you have the power to bring good news to someone who needs it, or if you have the power to do a good deed – do it now! Do it fast! For tomorrow may be too late.

And there is a third story that is found in the Midrash about a time when Naftali ran.

The Torah says that when Jacob died, Yosef received permission from the Pharaoh to go back to Canaan in order to bury his father. Four hundred Egyptian soldiers accompanied the funeral procession – perhaps to pay honor to Jacob, or perhaps to make sure that the sons came back to Egypt. We cannot say for sure which it was.

The sons of Jacob arrive at the Ma'arat Hamachpela, the burial cave where Abraham and Sarah, Isaac and Rebecca, are buried. And much to their surprise, they find their uncle, Esau, waiting for them there, with his armed guards, blocking the entrance to the cave.

Esau says to them: "Excuse me, gentlemen, but this cave is now mine. And there is no way that I am going to permit the body of your father, Jacob, to be buried here. Do you know what he did to me years ago? Do you know how he conned me into selling him my birthright? Do you know how he disguised himself as me, and got our father to give him the Blessing instead of me? Yes, I forgave him for what he did when we met after many years of separation, but I have thought it over and changed my mind. And so, I am not going to let you bury Jacob here in this place."

What should the brothers do?

What would you do if you were in their situation?

Picture the scene: the sons of Jacob are standing out there, in the heat, in front of the cave, standing there with their father's coffin – and there is no way that they are going to be able to persuade their uncle to let them bring it in.

And then one of them remembers. He says: "Wait a minute! There is a deed to this cave!" Just as we nowadays arrange for the purchase of a grave and for the details of a burial on a pre-need basis, so Jacob had done the same thing. He had brought the deed to the cave in Hebron with him when he went down to Egypt. He had put it in the vault, together with all his other important papers – his property will, his living will, and all the rest. And somehow, in the confusion, in their haste, when they were leaving Egypt, they had forgotten to take the deed with them.

What should they do?

Naftali said: "I'll get it!" And quick as a flash, before anyone could try to argue with him, before anyone could try to tell him that it might be dangerous to go back to Egypt, or that it might take too long to go there and back, Naftali had turned around, made sure his Nikes were properly tied, and was on the way.

He must have run for many days and nights, but he got there. When he arrived, he must have been out of breath and exhausted. But he went as quickly as he could to Jacob's safe, dialed the combination – which fortunately he knew by heart – opened the safe, pulled out the deed to the cave at Hebron, turned around, and raced back as fast as he could go.

He arrived, out of breath but triumphant. He rushed up to Esau, handed him the deed, and said: "Here it is! It says right here in black and white that this cave belongs to Father Jacob, that he got it from his father, Isaac, who got it from his father, Abraham. And it says right here that our father intended to be buried in this place. So would you kindly move aside, Uncle Esau, and let us bury him here, as he would want us to."

Esau read the document and realized that he had no choice. He moved aside, and the children of Jacob carried out the last good deed that they could do for their father. They buried him– in the same place as his father and his grandfather were buried – in the cave at Hebron.

What does this Midrash teach us?

I think it teaches us two things.

The first is that we better have OUR papers in order, and we better make sure that our children or our attorney or somebody knows where they are.

No one likes to think about these things – but death will come to each and every one of us – ready or not – and so we ought to prepare for it. And we ought to make sure that our children know our desires so that they do not have to guess what they are when the time comes.

And the second lesson that I think we should learn from this story is that we have a deed to the Land of Israel. We may not be able to occupy it all. There may be another people that lives there too. We may have to divide the land in order to live in peace with them.

That is a question for the people who live in Israel to decide, not for me. They may decide that it is worth the risk to give up some of the land in order to achieve peace. Or they may decide that there is no one to whom to entrust the land, and that they should keep it all for security reasons or until a generation of Arabs that is more trustworthy and more peaceful arises. That is for them to decide, not for me. I am not so smart as to presume that I can tell them from here what they should do, when it is their safety that is at stake.

But this I do know: that we need to remember that the Jewish people has a deed to this land – and that we must not leave this deed to linger in some forgotten safe deposit box somewhere. I am scared when I read the surveys that show that the young people of our community do not seem to feel the same intense connection to the land of Israel that our generation feels. I am worried when I realize how many young American Jews have never been to Israel. And I am concerned when I realize that their earliest memories of Israel are not the War of Independence or the Six Day War, which were both triumphant and dramatic events, but that their earliest memories of Israel are the Lebanon Wars or some other events that were not so dramatic or so triumphant. And that is why I think that projects like Birthright Israel and Masa and the gap year programs, and all the other educational programs that teach our young people to understand the connection between the land of Israel and ourselves are so important.

Naftali had to run all the way back to Egypt and rummage around in a safe deposit box in order to find the deed to his father's heritage. We don't have to do that, for we have the Torah, and we have many educational programs through which we can make the connection between us and the land of Israel real to our kids.

And we should take advantage of these programs, so that our claim to the land will not get lost – not among our children, and not among the children of the Israelis – who sometimes forget what the connection is between them and this land.

These then are the three lessons that I would have us learn today from "Naftali the Jogger," as I like to call him: that when someone needs help, you should run, not walk, to bring him help; that when you have good news to announce, you should run as fast as you can in order to bring it; and that there is a claim and a link between us and the land of Israel that must never get lost. And one more thing you should know: you should know that you have a deed to a heritage – to a heritage that has great wisdom in it – a heritage that has been guarded for you and transmitted to you down through the centuries, and therefore, you ought to know where that deed to that heritage is, so that you can produce it whenever and wherever it is needed.

And so the next time you drive with me, and you see me put my foot to the pedal a little bit more firmly than I should, remember that I am a descendent of Naftali, and do not be alarmed. Who knows? I may be on the way to doing a *mitzvah*, and therefore I may have the right to speed. Or I may be on the way to deliver some good news, and therefore I have the right to speed. Or I may be on the way to teach, which is a way of delivering a deed to someone who needs it, and so I may have the right to speed.

At least that is what I will try to tell the policeman if he catches me and wants to give me a ticket.

I hope that if this happens, that he will believe me, and let me off with just a warning.

And to this, let me add just one last word:

Let me say: Good luck and God bless to all of the joggers who are here today. May you run speedily, and may you run safely. And may you reach your goals – in the marathon, and in all the other races of your lives. May you, and we too, run to do many good deeds. May you, and we too, run to bring good news to those who wait so desperately to hear such news. And may you, and we too, know where our heritage is located, and know how to find it, and how to live by it for all the days to come.

Amen and Amen. And run well!

I Want Patience – and I Want it Now!

VA'EIRA

THIS MORNING'S SERMON – for reasons which will become clear in a few minutes – is dedicated to two groups. It is dedicated to the fans of the Chicago Cubs, and to the Jewish people.

Does everyone here know what these two groups have in common?

If not, listen to the sermon and you will find out.

But first, does everyone here remember where we left off in the reading of the Torah last week?

We left off at one of the saddest points in the life of Moses. Moses comes to Pharaoh and asks him to let the people of Israel go, and Pharaoh says: absolutely not. Pharaoh says to Moses: "Who is this god that I should listen to him?" And he orders Moses and Aaron thrown out of the palace. That would have been bad enough, but then Pharaoh summons the taskmasters of the Israelite people, and he says to them: "The reason why the Israelites listen to these outside agitators is because they have too much spare time." And so Pharaoh doubles the work load of the people. He says to them: "From now on you are going to have to produce the same number of bricks as you did before, but now you are going to have to gather the straw with which to make the bricks yourselves. And if you don't reach your daily quota of bricks, you will be beaten."

The leaders of the Israelites come out of the palace of Pharaoh after they have received these new orders, and they meet Moses and Aaron who are on their way into the palace. And they say to them:

"May the Lord judge you, for you have made us disgusting in the sight of Pharaoh and his servants. You have given them a sword with which to slay us. "

Can you imagine how Moses must have felt at that moment? Here he had given up a peaceful life as a shepherd in Midian in order to fight for his people – and now look at the results. Not only does Pharaoh refuse to listen to him; the people of Israel do not listen to him either.

And so Moses cries out to God: *Lama hareyota la'am ha'zeh, v'lama zeh shilachtani?*

He says to God: "Why have You brought harm upon this people? And why did You send me?

Ever since I came to Pharaoh to speak in Your Name, he has dealt worse with the people."

Vihatzeyl lo hitzaltah et amecha! – "And still You have not delivered Your people!"

And on that note, with that ringing accusation of God, the *sedra* ends.

When you read the last lines of that *sedra*, you are left with an image of Moses in total despair. He came to do good for his people, and he has only made things worse. And so Moses is ready to quit. He is ready to throw in the towel, and let God find somebody else to take his place if He wants to. He has had it with this frustrating task, in which not only Pharaoh but the people of Israel have turned against him. And so he screams out: "Why did You send me?"

And then comes the most striking line in this bitter accusation that Moses makes: *Vihatzeyl lo hitzaltah et amecha.* Let me translate it literally: *Vihatzeyl?* "You promised me that you would save them." *Lo hitzaltah,* "and You have not done so. Therefore I want to quit."

How long has Moses been at his task when he makes this statement? A week? A month at the most? He has not yet unleashed even the first of the ten plagues. And yet, he seems to feel that if he has not made an impact on Pharaoh and on his court by now, and if he has lost the confidence of the Israelites, and if he has ended up making things worse for them, and if God has so far done nothing to back him up, if, so far, God has not done any of the things that

He promised him that He would do, then he is disgusted, and he wants to quit.

And what is God's answer to this bitter speech of Moses'?

He says in the opening lines of this week's *sedra*: Oh, how I miss Abraham and Isaac and Jacob! Because I made many promises to them, and they never saw even one of those promises fulfilled and yet they had faith in Me.

I promised them that their people would be many. It did not happen in their lifetimes.

I promised them that their people would possess the Land of Canaan. Not in their lifetimes.

I promised them that their descendants would be a source of blessing to all the nations of the world. Not in their lifetimes.

None of the promises that I made to Abraham, Isaac and Jacob ever came true – at least not in their lifetimes.

And yet, they did not talk to me the way you do, Moses. They did not claim that I do not keep My word, the way you do, Moses. They trusted in Me, and they had faith that eventually I would fulfill the promises that I made to them, unlike you, Moses.

What is God saying in these opening words of today's Torah reading?

He is saying that if you want to be a leader of the Jewish people, you need to have the quality of patience. If things go slowly, if you do not succeed immediately, if you do not win on your first try, you must not give up and quit.

He is saying: Moses, you need to understand that you have signed up for a long hard battle. You have signed up to take the Israelites out of Egypt, which is very, very difficult, and you have also signed up to take Egypt out of the Israelites, which is even more difficult. And if you do not understand that this is only the beginning of the struggle, if you want to quit just because the first round has not gone well, then you are not fit to be the leader of the Jewish people.

Now do you understand why I said at the beginning of this sermon that this sermon is dedicated to the fans of the Chicago Cubs and to the Jewish people?

The reason is that the fans of the Chicago Cubs and the Jewish people have one thing in common. They have both demonstrated enormous patience.

The Cubs have failed to win the pennant or get into the World Series over and over and over again for many years. In fact, they hold the world record for the team that has failed to get to the World Series more times than any other team in either league. And yet, year after year after year, Chicago Cubs fans go out to cheer for their team. Year after year they keep hoping that this will be the year. And for this, they deserve our respect and our admiration.

And the Jewish people have shown that same quality of patience. When the whole world worshipped Caesar and claimed that he was a god, the Jewish people said no. When people claimed that a certain teacher who lived in Nazareth was the messiah, the Jewish people said no. When millions of people claimed that a man from Mecca was the messiah, the Jewish people said no. When people claimed that Shabtai Tsvi was the messiah, the Jewish people wavered and then said no. When people claimed that Karl Marx was the messiah, and that his torah would bring redemption to the world, the Jewish people said no.

We have held on to two claims down through the centuries. The first is that the messiah will someday come – and the second is that the messiah has not yet come. And it is that quality of patience, that ability to hold on and to wait, that has made the Jewish people what they are until this day.

And so, the lesson that I would have you learn today from the life of Moses is to be what he was not – at least not at the beginning of his career. The lesson that I would have you learn from the opening lines of today's *sedra* is to be patient if the goal is important, for great causes can never be achieved quickly.

If the goal had only been to bring the people of Israel from Egypt to the Promised Land, they could have gotten there in two weeks of hard marching at the most. But that was not the goal. The goal was to train a generation that would not panic when they entered the land. The goal was to train a generation that would be fit to live in the land. And to train this kind of a generation took forty years to achieve. Moses learned the hard way that there are no short cuts when you have a mighty and a complex goal.

And we must learn that lesson too. Many of us thought that all we had to do was remove Kaddafi and Iraq would be in order. And so we did, and we left a country that was so terribly divided that it could not be governed. And so it was with Syria and with Afghanistan. We thought we could win a victory and then go home. And we learned the hard way that every solution leads to new problems, and that it is sometimes easier to go into a country than it is to get out of it.

I am not going to talk about politics or international affairs today, for what do I know about these things? I am here to talk about the one task that every one of us struggles with all the days of our lives. I am here to talk about the task of becoming a *mentsch*. I am here to talk about the task of doing *teshuvah*. I am here to talk, not about the task of defeating others but about the task of perfecting ourselves. And I am here to tell you that there is no greater task, and there is no more difficult task than this.

Sometimes the task of perfecting ourselves is two steps forward and one step back. And sometimes the task of perfecting ourselves is one step forward and two steps back. And so it takes enormous patience. It means falling – and getting up again. It means trying and failing – and trying again. It means realizing that there are no quick solutions. That is why the *Mussar* literature of our people is so full of instructions on how to discipline ourselves, and on how to overcome the drives within us. If it were easy, we would not be told how to fight the pressures inside us in so many ways. As Rabbi Israel Salanter, the founder of the *Mussar* movement, put it: "It is easier to go through the sixty-six volumes of the Talmud than it is to overcome one bad quality."

Even patience is a quality that only comes to us, if we try for it again and again and again. I am sure you all know the old joke about the man who comes to realize how important patience is, and so he cries out to God, and says: "Lord, please give me patience – and please do so immediately!"

There is a legend in Jewish history that very few people know about. It is the legend of the tribe of Ephraim. The legend is that when God decreed that the people must stay in the wilderness for a whole generation, the tribe of Ephraim refused to accept this decree. And so they broke loose and headed for the Promised Land.

They decided that they would conquer the land – with or without the permission of God. You can understand why they did it. Who wants to stay in the wilderness for a whole generation until they have improved their character and learned how to live? They went – and they were defeated on the way. And their bodies remained in the wilderness ever afterwards in order to serve as a warning and a lesson to others who might make their mistake.

Let me be clear: There is a time for impatience. When your people's suffering is unbearable, you cannot, and you should not, preach patience. When your people need water, you cannot and you should not tell them to be patient. But if the struggle is for a mighty goal, if the struggle is for a goal that can only be achieved by enormous hard work, then you should and you must teach them to be patient.

And so this is my message to you today – to you and to myself: that we should try, and when we fail, that we should try again, that we should work upon ourselves, and not give up, no matter how frustrating or difficult the task may be. My message is: ask the person who used to be a chain smoker and who no longer smokes; or ask the person who used to be addicted to drugs or to alcohol, and has overcome these temptations; ask them and they will tell you. They will tell you that you cannot quit in a day. They will tell you that it took hard work and that it took determination. They will tell you that it took patience and the ability to try again in order for them to finally overcome these destructive drives. And they can tell you that the battle is never over. I know one person who gave up smoking twenty years ago, and yet she tells me that there is no day in which she does not feel the temptation to smoke again. And she says that she knows that if she gives in to the temptation just once – she would soon be a chain smoker again.

So patience is what I ask of you today.

And now, to those of you who have listened to this sermon patiently, and who thought that it would never end, let me reward your patience by saying that this sermon is now over.

A "Fowl" Matter

BO

BEFORE I BEGIN, let me ask you this question: Does everyone here realize how lucky you are to have me as your interim rabbi?

Does everyone here realize that, for the paltry half a million dollars a week that you pay me, that you get a rabbi who is renowned throughout the area for his wisdom and for his judgment – not to mention his modesty?

Does everyone here realize that I am known throughout this area for my ability to resolve controversial issues?

Just in case there is someone here who is not aware of my virtues, let me tell you about a case that I have been called upon to mediate this week.

I was sitting at home last Sunday, minding my own business, when the phone rang.

I answered it, and I said: "Hello."

I figured that that was a good way to begin a conversation.

The man on the other end of the telephone said: "Is this Rabbi Jack Riemer?"

I said: "Yes."

Then he said: "Are you the Rabbi Jack Riemer who is the interim rabbi of Congregation Anshe Shalom?"

I said: "Yes I am." I love when people ask me questions that I can answer either yes or no. Usually, when they ask me a question in Jewish Law, I have to say that there is a majority opinion and a minority opinion, or some people say it is permitted and some people say it is forbidden, but to this question I could answer without equivocation: yes.

Then he said: "I am calling on behalf of our condo association in order to ask if you would help us resolve a dispute. We would like you to agree to serve as an arbitrator, because we have heard that you are a very wise man."

I didn't know what to say when he said that he had heard that I was a very wise man. If I said yes, I would be boasting. And if I said no – I would be lying.

So I said: "What is this dispute that you want me to arbitrate? And why would you want me to be the mediator? I am not a lawyer, and I am not the son of a lawyer, and I know very little about condo laws and regulations."

I said: "Why don't you try Senator George Mitchell instead? He just made peace between Northern and Southern Ireland. Maybe he can make peace within your condominium association."

The man on the telephone said: "We thought of him, but we decided that anyone can make peace between the North and the South in Ireland. This job is much more difficult and requires more skill than that job did."

I said: "Well, in that case, why don't you try to get Richard Holbrook? He just made peace in the Balkans, and so I am sure that he must be very competent."

And the man on the telephone said to me: "We thought of him too, but we decided that making peace in the Balkans was easy. Anyone could do that. We are looking for someone who is really smart, someone who is so smart that he can make peace within our condo association. And besides, we checked, and neither George Mitchell nor Richard Holbrook is available, and we found out that, if they were available, they would charge a lot of money, and so, we decided to ask you instead."

I did not think that was such a big compliment, and so I said: "You think that George Mitchell and Richard Holbrook are busy???? I am the interim rabbi of Congregation Anshe Shalom and that is a much bigger job than making peace in Ireland or in the Balkans is any day! Do you realize how big a job I have? Do you have any idea how many questions of Jewish law I get every day? Do you realize how many responsibilities I have in my pastoral work alone? So, I am sorry but I don't think I can take this case."

I was about to hang up, when this man tried one more argument, and this one persuaded me to take the case. He said: "Rabbi, you have to do this, because this controversy is tearing our condo association apart. If we don't resolve this matter, it will go to court. And if it goes to court, it will be a *shandeh* for the whole neighborhood. And besides – do you know who will benefit if we go to court?

The lawyers!

So will you, please, please, please agree to serve as the arbitrator of this case?"

To that, I had no answer, and so, reluctantly, reluctantly, reluctantly, I agreed to serve as the arbitrator of this case. And we are going to have our first – and I hope our last – meeting tomorrow afternoon at three o'clock.

My wife gave me permission to do this – but only on one condition. The condition is that the hearing has to be over no later than six o'clock, because that is when the Super Bowl begins, and she says that the Super Bowl is a holiday that is more important than any condo association or anything else, and so she said that I better be home in time for that – or else.

And so, tomorrow at three o'clock, I, together with two lawyers, who will represent the two parties involved in this dispute, are going to have our first meeting.

And it is going to be our task to bring about peace and harmony within this condo association. I have a hunch that compared to accomplishing that, Mr. Mitchell's job making peace in Ireland, and Mr. Holbrook's job making peace in the Balkans, is going to seem easy.

I can't give you all the details . . . but I will tell you that this dispute is a fowl matter. A fowl matter. Fowl is spelled "f-o-w-l," not f-o-u-l. This is a dispute that has come about over the behavior of certain ducks.

Does everyone here know where and what Boca Pointe is?

Boca Pointe is a community made up of many different developments. Some of these developments have been planned as homes for young families and some of these developments have been planned as homes for senior citizens. This is what the heads of the Boca Point Condo Association explained to me when they asked me to take the case.

They said: Boca Pointe is a development that has many subdivisions within it. One of these subdivisions is a place called Princeton Place, and another one of these subdivisions is a place called Palm Shores. Princeton Place is a subdivision which is intended for young families who have children. It has two-story houses, and its yards have jungle gyms and swings and sand boxes in them. If you drive up or down the streets of Princeton Place you will see kids riding bicycles and nannies wheeling baby carriages. It is a place that was built for families that have children.

On the north side of Princeton Place – just across the lake – is a development called Palm Shores. This is a development that is intended for seniors. In fact, you cannot buy a home in Palm Shores unless you are fifty-five years of age or older. The houses in Palm Shores are smaller. And there is not a single swing or sandbox in sight. If you drive up or down the streets of Palm Shores you will not see a single child on a bicycle or a single nanny wheeling a baby carriage. You may see people walking with canes, or you may see people being wheeled about by their caretakers, but you will not see anyone on a bicycle or on skates or in a baby carriage . . . not in Palm Shores.

On a warm afternoon, the streets of Princeton Place hum with kids skateboarding, bicycling, or just hanging around. Palm Shores, however, is quiet during the day, except for the occasional car going in or out.

The two communities got along fairly well until recently. And then the trouble started. An incident took place a few months ago which threatens to tear the two communities of Princeton Place and Palm Shores apart. This is what happened:

There is a woman whose name I am not going to mention. Let me just call her Plaintiff A. Mrs. Plaintiff A lives in Princeton Place. Mrs. Plaintiff A is a lawyer by training, and she is now a stay-at-home mom. When she and her family moved into this area a few years ago, one of the big attractions for them was the lake.

"We love to walk to the lake with our two-year-old child in order to feed the ducks," Mrs. Plaintiff A says. "It reminds me of when I was a child, and my father used to take me to feed the ducks. He was the one who taught me to love nature."

One day, a few months ago, she says that she and her child were innocently minding their own business, tossing pieces of bread to the ducks, when a woman in a golf cart drove up and, according to Mrs. Plaintiff A, this is what happened:

This woman, whom I shall call Mrs. Plaintiff B, started yelling at Mrs. Plaintiff A and her child. "You're trespassing!" she said. "Get out of here! And don't let me ever catch you feeding the ducks again! It is against the condo regulations."

I must tell you that I wish that some of these people kept the Torah as strictly as they keep the condo regulations, but this is what this woman is reported to have said. It is claimed that she said these words in a loud and angry voice: "Feeding ducks is forbidden because it encourages them to stay, and if they stay, they will end up spoiling our lawns," she said. And as she said this, it is claimed that she pulled a big thick book out of her purse, and opened it up, and pointed to the page in the condo regulations that forbids feeding the ducks. "Do you see what it says here," she said, pointing her finger at this woman and her child, "right here in black and white, on page 537, it says that you are not allowed to feed ducks within this development!"

This woman evidently carried this book around with her wherever she went – just in case something came up that was a violation of the rules of the condo association.

Mrs. Plaintiff A claims that this woman's voice was so loud, and that her attitude was so hostile, that her little boy burst into tears.

We don't know if this is true or not. Mrs. Plaintiff B denies it. She claims that she spoke nicely at first, and only after Mrs. Plaintiff A refused to stop feeding the ducks did she raise her voice. And we don't know which one of them to believe – because there were no witnesses to this altercation – none except the two-year-old child, and we don't know whether he can testify or not. We don't know if he is too young to testify or whether it is age discrimination if we don't let him testify. That will have to be determined by the arbitration committee when it meets tomorrow.

The woman turned out to be one of those whom people living in Florida call "the condo commandoes." Do you know what a condo commando is? These are people who see it as their self-appointed task in life to make sure that all the laws of the condominium are strictly observed.

Do any of you have condo commandoes where you live? If so, you know what I mean.

Mrs. Plaintiff A says that she feels very badly that her efforts to teach her child the joys of nature are being thwarted. But the problem is that what she and her friends who live in Princeton Place, see as communing with nature, the people who live in Palm Shores see as a great nuisance.

Mrs. Plaintiff A went to the meeting of the condo association to complain about what happened to her and her child. She threatened to sue for trauma and psychlogical damage that had been done to her child by this condo commando. But the President of the Palm Shores Homeowners Association told her that the woman who tried to stop her from feeding the ducks was right – according to the condo regulations. He said to her: "I am sorry, but these ducks damage our lawns. And they frighten people. And feeding them encourages them to stay. And therefore, it is against the condo rules to feed them. And if you continue to feed these ducks, you are going to be fined – each and every time that you do!"

And so there began a "fowl" campaign between the young people who live in Princeton Place and the older people who live in Palm Shores. The young people who live in Princeton Place have accused the older people who live in Palm Shores of putting out poison for the ducks. But the older people who live in Palm Shores vehemently deny the accusation. And they too are threatening to sue – for the damage to their lawns and for the stress and the emotional trauma that this incident is causing them.

Now it gets interesting. Lawyers – and people in the congregation who live in condominiums – please pay attention. It turns out that the lake which divides the people of Palm Shores and Princeton Place – physically and legally – is under the jurisdiction of a "master association," which has authority over the boards of directors of both Princeton Place and Palm Shores. And therefore, at least according to the ruling of the board of the Master Association, Mrs. Plaintiff A and her child were not trespassing – not at all – and therefore no condo commando had the right to tell them that they were.

But that ruling is being contested by both sides. The woman from Princeton Place says: "What kind of a role model for my child was this condo commando who yelled at us?" But the condo commando says: "I spoke politely at first, and only afterwards did I yell. And what kind of a role model is a mother who is told not to do something, and just goes ahead and keeps doing it?"

As I said, there were no witnesses – except the child – and so it is hard to determine the facts in this case. Did the condo commando identify herself as an authority first? And did she speak politely first before she began to yell? And if she did, would the mother have listened? We cannot really say for sure.

But the young people of Princeton Place are threatening to sue the people of Palm Shores, and the people of Palm Shores are threatening to sue the people of Princeton Place. And that was what led the Condo Association to ask me – together with two lawyers – one representing each side – to see if we could resolve this matter without it going to court, because both sides agree that if it went to court it would be a *shandeh* for all of Boca Pointe – and no one wants that.

And so this is why they came to me and my colleagues and asked us to mediate this "fowl" matter.

It is our job to try to somehow resolve this matter, without – if you will excuse the expression – without "ruffling any more feathers."

And so I have been thinking all week about what I should do when this case comes before us tomorrow.

I don't know anything at all about condo rules and regulations, but I do know a little bit of Torah, and so I thought about this question, and I asked myself: What would the Torah say to the two parties in this dispute?

And when I meet with the two sides in this dispute tomorrow, do you know what I am going to tell them?

I am going to tell them that I believe that if both sides in this controversy had been in *shul* today, and that if they had paid attention to what it says in today's Torah reading, that I believe this whole matter could have been resolved peacefully – without lawyers and without law suits and without fuss and without feathers. Well, maybe not without feathers, but certainly without fuss.

Do you remember the scene that we read about in the Torah this morning? It is the one in which Pharaoh is on the ropes. He is battered and bruised and exhausted. Plague after plague after plague has devastated his country. His people are suffering beyond description. The economy of Egypt has been demolished. And so Pharaoh is finally ready to negotiate. He says to Moses: "Ok, ok, ok already. You can go for three days to worship your God as you have asked. But tell me: *mi vami haholchim*? Who exactly do you want to take with you?"

And Moses answers: *Binureynu u'vizkeineynu neylech* – "with our young and with our old together we will go."

At which point, Pharaoh says: "Out of the question!" And he throws them out of the palace.

Moses evidently believed that you cannot worship God, and that you cannot have a real community, unless both groups – the young and the old – work together and serve God together and respect each other, and recognize each other's rights and needs.

And so it seems to me that the older people who live in Palm Shores have to understand that the young people who live in Princeton Place need to have the lake, and need to have the ducks. For them, the ducks are a delight.

But the young people who live in Princeton Place have to understand that for the older people who live in Palm Shores, these ducks are not a delight. They are a detriment.

One side is right. There is something wrong with a community that values its lawns more than it does living creatures. There is something wrong with a community that values perfect lawns more than it does a child's opportunity to interact with the nature. But the other side is also right! There is no reason why so many ducks should be permitted that they become a danger or an annoyance to the residents on the other side of the lake. There has to be – in Princeton Place and in Palm Shores – and in many other places in our society as well – a willingness to compromise, and a sense of respect for each other's rights. Both sides have to understand what Moses said centuries ago: that if you want to serve God, you must go with your young and your old together.

And therefore, this is the proposal that I am going to make when our arbitration committee meets tomorrow afternoon:

I am going to propose that the people of Palm Shores agree that there should be ducks, so that the children can play with them. And I am going to propose that the people of Princeton Place agree to limit the number of ducks that are permitted in the lake, and that the people of Princeton Place agree to pay for a fence to be put in the middle of the lake, so as to keep the ducks from getting out and doing harm to the lawns of the residents of Palm Shores. If the Israelis can put up a wall to prevent the Arabs of the West Bank from entering their land and endangering their lives, and if the United States can think about putting up a wall to keep illegal immigrants from coming in from Mexico, I see no reason why the people of Princeton Place should not be able to put up a wall in order to prevent the ducks from entering an area where they can do harm and cause damage. And I think that they should be the ones who pay for this divider.

I believe that if these two proposals of mine are accepted – both sides can come away feeling that they have gained something and given up something so that they can live together in peace and harmony.

And now, will you permit me to take this teaching and apply it, not only to the people who live in Boca Pointe, but to all of us who are here today.

When you and I were growing up, there were no such things as planned communities – one only for the young and one only for the old. We lived on streets that were a mixture of young and old, and so we learned to get along. For example, if I was bad, and my parents were busy, Mr. Pinuchi, who was our next door neighbor, would hit me for them. I grew up on a block where Jews and Christians, Republicans and Democrats, young and old, all lived together, and we learned to get along. But now, we live in these carefully segregated communities, separated not only by age but by race and by income as well. We drive to work from the suburbs on these highways, and we are scarcely aware of the slums that we whiz by that adjourn the highways on which we travel. The only way you can tell that you are driving by a neighborhood where Blacks live is by the

sign that you see that says: 'Next exit: Martin Luther King Drive.'"
By living in these segregated neighborhoods, whether they are segregated by income or by age or by race – we make ourselves less
aware and less able to understand each other's needs and rights and
concerns. This is what happens – forgive the pun – when birds of a
feather flock together.

But that has to change. Do you know that California is already
a state in which the Whites are no longer the majority? Asians and
Blacks and Hispanics make up more than half the population of the
state. And demographers predict that by 2050, the rest of the country will be that way too. There was a time when New Yorkers would
go to Puerto Rico for vacation. Now they don't have to. Puerto Rico
has come to New York.

Do you remember one of the most famous sentences of recent
years? It was at the Democratic convention of 2004. A young,
unknown, newly elected Senator from Illinois named Barak Obama
gave the keynote address. And in it he said: "The time has come to
understand that there is no longer a blue state America and there
is no longer a red state America. There is only a United States of
America." That man went on to become the President of the United
States four years later, and that unforgettable line is one of the reasons that he rose to national attention.

And so this is the line that I would have us learn from today's
Torah reading. Whether we live in gated communities, or in
planned communities, or in the city or in the suburbs, we all live in
one society. We live in an America that now has more Hispanics in it
than it has Blacks, and that has more immigrants coming to it from
Asia and Africa every year than it has coming from Europe. And
therefore every group in this land – the old and the young, the rich
and the poor, the white and the black – must learn how to compromise and dialogue with each other or else we will not survive.

So let the words of Moses in today's Torah reading speak to us all
today. Whether we are young parents with small children, or older
people who have chosen to live in a neighborhood that caters to our
needs – let us learn from Moses to go through life *binureynu u'vizkeineynu* – "with our young and our old," working together, respect-
ing each other's needs, and recognizing each other's concerns.

So this is the two part proposal that I am going to make to the people of Princeton Place and Palm Shores when we meet tomorrow: that the ducks be allowed to stay, and that the young people be allowed to feed them – but that there be a fence in the middle of the lake and that the young people pay for it. I think it is a reasonable proposal, and I hope that both sides accept it.

I will let you know how my proposal is received next Shabbat when we meet again. Wish me luck, for I know that my task is much harder than the one that was faced by George Mitchell or Richard Holbrook. They only had to make peace between countries that had been at war for centuries. I have to make peace within a condominium and that is probably much harder. But pray for me, and wish me well.

The 'You-Can-Do-It'ers

I MADE UP A NEW WORD today.

But before I tell you what it is, I want to ask you a couple of questions.

The first one is an easy one: Who was Aaron?

That was easy. He was the Kohen Gadol, and he was the brother of Moses.

Now let me ask you a question that is a little bit harder. Who was Nachshon?

Nachshon was the first person who went into the sea before it split. He is the hero of today's *sedra*.

Now let me ask you a really hard question.

Who was Elisheva?

Hardly anyone raised their hands, and I am not surprised. And yet I think that Elisheva was one of the most important people of the generation that went out of Egypt. She is important for two reasons: first, because of her *yichus*, and second, because of her character.

Listen to her *yichus*:

First of all, she was the daughter of Aminadav, who was the head of the tribe of Judah. His tribe was the one that marched in front when the Israelites travelled through the wilderness. And so I picture her walking next to him, right up front, holding his hand, and feeling so proud to be travelling next to her famous father.

Second, she was the wife of Aaron, the Kohen Gadol, the one who was in charge of the *Mishkan*, and the one who officiated at the sacrifices. I picture him going by on Yom Kippur on the way to the *Mishkan* to perform the special sacrifices of the day, dressed in all his splendor, and I picture her standing with the crowd along the way, waving and cheering for him as he went by. I picture her turning to the people around her in the crowd, and saying: "That's my husband there!" as he went by.

And third, she was the sister of Nachson ben Aminadav, the person who went into the Red Sea first, before it split open. He was the one who was the hero on that day. He went in first – and then all the people followed him. And I imagine her standing on the beach that day, beaming with pride as her big brother went into the water. And I picture her breathing a sigh of relief when the waters opened up before him.

That is what you call *yichus*, isn't it? To be the wife of the High Priest, to be the daughter of the head of the tribe of Judah, and to be the sister of the hero who saved the Jewish people? That's *yichus*! If someone today was the daughter of the governor of New York State, and was also the wife of the most famous minister in the country, and was also the sister of Neal Armstrong – the first man to ever set foot on the moon – can you imagine how famous that person would be? That person would need a full-time staff just to handle the requests for interviews that she would get from the media every day. Isn't that so?

And yet, we know almost nothing at all about Elisheva. We don't know how her father felt about her. We don't know why Aaron chose to marry her. We don't know anything at all about her relationship to her brother, Nachshon. We don't know anything about Elisheva – not from the Bible, and not from the Midrash. We know almost nothing at all about Elisheva – up until our time.

And therefore, a few years ago, Danny Siegel – the poet and famous *tzedakah* teacher – wrote a midrash about Elisheva that I want to share with you today. He wrote it because he was bothered by the almost total silence about her that is found in the tradition. And I want to share his midrash with you today, because I believe that there is a lesson in the life of Elisheva that we all need to learn if we are to live good lives.

Danny Siegel says that Elisheva started out as Nachshon's kid sister. She was a few years younger than he was, and so he took care of her. He walked her to school. He looked out for her when other kids picked on her. He helped her with her homework. And whenever she was upset, he would calm and comfort her. After all, travelling through the wilderness, together with thousands and thousands of other people, and with cattle and goats and sheep to look after, was enough to cause anyone to go a little bit crazy once in a while. And so, whenever Elisheva got upset, Nachshon was there to put a reassuring arm on her shoulder and calm her down.

And then do you know what happened? The same thing that happens to all little children happened to her: Elisheva grew up! Nachshon did not know exactly when it happened, but one day he looked up – and his little sister was no longer so little. And she no longer cried or misbehaved the way little children do. All of a sudden, Elisheva had become a young woman, who was smart, and mature, and able to take care of herself!

And then came the day when the people of Israel stood in front of the Red Sea. The Egyptians were chasing after them, and the sea was in front of them, and they were trapped in between.

What should they do?

If they stayed where they were, the Egyptians would recapture them. If they went forward into the sea, they would drown. What should they do?

According to the Midrash, Nachshon ben Aminadav took his life in his hands and jumped into the water. And then, and only then, only after he had jumped into the water, did the waters split and dry land appear.

The question is: Where did Nachshon get the courage that it must have taken for him to go into the water? I don't know about you, but if I had been there, I don't think that I would have had the courage to go first. Once he went in, it was easy for others to follow after him, but where did Nachshon get the courage that it must have taken to go first?

Danny Siegel's answer is that Elisheva was standing next to Nachshon at that moment. She looked up at him with those admiring eyes with which she had always looked up to her big brother, and she said just four words to him. She said: "You can do it!" And when he heard those four words: "You can do it," Nachshon jumped into the sea, without hesitation, because he did not want to disappoint his kid sister. If she said that he could do it, then he felt that he could do it, and so he jumped into the water, and, sure enough, the waters split, and the people of Israel were saved – all because of Elisheva.

And that is why Aaron, the Kohen Gadol, married her. Most people saw him as a very dignified person. They saw him dressed in his royal robes. They saw him with the miter, and the *urim v'tumim*, and the breastplate, and all the other finery that he wore. They had no idea that underneath his robes, Aaron was a human being who had all the insecurities that every human being has. "What if I make a mistake?" he often asked himself. "What if I do something wrong? Won't I bring disgrace down, not only on myself, but on the whole people of Israel who depend on me?"

Aaron was an insecure, apprehensive person, as any of us are, and so, when he met Elisheva, and when he heard about what she had done for her brother, he said to himself: This is the kind of woman that I need! And this is why he married her.

That is Danny Siegel's theory as to why Elisheva is so important to the story. He suggests that she was the one who gave her brother the courage to go first, and that she was the one who gave Aaron the courage that he needed in order to be the Kohen Gadol of the people of Israel.

According to his midrash, Elisheva was the first "you-can-do-it'er" in Jewish history. And so that is the word that I have created with which to describe her.

I don't know if Danny Siegel is right or not, but I would like to say that all of us need someone like Elisheva in our lives today. We all live in such complicated and such demanding times that we need someone who believes in us, and who gives us the courage and the confidence that it takes to believe in ourselves.

And I hope that I don't get into trouble for saying this: I don't mean to denigrate the equal rights that women have achieved in our time, and I don't mean, *chas v'shalom*, to minimize or criticize feminism – I really don't – but I must say that down through the centuries, and even today, it is the women who have been the ones who have said: "You can do it" – to their husbands, to their children, and to their grandchildren.

Think of Pat Nixon or of Rosalynn Carter or of Nancy Reagan – and what image comes to your mind?

You think of adoring women, looking up soulfully at their husbands, while they spoke. But Hillary Clinton and Michelle Obama are of a different generation. They do not stand docilely by, while the spotlight is on their husbands. They speak too – and sometimes they speak as well as their husbands – or even better.

And yet, I still think of the image of these women of the previous generation, who, at least in public, seemed to be such docile admirers and unquestioning followers of their husbands. And I wonder: no one can say for sure, because none of us were there, but I wonder if these presidents ever had moments of self-doubt, moments in which they were just not sure that they were up to the enormous demands that the office of the presidency imposed on them – and if so, I wonder if these women were the ones who said to them: "you can do it."

I hope they were, because every person who takes on supremely difficult and demanding tasks has to have such a person at his side, who gives him strength and who tells him that he can do whatever he has to do.

Mothers had this role in the lives of many of us. Do you remember what it was like when you had to play a solo at a school assembly, or when you had to say a few words in front of the whole school when you were a child? You were nervous, but then you cleared your throat, and looked over to where your mother was sitting, and caught her glance of encouragement, and when you saw that glance on her face, you were able to calm down and do what you had to do.

And perhaps this is the role of grandparents. All children may not be above average, but all children who have a grandparent rooting for them know that there is at least one person who thinks they are special, and who believes that they can do whatever they have to do – no matter what.

And now, let me make one more point. I say this, because I do not want to be criticized by the women who are here today, and because I do not want to be accused of believing that women, and only women, have this role of being the encourager. In an age when women can do anything they want, I can understand why they might be offended if they thought that this was my only image of their role in our lives. So let me tell you this story, which demonstrates that you don't have to be a woman to be an Elisheva in somebody's life.

We had a close friend, Rabbi Bernard Lipnick, *zichrono l'vracha*. Bernie was a very talented person in many areas of life. He was a fine rabbi and a good educator. He was an excellent administrator and he was very capable with his hands as well as with his mind. When he retired, he moved to California, and there he built his own home, with his own hands, doing the electrical work and the carpentry and all the other things that go into building a house, and he did each of these things very well.

And then, some years later, we moved here, and we bought a home. It was a lovely home, but it needed considerable work. It needed repairs and reconstruction. It needed a whole new kitchen, and lots of other things. And so, my wife Sue was overwhelmed by the demands of the house. How was she, who had never done any of these things before in her life, going to supervise the reconstruction of this house?

And then the Lipnicks came to visit. Sue told Bernie how overwhelmed she felt at this task, and she said that she was going to hire a contractor to supervise this project, even though she knew that contractors are expensive.

Bernie was not the kind of person who was given to flattery or to giving someone undeserved praise. But he knew Sue well, and he had great respect for her intelligence and her ability to organize things. He had seen her undertake many projects before, and he had seen her do them very well.

And so he looked at her, and just said in a calm and reassuring voice: "Sue, you can do this." And when she heard him say these words, the fear inside her subsided, and Sue said: "Okay. If you really think that I can do this, then I will."

And she did.

The house we live in is a testimony to Sue's ability to organize and direct and plan. But if you ask her, I think that she would say that it is also a tribute to Bernie Lipnick's judgment of her abilities, and to his confidence in her. When he said: "You can do this," the butterflies inside her calmed down, and she decided that, if he, who knows so much about building, thinks that she can do this, then perhaps she can. And so she did.

I tell you this story today, not only in order to boast about my wife and her talents, but in order to make the point that all of us need an Elisheva in our lives, and that all of us can be Elishevas to each other, and that men can be Elishevas just as much as women can.

And so, if you know someone who has ability, but who is not sure that he or she can do the task that faces them, think of what Elisheva did for her brother and for her husband. Think of how she was the one behind the scenes who gave Nachshon the courage and the confidence to leap into the waters before they split. And resolve that you will be an Elisheva to others who need an encouraging word from you, and pray that if and when you ever need an Elisheva in your life, that there will be someone – male or female does not matter – but may there be an Elisheva in your life. May there be someone at your side who says to you: I bet you can!

And one last thought, if I may. There are lots of definitions of God, and there are lots of different definitions of what God does for us, in our tradition. This morning, may I add one more? God is the great "you-can-do-it'er" in our lives. God is the One who gives us the courage and the confidence to do what needs to be done, even when we are afraid to try. God does not do things for us, and God does not do things instead of us, at least not very often. But God is the One who encourages us, and who enables us, and who gives us the strength and the will to do that which is right and necessary to do.

God is the great "You-can-do-it'er" in our lives.

The Super Bowl and the *Sedra*

YITRO

I WANT TO TALK TO YOU today about the great catastrophe – the terrible catastrophe – that took place this past Sunday afternoon.

If you are one of the hundred thousand people who were there, or if you are one of the hundred and forty million people who watched the Super Bowl this past Sunday, you know what I am referring to.

Some of you are laughing, but I am very serious. For the people of Seattle, what happened this past Sunday afternoon was a calamity – and a catastrophe. The Seattle Seahawks were four points behind as the fourth quarter drew to a close. And then, by a fluke, one of their players somehow caught a ball that bounced around and that no one believed he could catch, and a few minutes later, they were on the Patriot's one yard line – with thirty seconds left in the game. They had one of the very best runners in the country in Marshawn Lynch. If Lynch could just push his way across the line and fall forward, the Seahawks would be the winners of the Super Bowl.

A hundred thousand fans who were at the stadium, and a hundred and forty million people who were watching the game on television, held their breath. It was second down, and only a yard to go.

And what did the Seahawks do?

Darrell Bevell, who was the offensive coordinator of the Seahawks, gave the signal – not to run – but to pass. Russell Wilson, the Seattle quarterback, obeyed instructions, and threw the ball. And Malcom Butler of the Patriots – who had never intercepted a ball before in his entire career – Malcom Butler intercepted the ball half a foot away from the goal line, and in twenty-five more seconds, the game was over. The Patriots had won. The Seahawks had lost.

There was great mourning in Seattle on Sunday night. The team slunk back in the middle of the night. No one was there to welcome them at the airport. There was no cheering and no excitement when they got off the plane. They pulled their hats down over their faces, and hoped that no one would recognize them as they went to get their luggage. The Seahawks came home in disgrace.

Meantime, on the other side of the country, there was a ticker tape parade to welcome the Patriots home to Boston. The parade had to be postponed for two days because of the snowstorm that hit Boston on Sunday, but there was no way that Boston was going to cancel this historic occasion when their team came home. The weather in Boston on Wednesday was seven degrees below zero, and there were piles of snow all over the streets, and yet more than a hundred thousand people came out and stood in the cold for hours to cheer for their team. And if you saw the crowd go wild with enthusiasm when Malcom Butler went by, you would agree that if he had announced that he was going to run for President of the United States that day, he would have won by a landslide – at least in the city of Boston. There is no doubt in my mind about that.

And Darrell Bevell, the coordinator who called that play? Do you know where he is today?

Neither do I.

No one knows where he is today.

Rumor has it that he slunk back to Scottsdale, the town where he was born, which is about twenty miles away from Glendale, where the game was played, and that he has not been seen since. No one answers the phone at the house where it is believed he is staying. No one comes out to get the mail. Darrell Bevell is evidently in hiding. All the good plays that he called in his long and distinguished career as an offensive coach have been forgotten, and he is now in permanent disgrace because of that one play that he called that went wrong. If that play had succeeded, he would have gone down in history as the smartest coach in the history of the league. But because the play that he called failed, he can no longer show his face in public.

Why do I talk about Darrell Bevell today and the mistake that he made? What does what this man did have to do with the Torah that I am supposed to teach on Shabbat? Am I *meshugah*? Or is there a connection between this sport event and the portion of the Torah that we have read today?

I think that there is a connection.

This is the day when we read the *Aseret Hadibrot* – the Ten Fundamental Statements on which all of human civilization is based.

Nine of the Ten Commandments we all understand and we all accept. That you should not murder, that you should not steal, that you should not commit adultery, that you should honor your parents, that you should not envy, that you should not take God's Name in vain, that you should honor the Sabbath – these commandments we all understand and accept.

But there is one commandment in the list that seems trivial and irrelevant to many of us. The Second Commandment is: "Thou shalt not make a graven image of anything that is on the face of the earth or in the sky above or in the sea below – you shall not bow down to it, or worship it for I the Lord am a zealous God." That commandment seems to many of us to be outdated, and even, if I dare say so, petty. Who do you know nowadays who makes an idol and bows down to it? Who do you know who makes a graven image? And if nobody does, then why do we still need this commandment?

The answer is that long ago the Sages of the Talmud taught us that this is not what the Second Commandment means. You are allowed to make a statue, if you want to. You are allowed to make a painting if you want to. Of course you can. That is not forbidden. What you cannot do is take anything of this world – anything on the earth or in the sky or in the sea – and worship it. You cannot take anything of this world – and make it the be-all and the end-all of your existence. And if you do, you violate the Second Commandment.

This is the definition of idolatry.

I have given some controversial sermons in my day, but I think that what I am about to say may be the most controversial sermon that I have ever given. But let me stick my neck out, and let me say what I believe – and if I get fired for what I am about to say. . . *nu*.

Does everyone here know where the word "fan" comes from? We talk about a football fan or a baseball fan, but where does the word "fan" come from? Do you know?

The word "fan" comes from the word "fanatic."

And do you know why some people are called fans?

It is because, even though they may say that they are not religious, even though they may say that they are non-believers – it is clear if you watch the way that they behave at the stadium, that they are fanatics. If you listen to the way they scream when their team scores a touchdown, and if you watch the way they carry on when they disagree with the referee, and if you watch the way their faces turn red, and the way their blood pressure goes up when their team loses, you will know that these people are fanatics.

I learned this truth from one of the local undertakers recently. We were driving out to the cemetery together for a funeral, and I happened to mention to him that in my opinion, some of the people who go to the games have become fanatics. And he said to me: "Oh, really, if that is what you think, let me show you something when we get to the cemetery."

And sure enough, after the burial service was over, he took me for a walk, and he showed me some of the tombstones that are found at the Star of David Cemetery.

He showed me a number of tombstones that I had never noticed before. He showed me tombstones – of Jews – in a Jewish cemetery – that have the insignia of the Yankees or the Marlins or the Dodgers or the Giants inscribed on them. He showed me tombstones that have a gold club or a catcher's mitt inscribed on them. And I must tell you: when he showed me these tombstones, I was shocked.

I can remember – perhaps some of you can too: There was a time – not so very long ago – when *Kohanim* were buried with a sign of the way they blessed the people on their tombstones.

I can remember – perhaps you can too: There was a time not so long ago – when merchants had a scale inscribed on their tombstones, to signify that they ran their businesses with just weights and just measures.

I can remember – perhaps you can too: Not so long ago there was a time when scholars were buried, with their coffins made out of the *shtenders* at which they stood when they studied.

And now?

Now we have people in Jewish cemeteries, who are buried with the insignia of their favorite football team or with gold clubs or catcher's mitts inscribed on their tombstones???

That to me is a violation of the Second Commandment: "Thou shalt not worship anything on the earth, or in the sky or in the sea."

And I ask you: What should you call it when people spend thousands of dollars at an auction for a keepsake that was touched by an athlete as if the object were magic, and as if some of his power would rub off on them if they touched it? That to me is idolatry.

And what do you call it when people stand out in the snow for hours in weather that is seven degrees below zero, just for the opportunity to wave at an athlete going by – as if he were royalty? That to me is idolatry.

And what do you call it when people will not forgive a player or a coach because they made an error in a game – even in a crucial game? What do you call it when people hoot and jeer and boo a player who made a mistake during a game – and persecute that player for the rest of his life – as if he had committed a crime? That to me is idolatry.

There is one man I know who identified with Darrell Bevell this past Sunday. His name is Bill Gilson, and he was the offensive coach of the Giants in a Superbowl that took place many years ago. There was only one minute left to play. The Giants were in the lead. And they had the ball on the fifty yard line. And Bill Gilson – for some reason that I do not begin to understand – ordered the quarterback to run the ball instead of kneeling and letting the clock run out. The quarterback fumbled, and a member of the other side picked it up and ran it fifty yards for a touchdown.

Do you know what happened to Bill Gilson?

He was fired that evening! The Giants did not even wait until the next morning to fire him. And he never worked another day in professional or college football from that day on. He never went to another football game, for fear of being jeered or hooted or even harmed physically. He opened three businesses in the town in which he lived: first a bait shop, and then a restaurant, and then a market, and each business closed in two months, because no one wanted to buy from him, or even to be seen with him.

Bill Gilson is an old man now. He watched the game from his hospital bed, and he did not say a word. But if anyone understands how Darrell Bevell felt when the Superbowl ended on Sunday afternoon, I am sure it was Bill Gilson.

I feel for Darrell Bevel who is in hiding today. I feel for this man who will be remembered for the rest of his life for the one mistake that he made. I really do.

And therefore, let me say it clearly and hear me well:

I believe that sports are a good thing, and that we should all enjoy games whenever we can. I believe that sports are a healthy pastime. And I believe that watching them can add pleasure to our lives.

But – and here is where I am going to stick my neck out and risk my job – I believe that sports are not . . . and should not – be a religion. And I believe that a game is only a game. And therefore, when a player or a coach makes a mistake – even if it is a costly mistake – even if it is in a crucial game – they should not be booed or jeered or threatened with bodily harm or ostracized forever.

And I believe that anyone who lives for the game to the point where it becomes an obsession, to the point where it becomes the be-all and the end-all of his existence, is guilty of idolatry. I believe that a person who eats, drinks, sleeps and lives for the game is guilty of violating the second of the Ten Commandments.

And therefore, on this, the day when we mark the giving of the Ten Fundamental Statements on which human civilization is based, let us not make the mistake of thinking that only nine of the Commandments are relevant in our time, and that the second one is irrelevant and trivial.

But instead, let us treasure this Commandment, together with the other nine, so that we may live sane and sacred lives, so that we can be faithful to God, and so that we can be respectful to other human beings, and so that our lives may have balance and purpose and direction and not be devoted to trivia.

I hope that you will agree with what I have said to you today.

And I hope that if the board of directors decides that it wants to fire me for what I have said today, that you will speak up for me, and that you will defend me. Will you please?

A Lesson from a Six Year Old

MY SERMON THIS MORNING is addressed to me. It deals with a sin that I admit that I have committed more than once, and that I need to atone for.

And my sermon today is also addressed to you, because I am sure that I am not the only one here today who has committed this sin. This sermon is addressed to the parents, and the teachers and the counselors who are here today in particular, for it is a sin that those of us who are in these groups are especially liable to commit.

I want to tell you the story of a rabbi who started out intending to give *mussar* to two of his congregants, and who ended up receiving *mussar* instead. But before I tell you this story, I want to study with you a strange phrase that appears at the end of the *sedra* of this week – a phrase that, when you first look at it, seems to be unnecessary.

After the moment at Sinai, at which God gave the Torah to the people of Israel, Moses is offered a private tutorial by God. He is invited to go back up to the top of Mount Sinai, and to study there for forty days and forty nights with the greatest Teacher of them all.

God says:

Aley aylai ha-harah – "Come up to Me on the mountain."

Could there be a greater honor than this – to study Torah with God Himself?

Could there be a greater honor than this: to have the Giver of the Torah teach the Torah to him?

If you were Moses, would you not be flattered beyond words to receive this opportunity?

What would you expect Moses to say?

You would expect Moses to say: "Yes! By all means! Thank you for the invitation. What time do you want me to be there?"

Instead, The Torah adds two words to this invitation, two words that seem gratuitous. God says to Moses: "Come up to Me to the top of the mountain" – *v'heyei sham* – "and be there."

What do we need these two extra words for?

Why does God have to tell Moses to be with Him when He teaches him the Torah? Would it occur to Moses to be anywhere else? Can you imagine Moses saying to God: "I can be with you from two to four o'clock, but then I have a card game scheduled, and so I will have to leave then?" Can you imagine Moses saying to God: "I would love to stay with you longer if I could, but the budget committee is meeting at six o'clock, and I have to be there?"

Why then does God have to say to Moses: *v'heyei sham* – when you come up to study with me, "be there"? In a book that does not usually waste any words, why does God have to say: Come up to Me on the mountain – and be there?

There are many different explanations of this extra phrase that are found in the commentaries. This morning, I want to offer one of my own. It is an explanation that might never have occurred to previous generations, but I think that it speaks directly to ours.

Perhaps *v'heyei sham* – "be there" – means: be with Me with your whole mind during this lesson. Concentrate on what I am going to teach you, and do not let anything distract you during the lesson.

What could possibly have distracted Moses during his time alone with God?

I don't know, but perhaps he was worried about his wife and his children. Perhaps he was wondering about how they were managing without him while he was up on top of Mount Sinai?

Or perhaps he was worried about the people of Israel. Could they be trusted to manage on their own while he was away? Or would they get into trouble if he was not there to watch over them and make sure that they behaved?

I can't say for sure, but perhaps God was concerned that Moses would be distracted by concerns like these, and so He had to warn him: *heyei sham* – "be present" during the lessons, and do not let anything else distract you from concentrating on what I am going to teach you.

It could be.

I know that, if God were to appear in our synagogue today, and if God were to announce that He would like to teach us some very important things, do you know what the first thing that He would have to say to us would be?

Anyone?

I think that the first thing that God would have to say to us before He began the lesson would be: "Will you please disconnect your cell phones, or put them on vibrate, until the end of the lesson."

We live in a very pressured world. The truth is that even if I turn off my cell phone, I still find myself thinking about the fact that somebody may be trying to reach me, perhaps with an important message. Even if I put my machine on vibrate, I find myself still thinking about the fact that somebody may be trying to text me, and so it takes all my will power to concentrate on what the teacher is saying, and not steal a look at my cell phone.

Are you like that too?

If God had to say: *V'heyei sham* to Moses, how much more would God have to say that to us, if He wanted to give us a message today.

And that is the background for the story that I want to tell you today. The story comes from Rabbi Ron Yitschak Eisenman, who is a rabbi in Passaic, New Jersey.

He says that a couple had made an appointment to see him for counseling two weeks before. He knew how difficult it was to coordinate their schedule with his, and how hard it was for them to get a babysitter, so when the wife called in the morning to say that their babysitter had cancelled at the last minute, and would he mind if they brought along their six-year-old daughter, he could not say no, although he was a little bit hesitant at having her join them at their meeting.

He was hesitant, not only because he was worried that the child would listen in on the sensitive matter that they would be discussing, but because he was afraid that the parents would end up having to pay more attention to their child than to the problem that they were coming to discuss.

He was afraid that every minute or so, they would be looking over at little Serelle to make sure that she was happy with the toys that they had brought for her, or that she was eating or drinking the six bags of Super Snacks and the three boxes of juice that they had packed for her to enjoy during the "outing" to the rabbi's office.

He was sure that just as he was about to make his point about what he wanted this couple to do, little Serelle would jump up and ask for her crayons, and the gravity of his message would fall on inattentive ears.

But as it turned out, the rabbi's fears were unfounded. Serelle behaved beautifully the whole time. There was not a peep out of her during the entire counseling session. She sat quietly in a corner of the office, playing with her toys, and never interrupting the adults who were talking just a few feet away from her.

The meeting ended and the rabbi felt very good. He felt that he had delivered his *mussar* message very well. But his pride did not last very long.

As he was gathering up his papers and getting ready to go to his next appointment, the young mother said to him: "Oh, Rabbi, before we go, Serelle has a question in Chumash which she wants to ask you. We told her that she could ask you tonight, at the end of our meeting. Is it okay if she asks you now?"

The rabbi was tired, and not in the mood to be cute or playful with a six-year-old, but he contained himself, and asked Serelle to ask away.

With her mother's prodding, Serelle timidly approached the rabbi's desk. She hid behind her mother's skirt as the rabbi straightened out his papers.

"Go ahead, Serelle," said her mother. "Now is the time to ask the rabbi the question that you prepared for him."

Serelle said: "But, Mommy, he's not listening."

"Of course I'm listening," said the rabbi. "Please go ahead."

Serelle's mother said, "See, Serelle, the rabbi is listening. Go ahead and ask him your question."

And then Serelle looked at her mother, and said the words which seared the rabbi.

"No," she said. "The rabbi is listening with his ears, but he is not listening with his eyes."

Rabbi Eisenman says that he sat back down in his chair, put down his papers, apologized to Serelle, and listened to her question carefully.

And ever afterwards, he says, when someone comes to ask him a question, he tries to listen with both his ears and his eyes.

And he says that he thought that the purpose of this meeting was so that he could give *mussar* to two adults, but in the end, he was the one who received *mussar* – and from a six-year-old at that!

I think that is a great phrase, is it not? A person should listen – not only with his ears – but with his eyes as well. And if you don't, you should know that the questioner can tell. Even if the questioner is only a six-year-old, he or she can tell the difference between someone who just listens with his ears and someone who listens with his eyes as well.

I confess that I have sometimes listened the way that Rabbi Eisenman says that he listened that day – only with my ears or with half a mind instead of with full concentration. And I suspect that many of you have committed that sin too. And so this is the lesson that I would have you learn today.

If the Torah added two seemingly unnecessary words to the story of how God invited Moses to study with Him, if the Torah had to remind even Moses to concentrate on what he was doing and not let himself be distracted by anything else, then surely we need to learn this lesson too. And therefore, I ask you – and I ask myself – to learn this lesson and to take it to heart: when someone comes to you for help or for advice, listen! Listen, listen well, listen with your eyes as well as with your ears, so that you can fulfill the *mitzvah* of giving advice wisely and well.

Let me finish by telling you just one more story. Martin Buber was one of the greatest thinkers of the twentieth century. He was the founder of what we now call Dialogic Thinking. And he tells this story about himself.

Many years ago, when he was just starting out, a student once came to him, and asked him what he thought was an abstract, philosophical question. The student asked him: What is the meaning of life? Professor Buber gave him an answer, an answer that drew upon the insights of Kant and Hegel and other thinkers, but that did not really come out of his own innermost soul. He thought that it was a good enough answer, and so he gave it, and then he dismissed the student, put the matter out of his mind, and went back to the research that he was working on.

The student thanked him for his time, and left. And a few hours later, the student committed suicide. Dr. Buber regretted for the rest of his life that he had not really heard what the student was asking. He had misunderstood. He had thought that the student was asking him an abstract, theoretical question. He did not realize that the student was asking him a life and death question, and so the answer that he gave him was a superficial and inadequate one.

He heard his question with his ears – but he did not listen with his eyes, to quote the six-year-old girl whom we learned about today. And so he had to live for the rest of his life with the knowledge of the harm that he had done. He said that, for the rest of his life, whenever someone came to him for advice, he tried to listen with all his being.

There is no greater compliment, and there is no greater responsibility than when someone asks your advice in an important matter. It is an even greater honor and an even greater responsibility than being asked to study Torah with God.

And therefore, may none of us ever make the mistake that Martin Buber did. Instead, let us resolve today that if we are asked for advice, that we will listen with our whole being. Let us resolve to "be there" when we are called upon, as God called Moses to be.

Let us focus our hearts and souls on what we are doing, and not let ourselves be distracted by anything else.

And may God bless us in our efforts to listen and to help.

Sports Illustrated and the *Sedra*

TERUMAH

DOES EVERYONE HERE REALIZE how lucky you are to have me as your rabbi?

Just in case you don't, let me tell you.

You are lucky to have me, for at least two reasons. The first reason, as I think I have told you before, is because of my modesty. I am world famous for my modesty. I have more modesty in my little finger than most people have in their whole bodies. And so, for my modesty alone, this congregation is very lucky to have me.

But the second, and the more important reason why you are lucky to have me is because of the enormous amount of research that I do every week in preparing my sermons.

For the measly ten thousand dollars a week that you pay me here, do you have any idea of the amount of research that I do in preparing my sermons?

Some rabbis just pick up the Etz Chaim commentary during the Torah reading, and summarize what it says – and call that a sermon. But not me. I study the Chumash with Rashi and with Ramban and with Ibn Ezra, and with Abravanel, and then I study the modern commentators as well every week.

And some rabbis just read the local newspaper and talk about what it says. But not me. I read all the newspapers of Europe and Asia and Africa and South America and North America every week in order to prepare my sermons. And I do research every week on different aspects of the culture around us. I study the latest findings in economics and in literature and in philosophy and in psychology and in political science every week in order to prepare my sermons.

And this morning, I want to give you just one example of the kind of research that I do.

In order to prepare my sermon for today, do you know what I have done? You will never guess. In order to prepare my sermon for today, I have studied intensively the February issue of *Sports Illustrated*.

How many rabbis do you know who would do that?

Does anyone here know what is special about the February issue of *Sports Illustrated*?

The February issue of *Sports Illustrated* is the annual swimsuit issue. This is the issue in which they publish pictures of the most beautiful women in the world, dressed in their bathing suits – although why they are called bathing suits I have no idea – women wear these suits in order to be photographed, they wear these suits in order to walk up and down the runway in them. They don't wear these suits in order to take a bath – or even to go swimming. And so I don't understand why they are called bathing suits. But that is another matter which we can discuss some other time.

I bought this annual issue of *Sports Illustrated* – with my own money by the way! I didn't even charge it to the shul – and I didn't even list it as a business expense on my taxes – even though I could have, and probably should have – and I have been studying it all week, in order to see what it has to teach us about this week's portion of the Torah.

And this is what I found:

I found that of all the beautiful women in the world whom they could have chosen, the editors of *Sports Illustrated* have chosen, not one but two – two Jewish women!!

They chose Bar Rafaeli of Tel Aviv to be on the cover a few years ago, and now they have chosen Esti Ginzburg of Hadera for inclusion in their annual swimsuit issue.

Can you imagine that? Israel is one of the smallest countries in the world. The total population of Israel is less than a statistical error in the annual birth rate of China. And yet not one but two Israeli women have now been chosen for inclusion in the annual swimsuit issue of *Sports Illustrated*.

I ask you: How do you feel about this achievement?

Are you proud?

I am.

But how do you think your parents would have felt about this achievement?

I don't know about your parents, but I am pretty sure that I know what my parents would have said. I think that they would have said: "past nisht." They would have said: How does it look for a Jewish girl to appear in a national magazine, wearing only a swimsuit?

They would have said: It's not tzniesdik. It is immodest. And they would have been right. I have the issue, but I am not going to hold it up for you to see today, because the picture of a young girl in a bathing suit that is held together by a pair of strings is not something that should be shown from the bimah of this synagogue.

And therefore, if you want to see what Ms. Rafaeli or Ms. Ginzburg look like, you will have to go to the store and buy your own copy.

I am serious about what our parents would have said. Tznius is a basic Jewish value. And so they would have been offended, and rightly so, by the costume – or should I say – by the LACK OF COSTUME – that these two young women are wearing.

My father would have said: "past nisht." And my mother would have said: "Nebech, give her a blanket quick. This poor girl is liable to catch a cold."

But the two questions that I want to ask you today, in all seriousness, are:

1. Is it good for the Jews? Is it good for the Jews that we now have, not one but two, young ladies featured in the February issue of *Sports Illustrated*?

And 2. What on earth does this topic have to do with the sedra of Terumah that we read from the Torah today?

Is your rabbi crazy? – Don't answer that!!

Or is there a lesson in this issue of *Sports Illustrated* that is connected in some way to what we read in the Torah today?

First: Is it good for the Jews or not?

I think that the answer to that question is: yes it is.

Because Jews have always appreciated beauty.

When Sarah, the wife of Abraham, is mentioned in the Bible, the Torah says:

isha tovat mar'eh at. . . "you are a beautiful woman."

When Rebecca is introduced to us in the Bible, the Torah says:

v'ha'na-arah tovat mar'eh me'od . . . "the maiden was very beautiful."

When Rachel is introduced to us in the Bible, the Torah says:

Rachel hayeta yifat to'ar, v'yifat mar'eh. "Rachel was beautiful and shapely."

Esther, the woman whom we will read about in just a week and a half was surely one of the most beautiful women in all of Persia.

And there is a whole book of the Bible in praise of beauty – *Shir Hashirim* – The Song of Songs.

And so it is clear from the Torah that there is nothing wrong with a woman being beautiful. Nothing at all. In fact, did you know that there is a special *bracha* that you are supposed to say, according to the Jewish tradition, when you see a beautiful person? Did you know that? It is my favorite *bracha* in the whole *siddur*.

When you see anyone beautiful, you are supposed to say: *Baruch attah Hashem, Elokeynu melech ha'olam, SHEKACHA LO B'OLAMO.* "Blessed are You, O Lord our God, Ruler of the universe, who has created something as beautiful as this in His world."

I say this *bracha* every morning when I wake up. And may I suggest to you, in all seriousness, that, when you wake up in the morning, and look at your wife, that you say this *bracha* every day too. If you do, I promise you that your married life will be much better. Trust me, it will.

And so it is clear from the Bible and from the Talmud that Jewish women were often beautiful, and were admired for their beauty – up until modern times.

And then, something changed.

For some reason – I don't know why – two things happened.

One was that those Jewish women who were beautiful began to believe that they had to deny their Jewishness and drop out of Jewish life in order to be appreciated. And the other was that those Jewish women who stayed within Jewish life were mocked and maligned for their appearance and were not considered to be beautiful.

So you have women like Sarah Bernhardt, the great matinee idol of the 19th century, who denied or de- emphasized her Jewishness.

And you have women like Theda Bara, the matinee idol of the silent film era, whose real name was Theda Goodman.

And you have a woman like Betty Persky, who was Humphrey Bogart's girlfriend. You may know her better by her stage name, which was Lauren Bacall.

And you have Gwyneth Paltrow, who is descended from a family of rabbis, but you would never know that from reading her resume.

And you have Winona Ryder, whose real name is Winona Horowitz.

And you have many, many more women like them. These are Jewish women, who have changed their names, and denied their identity and their heritage, because they believed that if you wanted to be a success on Broadway or in Hollywood, you had to perform a lobotomy on your identity, and deny your Jewishness.

And do you know what happened to those who stayed Jews?

The image of Jewish women which Hollywood has promoted is that Jewish women are fat and frumpy, and demanding, domineering, and *kvetchy* – anything but beautiful.

The best example is the movie called *The Heartbreak Kid*. Do any of you remember that movie? It was a really anti-Semitic movie, in which the hero – if that is the word – goes off on his honeymoon with his Jewish bride, and she immediately gets a bad case of sunburn, and all she does is *kvetch* and *kvetch* and *kvetch*. So the groom leaves her in the bridal suite to recover, and he goes out to the beach without her, and he falls in love with a really gorgeous girl there, who is, of course, not Jewish.

The message that Hollywood sends in this movie, and in many other movies, the message that it has sent out for years – the message that it has sent out to Jewish boys – and to Jewish men, who are often as immature as boys – is that Jewish women are not beautiful.

And that is why I believe that, at one level, this issue of *Sports Illustrated* is good news. It sends a message to Jewish men that Jewish women ARE really beautiful, that they are just as beautiful as any other group of women. If two Jewish women can make the pages of the February issue of *Sports Illustrated*, no one will ever be able to say again that Jewish women are not beautiful.

And so, the answer to the question: is this issue of Sports illustrated good for the Jews or not, is: yes, it is good for the Jews.

And so, if you have a teenage grandson I suggest that you buy him a copy of this issue of *Sports Illustrated*, and if he asks you why – you can tell him that the rabbi told you to do it.

And now comes the question that I am sure you have all been waiting for:

Which is: What on earth does this have to do with today's Torah reading?

I think that it has two things to do with today's Torah reading.

The Torah in today's reading describes in great detail the making of the Ark, which was the central object in the Mishkan.

And it says two things about the Ark.

First of all, it says that the Ark had a curtain. The Ark had a *parochet*. And then it says that the Holy of Holies, in which the Ark was placed, was only entered once a year, by the holiest person on earth on the holiest day of the year.

And notice one thing more. Notice that the Torahs in our Ark, like the Torahs in every other synagogue that you have ever been in, each have a covering. In fact, they have two coverings. They have a curtain, and behind the curtain they have a door, and not only that, but every single Torah inside the Ark has a covering.

Why?

Because, say the Sages of the Talmud, anything which is holy has to be covered. And since the Torah is the holiest object that we have, it is triply covered: once by the curtain, and then by the door, and then by the covering that is on it.

That is the law: The holier an object is, the more it should be treated with respect. And one of the ways in which we show respect for something holy is: we cover it.

That is why an *etrog* is always kept in a box – until it is time for it to be taken out and used.

And that is why the challah is always covered until it is time to make a *motsi*.

And that is why the *Tefillin* are always kept in two boxes, and these two boxes are always kept in a bag.

And that is why the *Tallit* is always kept in a bag, until it is ready to be worn.

Because: The holier an object is, the more it should be treated with respect.

And therefore – and now I am being very serious – therefore, since we Jews believe that the human body is sacred, the kind of clothing – or to be exact – the lack of clothing, that these women wear in the swimsuit issue of this magazine is immoral and improper, and therefore you should not look at this issue of the magazine.

That is the first connection between this magazine and the Torah portion that we have read today. Whatever is holy should be covered, and the human body is holy, and therefore it should be covered.

And there is another connection between the magazine and the *sedra* that I want to point out to you.

The Torah describes this week in great and loving detail the building of the *Mishkan*, the tabernacle in which the Israelites worshipped in the wilderness. And it is clear to anyone who reads this *sedra* that the *Mishkan* was a work of great beauty. No doubt about it. The Torah describes the Ark, the Altar, and all the other holy objects in the *Mishkan* in loving detail, in order to show us how carefully and how beautifully they were made.

And then comes the passage that contains what I believe is the key to the Jewish definition of beauty. It says that the Ark was covered over with pure gold – both on the inside AND on the outside.

That there was gold on the outside, that I can understand. The outside of the Ark was visible to everyone who entered the *Mishkan*, and so it made sense to use gold on the outside.

But why was there to be gold on the INSIDE? Why would you waste money and effort putting pure gold on the inside of the Ark, where no one would ever see it?

To which the Sages of the Midrash say: In order to teach us that a human being must be the same – inside and outside. A person must be the same – on the outside where everybody can see whether he or she is beautiful or not – and on the inside, where no one can tell but God.

That is why we sing the *Eshet Chayil* to our wives every Friday night at the Shabbat table. The song says almost nothing about the woman's physical appearance. It only talks about her character, about her generosity, and about her goodness. And it ends with the words: *Sheker ha'chen, v'hevel hayofi, isha yirat Adonai hi tit'halal.* "Charm is deceitful, and beauty is brief – but a woman who serves the Lord, she is to be praised."

I must tell you those words are terribly true – not only for women but for man as well.

How do I know? I know this truth because of an experience that I had here in this synagogue a few weeks ago. Someone came running up to me after the services were over, and showed me a bulletin from my first congregation – which was the East Midwood Jewish Center in Brooklyn. He held it up proudly, and he said to me: Look what I have for you!

And he showed me a picture of me that was taken more than fifty-five years ago.

And do you know what? I couldn't recognize myself in that picture. I really couldn't. The person in that picture has black hair, and the person in that picture has no glasses, and the person in that picture weighs a lot less than I do now.

And looking at that picture taught me the lesson that the words of the *Eshet Chayil* – *sheker ha'chen, v'hevel hayofi* – that beauty disappears fast, and that charm does not last – is just as true for men as it is for women.

Beauty is precious. There is no question of that. Beauty is one of God's greatest gifts, but beauty, external beauty, is only temporary. No matter what you do, no matter what face powders or what lipstick or what cosmetics you use, no matter how much you exercise, no matter how many facelifts you have, no matter how many nips and tucks you go through, no matter what you do – physical beauty is only brief. The only kind of beauty that really lasts is the kind that is on the inside.

And that is the point of the Torah reading that we heard today. That is the reason why the Torah insists on putting gold on the inside of the Ark, and not just on the outside.

And that is the lesson that we need to teach our children and our grandchildren. We live in a world where women, and men too, spend over seven billion dollars a year on beauty aids. We live in a world that is obsessed with physical beauty, and therefore we need to teach our children and our grandchildren that physical beauty is wonderful – it really is – it is one of God's greatest gifts to humanity. It is worthy of a *bracha* – but only if, and only when, it is combined with inner beauty and with moral character.

Let me finish with one of my favorite Jewish stories. It is a story that I have told you once before, and that I hope to tell you someday again. It is a story whose punch line can only be told in Yiddish. And so, if you don't know Yiddish, ask the person sitting next to you, and perhaps he or she will be able to explain the joke to you.

Once a man who had moved from Europe to America heard that someone from his old village in Europe had arrived in America. And so this man eagerly invited the man who had just arrived to come to his home so he could get an update on what was doing back there.

He said to the man: "Tell me, do you know my friend, Reuven?" And the man told him. "Reuven? I know him well. He lived just down the street from me. And Reuven is doing well, thank God."

Then he said to him: "Tell me, how is my friend Shimon?" And the man told him, "Shimon? Shimon? I know him well. Shimon lived just around the corner from me. And I am happy to tell you that he is fine, thank God."

And then the host said: "Tell me, how is my friend Chaim?"

The man said: "Chaim? Which Chaim do you mean? I know a few Chaims."

"Do you mean the Chaim who walks with a limp?"

The man said: "Yes, yes, yes, that's the one."

The visitor said: "Do you mean the Chaim who has a scar on his face?"

The man said: "Yes, yes, yes, that's the one."

The visitor said: "Do you mean the Chaim who stutters and who is all bent over, and who walks with a cane?"

The man said: "Yes, yes, that's the one. How is he?"

The visitor said: "Ah, that Chaim! I know him well. *A sheiner yid.*"

A sheiner yid means: A beautiful Jew.

You can only tell that joke in Yiddish, because only in Yiddish is it possible to have a scar and a limp and a hunchback and a speech defect, and still be a beautiful Jew.

And so let me say one *mazel tov* to the two women from Israel who have made the cover of *Sports Illustrated*. And let me say that I hope that their parents have much *nachas* from them.

And let me say that I hope that these two women and all the women whom we know will have both the kind of beauty that wins prizes in the Miss America contest in Atlantic City AND the kind of beauty that the Torah describes today – the kind that is covered as the Ark is covered, and the kind that is beautiful on the inside as well as on the outside.

For this is what it means to be beautiful according to the Jewish tradition.

Meeting Natan Sharansky in the Bakery

I HAVE SOME GOOD NEWS from Israel that I want to share with you this morning.

I am happy to do so, because we don't usually get much good news from Israel these days. We hear stories of tension and turmoil. We hear stories of bickering between the political parties, and we hear stories of acts of terror. And so it is good to have some good news to share with you for a change today.

This is a story about Natan Sharansky, the freedom fighter who challenged the Soviet Union, the one who said: "Let us live as Jews or else let us leave as Jews" — and won. Sharansky is surely one of the very great heroes of our time. And so, let me tell you this story about him, Let me tell it to you precisely the way I heard it, and then let me share with you the three lessons that I think we should learn from it.

A friend of mine who lives in Israel sent me this e-mail this week. She wrote:

This morning I was in a bakery in Jerusalem when I happened to notice that I was standing in line directly behind Natan Sharansky. I summoned up my courage and told him that I had just cited his book this week in a class that I am teaching on the Psalms. I explained that I told my students the story of how he had kept a tiny book of Psalms with him at all times, and how he had fought with the authorities in prison to get it back each time they confiscated it.

Sharansky smiled when I told him this, and then he reached into his pocket and pulled out a tiny, tattered book of Psalms. I was stunned, and I asked him: "Do you still carry that with you wherever you go?" Sharansky did not even pause before he replied: "Actually, it carries me!"

And then my friend finished her e-mail with these words: "Don't you love Jerusalem! It is a city where famous people walk the streets, and where you can learn lessons in how to live while standing on line in the bakery!"

And then my friend signed her name, and wished us well.

I love this e-mail, and I love the story that it contains, because I think that it teaches us three important lessons, three lessons that all of us need to hear and that we need to take to heart.

The first is that this is how a Jewish hero behaves. Sharansky is a world famous figure – he has spoken at the White House and he has spoken at the United Nations, and at all kinds of important places – but when his wife sends him to the bakery, he goes to the bakery, and when he gets there, he stands in line, just like everyone else.

That is what it means to be a democracy.

I remember an incident that occurred here in America some years ago. America appointed a new ambassador to China, and this man – I am sorry but I don't remember his name – this man was standing at the airport, waiting for the plane that would take him to his new assignment. He reached into his pockets and saw that he was out of cigarettes, and so he walked over to one of the nearby stores and bought himself a pack.

And the picture of his doing that went viral in China!

The networks there played it over and over again, because they simply could not believe that a high-ranking American diplomat would go into a store and buy something by himself instead of sending one of his assistants to do it for him. They had never seen that happen before. In their country, that simply could not happen.

This ambassador taught the Chinese a lesson in democracy even before he got there.

There are countries in which the political or the military leaders are treated differently from everyone else. There are countries in which people bow and scrape before them, and where they are waited on hand and foot. But that is not the way it is in America and it is not the way it is in Israel.

I still remember the first time I went to Israel. I was on a guided tour, and one of the places that they took us to was an army base, and while we were there, we stopped to have a cup of coffee in the cafeteria. And I remember seeing one of the most famous generals in the army – I am not sure but I think it was Ezer Weitzman or Chaim Herzog – going through the line that day, getting his breakfast, and then holding his tray and looking around the room until he found am empty seat so that he could sit down and have his meal.

That is what it means to be a democracy. And that is the first lesson that I would have you learn from this story about Natan Sharansky standing in line at the bakery. It is a small incident, but I believe that it expresses what Israel is all about very clearly.

The second thing that I would have you learn – or relearn if you have heard it before – is the story of that book of Psalms.

Natan and Avital Sharansky got married in Russia, and then a few days later, she received the document that said that she was permitted to leave the country. She wanted to turn it down, because it was only for her, and not for her husband, but he insisted that she not lose this opportunity. And so she went and left her new husband behind.

When she arrived in Israel, one of the first things she did was send him this small book of Psalms as a gift. He says that when it arrived, he did not think much about it, because he was busy fighting for the rights of Jews and for the rights of others who were seeking freedom in the Soviet Union. But when he was arrested, he suddenly remembered the book of Psalms that he had received from his wife. And so he insisted that the KGB, which had confiscated this book when they arrested him, give it back to him. It took him three years to force them to return the book. They gave it back to him on the very day when he learned that his father had passed away. He felt terrible because he could not be with his mother and give her support at this sad time in their lives. So what did he do? He decided that he would start reciting these Psalms every day, even though he could not understand most of what he was reading. He was able to understand a word here and a word there, a phrase here and a phrase there, and soon he began understanding the Psalms. He decided that he would recite a Psalm every day in order to link himself to his heritage and to his wife and mother outside.

He says in his biography that the first psalm that he really understood was Psalm Twenty-Three, in which the poet says: "Yea, though I walk through the valley of death, I shall fear no evil, because You are with me."

When he deciphered that line, he suddenly felt that the long distance between the poet who wrote these words three thousand years ago, and himself, had been bridged. It was as if King David himself, together with his wife, and his friends, and his God, were all there with him in his prison cell, speaking to him and protecting him. The Psalm was sending him a message to be strong and not to be afraid. Saying this Psalm gave him courage and gave him comfort.

Sharansky says that he felt that as long as he had this book of Psalms, nothing could happen to him. And so he fought every time they took it away from him. He spent many days on hunger strikes and many days in solitary confinement in order to get them to give his book back to him every time that they took it away.

And then came the day when they took him out of prison and drove him to the airport and flew him from there to the border between East Germany and West Germany. There, they took away his prison clothes and gave him new clothes. He suddenly realized that something big was about to happen: they were about to let him go! But they still had not given him back his book of Psalms. And he refused to go without it. He lay down in the snow and refused to cross the bridge from slavery to freedom until and unless they gave his book of Psalms back to him. The reporters and the photographers were waiting on the other side of the bridge, and so finally the KGB had no choice but to give in. They gave him back his book of Psalms – and that was the only piece of property with which he left the Soviet Union!

What is the lesson of this story?

It is the power of the human spirit.

Who would have believed when Sharansky went to prison that the day would come when the most powerful empire in the world would break apart? Who would have believed then that today the

Soviet Union no longer exists and that the Jews of Russia have been able to leave?

This shows the power of inner freedom. This shows the power of people, when they unite, when they demand their dignity, and when they stand up for what they believe is right.

And this shows the power of a small book of Psalms.

And what is the third lesson that I would have you learn today?

I don't know how much Torah Natan Sharansky knows by now. When he arrived in Israel, I am sure that he knew very little, but he has been studying hard, and he has been trying to catch up on the education that he never got as a child in the Soviet Union. And I do know that, deliberately or perhaps not, what he said that day while he was standing in line at the bakery is an echo of a passage that is found in the Midrash on today's Torah reading.

This week's Torah reading tells the story of how Moses came down the mountain, carrying in his hands the two tablets of stone, on which were written the words of God. And then, when he came down off the mountain, he saw the people of Israel singing and dancing around the Golden Calf. The Torah says that he became so angry that he took the Two Commandments of stone that he had brought down from Mount Sinai and he smashed them.

The Sages ask: How could Moses have done that?

Here were the two holiest objects that ever existed. Here were the two tablets that contained the Word of God. How could Moses have dared to take them and smash them? How could Moses have dared to do such a thing, without at least asking permission from God first?

And this is the answer that the Sages give to this question. They say that as long as the Two Tablets were intact, they were not hard for him to carry. In fact, they say that Moses skipped down the mountain, carrying the tablets with ease. It was as if the tablets were carrying him. But when he came face to face with the Golden Calf, when he saw the people singing and dancing around the Calf, and calling out: "This is your God, O Israel" – at that moment, the letters on the Two Tablets came off the tablets and flew back to heaven.

And when the letters disappeared, the two tablets suddenly became too heavy to carry. Moses did not smash them, says the

Midrash. He dropped them. He dropped them because, when the letters disappeared, he was no longer able to hold them.

I have always felt that this Midrash is a parable of the Jewish situation. When Jews know the Torah, when Jews understand the Torah, when Jews live by the Torah, being Jewish is not a burden. It is a privilege. But when the letters fly away, when Jews can no longer even read the Torah, much less live by it, then the Torah and Jewish living become an impossible burden, and Jews drop it – not out of anger but simply because it is too hard to carry.

And this is what I think Natan Sharansky was saying that day in the bakery. When he was asked: "Do you still carry that book of Psalms with you wherever you go?" do you remember what he said? He said: "Actually, it carries me!"

I think I know what Natan Sharansky meant what he said those words that day. He meant that when he stood before cruel and brutal guards who tried to take away his inner freedom, the book of Psalms that he carried – carried him. That book gave him a sense of inner worth and a feeling of purpose in life. And afterwards, when he went around the world, speaking to heads of state and to people of power, on behalf of the Jewish people, when he could very easily have become smug and arrogant or vain, it was the book of Psalms that he carried with him that reminded him of who he was, and who he was not, and that enabled him to keep his perspective.

That is what I think he meant when he said that the book of Psalms that he carried with him in the gulag, and that he carries with him ever since, has carried him.

And so, this is what I want to ask of you today: Let this be the lesson that we learn from Natan Sharansky this morning, Let us learn from him to become literate Jews. Let us learn from him to understand that it is the books of our heritage that give meaning and purpose to our existence.

For if we do, the books will carry us, as they carried him, and as they have carried our people for all these many years. The books that we carry with us and inside us will make of our Jewishness a source of pride and a source of blessing, and a guide and a compass – for us as they have been for our ancestors, instead of a burden that weighs us down.

These are the three lessons that my friend learned that day while waiting in line at the bakery:

That everyone in Israel is equal, and therefore, that no one can go to the head of the line;

That if we fight for our rights and do not yield to our oppressors, we can win;

And above all, that if we carry the Jewish tradition that we have inherited proudly, it will carry us, and it will enable us to live a life of purpose and of meaning.

Imagine learning three such important lessons while standing on line in a bakery!

Only in Israel!

Mirrors Can Be Holy

I WANT TO TELL YOU two stories today.

One comes from the *sedra*. The other one comes from contemporary Israel.

Both deal with a question on which I do not claim to be an expert – namely how and why women should make an effort to be beautiful.

I tell you these two stories today, because I believe that they both teach a powerful moral lesson that I think we should all learn.

Let me begin with the story that is found in today's Torah reading:

The Torah says that Bezalel made the laver – in which the *Kohanim* washed their hands before they officiated at the sacred service – out of copper. And the Torah says that this copper came from the mirrors that the women of Israel donated for the making of the *Mishkan*.

Here, and only here, in the entire story of the making of the *Mishkan* do we have an account of who gave what. Everywhere else in the story, it simply says that the people brought gifts, but nowhere else does it say who gave what material for which object – except here.

And that leads Rashi, who is the greatest of all the commentators, to make this comment:

He says that Moses protested to God. He said: "Mirrors? Instruments of vanity? Should they be used in the making of the laver that the *Kohanim* will use when they begin their service? No way!"

To which God answered: *Kiblum! Ki hem chavivim alai min hakol.* God said: "Accept these mirrors, for they are more precious to Me than anything else."

Why?

Says Rashi: Because when the men came back from a day of back-breaking slavery, from a day of being treated as less than human, when they came back exhausted and demoralized and worn out, the women were there to greet them. And the women, with the help of their mirrors, had beautified themselves. And they were the one bit of beauty, the one bit of civilization, that these exhausted men had in their lives. And this beauty gave them morale, and dignity, and self-respect, and hope. And because the women had made themselves so beautiful, the men were moved to make love to them, and that is how come children were born during the dark years of slavery. If it were not for the women and their mirrors, the Israelites might have died out in Egypt. And therefore, God said to Moses: Accept these mirrors, for they are more precious to Me than anything else.

According to this Midrash, it was the women who kept up the morale of their husbands. Even in these difficult circumstances, the women would beautify themselves with whatever makeup and whatever rouges they could find or make. They would greet their husbands looking pretty, and by doing so, they kept their husbands from becoming completely dehumanized.

I love that Midrash for several reasons. One is because we think that the Torah and the tradition are male-centered, but here is a Midrash in which the credit for the survival of the people is given to women. And I love this Midrash because it teaches that the same object can be an instrument of vanity in one set of circumstances, and can be something sacred in another set of circumstances.

When a woman and her family live in luxury and comfort, and she concentrates only on her appearance, that is vanity. When a woman invests much of her time and energy and money in making herself beautiful instead of being involved in the welfare of her family or in the welfare of the world, that is vanity. But when a woman and her family live in the darkness of slavery, when they live in sub-human conditions, when they live in poverty and misery, and she strives to keep one tiny bit of beauty in that world, and uses her mirror for that purpose, then that mirror becomes holy. And that is why God commands Moses to accept these mirrors, and to use them in the making of the *Mishkan*, and to consider them more precious than anything else.

What is true of beauty is true of every other quality and characteristic in life. There is a time when atheism is bad, when it blinds us to the Presence of God. But there is a time to be an atheist. One of the Chassidic rebbeim says that when a poor man comes to you for help, you are not allowed to say to him: "God will help." At that moment you are supposed to act as if there is no God, and you – and only you – have the ability to help him.

And so it is with all the other vices. Stubbornness is usually considered a bad quality, but there is a time to be stubborn. If the Jewish people were not stubborn, we would not still be here today.

And there is a time to lie. Lying is usually considered a bad quality, but when your wife makes a bad meal – that has never happened in our house, but if it ever did – you are permitted to lie and say it was good, for the sake of *shalom bayit*. And if your wife buys a dress that is not returnable, and she asks you whether you like it or not, it is permitted, and even praiseworthy, to say that it is lovely.

And when you live in a dark and difficult world, it is permitted to keep alive a spark of civilization by making yourself beautiful, by means of rouge and makeup and mirrors. That is the lesson of this Midrash.

Now, let me tell you a story that comes from our own time. For one of the wonders of Jewish history is that things that happened centuries ago have a way of happening again in our own time.

I learned this story from a woman named Andrea Simantov, who lives in Jerusalem. Mrs. Simantov came originally from New York, but some years ago, she went with her family to live in Israel. She describes herself this way:

"I am religiously observant, civically active, often dieting, and hope to be a ballerina when I grow up." In addition to these talents and interests, Mrs. Simantov also happens to be a professional hairdresser – and that is the key to the story that I am about to tell you.

Do you remember what happened some years ago when the government of Israel removed the Jews from Gaza? It was a sad day for these people who had worked so hard there, who had settled there with the encouragement of the government, and who had built beautiful homes and lovely gardens there. But the government insisted that they must leave, and so they did.

The government sent buses to pick them up, and they took them to Jerusalem, and put them up in temporary housing while they determined what to do with them.

Can you imagine how these people must have felt when, after hours of driving in packed buses, they arrived in Jerusalem, and went to the no-star or the one-star hotels that had been assigned to them?

They were dirty and grimy from the trip. Their kids were tired and cranky. The parents were silent and sad, for they were giving up the homes that had been so precious to them for so many years. Yesterday, they had lived in spacious homes, with guest rooms and libraries. Now they were crowded together with their children and their belongings into one or two rooms in hotels. And they had no idea how long they would have to stay in these rooms, or where they would go from there.

They must have felt so disheartened and so depressed, as they tried to control their children and cheer up their husbands, and keep up their own morale.

"What can we do for these people?" was the question on the minds and hearts of everyone in Israel. Whether they agreed with the government's decision or not, the people of Israel felt for these disoriented and confused people, who had been uprooted from their homes, and were now sitting in these hotel rooms waiting for someone to tell them where to go and what to do with their new lives.

And at that moment, someone – I don't know who – came up with an idea. Someone figured out that it was not enough to bring them food and blankets, even though these hotel rooms were shabby, and the food they were serving was not very good. Money was raised with which to give these people toys for their children, and emotional counseling. Arrangements were made to take the children on field trips to the zoo, to the playgrounds, and to wherever else they might enjoy being, since they appeared to be dazed and depressed.

At that moment, someone came up with another idea. In addition to giving food and blankets, which were needed, and in addition to giving toys, and taking the children on field trips, which was appreciated, something should be done for the women in the group whose morale needed boosting. And so the call went out for beauticians and hairdressers to come to the hotels as soon as they could.

Andrea Simantov was a hairdresser. She knew that she could not take any of these people into her home, because she and her family lived in a small, crowded apartment. She had no money. In fact, she and her family were heavily in debt. They barely had enough blankets and clothing for themselves, so there was no way that they could donate blankets and clothing to these displaced people. All she could donate was a couple of cans of food that she put into the boxes that were set aside on behalf of the refugees from Gaza in every supermarket.

But she WAS a hairdresser! And so, for the next two weeks, after she finished working at her regular job, she would take her equipment, and go to one of the hotels that had been turned into a home for the people from Gaza, and she gave haircuts to the children and styled the hair of the women. She did it because she understood that these women, who had gone in one day, from being homeowners to being displaced people, had lost all their dignity, and their loss of dignity was reflected in their lack of grooming. And so by giving them facials and hairdos, she could enable these women to feel human once again.

Andrea Simantov did this for the several months that these families lived in these musty, run-down hotels in Jerusalem. And then, when the families were relocated elsewhere, she forgot about it. That is what you are supposed to do when you do a good deed. You are not supposed to strut around boasting about how good you are. You are supposed to do it – and then forget about it. And that is what Andrea Simantov did – until a few months ago.

A few months ago, a woman came to her door, bearing a present for her. It was a fancy mirror. Andrea Simantov had no idea who this woman was, or why she was bringing her such a nice present, but the woman explained.

She said: "I was one of the women who was stuck in one of those rat-traps of a hotel in Jerusalem after they took me out of Gaza. And you came to visit me. And you cut my hair, and put lipstick on me. I protested, but you insisted. You said to me that just because my world had fallen apart, I didn't have to look like a mess. You pointed out to me that my husband had enough troubles, looking for a job, and trying to find a home for his family, and that I should at least be something beautiful for him to look upon when he came home after a long day of failures. You were funny. I needed to laugh. I promised myself that if and when I ever had a simcha, you would be my hair stylist, and you would do my makeup. And I looked you up, and I am here to say thank you for saving my spirit during those awful days, and I am here to invite you to do my hair and my makeup for my child's Bat Mitzvah, which is next week. And I came to thank you for what you did for me by bringing you this mirror as a gift."

I don't know if this woman refugee from Gaza knew the commentary of Rashi on this week's *sedra* or not, but what she said and did is precisely what Rashi talks about when he explains why the women were allowed to bring their mirrors as their gift in the making of the *Mishkan*. Those mirrors enabled the Israelite women in Egypt to keep a bit of beauty in the minds and souls of their husbands during their darkest days, and in the same way, the makeup and the hairdo that this woman refugee from Gaza got from Andrea Simantov enabled her to stay human, and raised her morale and that of her family, during those first difficult days as they struggled to adjust to their new reality.

So here are two stories about mirrors. They are several thousand years apart in time, but they both teach the same spiritual lesson, which is that there is a time for beauty. There is a time when beauty is a *mitzvah*, and not a vanity. There is a time when mirrors and rouge and lipstick and makeup are sacred in God's eyes, and in ours as well.

And so, on this, the Shabbat when we read the story of how the women brought their mirrors and of how Bezalel used them to make the lavers in which the *Kohanim* washed before they began their sacred service, let us learn to appreciate the civilizing power of beauty. Let us learn that beauty can lift up broken spirits, and that beauty can give a bit of hope to brokenhearted people. Let us learn that there might not have been any children born to the Israelites in Egypt if it were not for the women and their mirrors. And let us learn to love beauty, and to use it for the glory of God.

Your Creation No Longer Belongs to You

THERE IS A STRANGE LINE in today's Torah reading, and I learned what it means from two people. One was David Ben-Gurion, and the other was Elie Wiesel.

The insight that comes from David Ben-Gurion I learned, not from him directly but by means of a story that was told about him by Shmuel Avidar Hakohen, and that I heard not directly from Rabbi Shmuel Avidar Hakohen but from my friend, Rabbi Peretz Rodman, who says that he learned it from him. But the insight that comes from Elie Wiesel I learned from him in person, as I will explain in a few minutes.

Let me begin with the lesson that I learned from David Ben-Gurion. This is the story:

In the spring of 1948, David Ben-Gurion arrived one day for a meeting of the Provisional State Council, which was the precursor of the Knesset. He was stopped at the entrance by security guards who had been given explicit instructions that no one was to be let in without I.D. and without an invitation to the meeting. Ben-Gurion was not just anyone. He was the person who had created the Provisional State Council! And he was the person who had called this meeting. And he was a very easy man to recognize – with his hair that went out in all directions. Nevertheless, the guards had their orders: no invitation – no admittance.

Ben-Gurion's guards were furious. How dare these stupid guards ask for an I.D. and for a copy of his invitation from the man who had created this institution, whose meeting he was about to attend?

But "The Old Man" silenced their objections. He told them that the guards were right, and he dug around in his pockets until he found the invitation, and then he showed his I.D., after which he and his guards were admitted into the meeting hall.

What Ben-Gurion was teaching his bodyguards that day was that it made no difference that he was the one who had created this Council. Once it was created, it had the right and the duty to formulate its own rules. It no longer belonged to him, and so he had to accept its rules, just like everyone else.

Rabbi Rodman says that he wonders whether Ben-Gurion, who was an avid reader of the Bible, was moved to obey the orders of the guards to the Council room by a passage in this week's Torah reading. It is possible.

Rabbi Rodman says that if you look at the five *sedras* of Terumah, Tetsaveh, Ki Tisa, Vayakhel and Pikudei, they deal almost exclusively with how Moses built the *Mishkan*. In the first three *sedras*, God instructs Moses on exactly how to build the *Mishkan*, and then, in the next two *sedras*, the Torah reports exactly how Moses built the *Mishkan*.

And then, in chapter forty, which is the last chapter of the book of Shemot, we read how Moses prepared the *Mishkan* for its official dedication, after it had been built. For fifteen verses, the instructions that God gives to Moses are spelled out in detail. God says to Moses: "You shall set up . . . ," "You shall spread . . . ," "You shall put . . . ," "You shall bring . . . ," "You shall take . . . ," etc., etc., etc. Then, in verse 16, we read: "And Moses did as all that the Lord had instructed him, so he did."

In Terumah, Tetsaveh and Ki Tisa, Moses is told what he must do. And then in Vayakhel and Pikudei, we are told that Moses did all that he was instructed to do. "He brought . . . ," "He put . . . ," "He spread . . . ," "He took . . . ," etc., etc., etc.

Rabbi Rodman says that, to be technical, Moses did not actually do everything in the making of the *Mishkan* by himself. As he puts it, "he outsourced the making of the *Mishkan*, its furnishings, and the vestments to others. Bezalel and Ohaliav were in charge of the construction, and all the men and women had a share in the making of the vestments and the making of the furniture. And yet the Torah describes the making of the *Mishkan* as if it were all the work of Moses, since he was the one who was assigned by God to build it, and he was the one who supervised its construction."

In verse eighteen, we read: "And Moses set up the Tabernacle," as if it were he who did all the work. The Torah then goes on to say: "He placed the sockets. He set up the planks. He inserted the bars. He erected the posts. He spread the tent over the tabernacle. He placed the covering of the tent on top of it – just as the Lord had commanded him to do."

And then it goes on to say: "Moses took the Pact and placed it in the Ark. He fixed the poles to the Ark. He placed the cover on top of the Ark. He brought the Ark into the Tabernacle. Then he put up the curtain for screening, and he screened off the Ark of the pact – just as the Lord had commanded him to do."

And then the Text goes on to say: "Moses placed the table in the Tent of Meeting, outside the curtain. He laid the show-bread before the Lord – as the Lord had commanded him to do. Moses placed the *menorah* in the Tent of Meeting opposite the Table. And Moses lit the lamps before the Lord – just as the Lord had commanded him to do."

And then the Text goes on to say: "Moses placed the altar of gold in the Tent of Meeting, before the curtain. On it Moses burned the incense – just as the Lord had commanded him to do."

And then the Text goes on to say: "Moses put up the screen for the entrance of the Tabernacle. And there, he placed the altar of burnt offering. On it, he offered up the burnt offering and the meal-offering – just as the Lord had commanded him to do."

And then, the Text goes on to say: "Moses placed the laver between the Tent of Meeting and the altar, and he put the water in it for washing – just as the Lord had commanded him to do."

And then the Torah says: "He set up the enclosure around the Tabernacle and the altar, and he put up the screen for the gate of the enclosure – just as the Lord had commanded him to do."

And then comes the climax: *Vayichal Moshe et hamelachah* – "Moses finished the work."

At this point you get the idea that Moses is the one who did it all. You get the sense from this chapter that Moses, single-handed, built and furnished the *Mishkan*. You get the sense from these thirty-three verses, in which Moses and only Moses is mentioned, that the whole task of the building of the *Mishkan* and the whole task of bringing in the furniture, and the whole task of arranging everything, was basically the work of Moses.

And then?

And then, just when you are psyched for the dedication ceremony to begin, comes this verse: *Vay'chas he'anan et ohel mo'ed, uchvod Adonai milei et hamishkan – vi'lo yachol Moshe lavo el ohel moed* – "The Cloud of Glory covered the *Mishkan*, and the Presence of the Lord filled the Tabernacle – and Moses could not enter the Tent of Meeting!"

How can this be?

For thirty-three verses we have been told, over and over again, that Moses built the Mishkan, and now that it is built, now that it is about to be dedicated, he can no longer enter it? Like Ben-Gurion, who created the Provisional Council and who now had to produce an invitation and an I.D. card in order to be allowed inside, Moses is not allowed to enter the *Mishkan* that he himself built? The man who built the *Mishkan* was banned from entering it at the very moment it was dedicated? How can this be?

Rabbi Rodman says that this passage teaches us a law of life, a law that we each have to learn at some point in our lives. The lesson is: Once you have created something, it no longer belongs to you!

The legislature may pass a law. But once they have passed it, they are bound by this law, just as everyone else is.

A novelist writes a book and sells it to Hollywood. How the director decides to adapt this novel for the movie is up to him, not to the author. The author can complain if he wants to, but the book is no longer his. The director has the right to interpret the story in the way that he sees fit.

A man may work for years to build up a company, and then he retires and turns the business over to his children. They will run it the way that they think is best. And the man has no right to say: I started this company and I want you to run it my way. It is no longer his, and he has to understand and accept that fact.

The clearest, and perhaps the most painful, example of this truth that Rabbi Rodman cites is the example of our children. We literally gave them life. We literally created them. And yet, there comes a time when these children of ours want to live their lives their way. And no parent has the right to say: I created you, and therefore you must live your lives the way I want you to. Our children are no longer ours, whether we created them or not.

Moses backed out of the *Mishkan* on the day that it was dedicated – and he never set foot in it again for the rest of his life! Aaron, not Moses, officiated at the *Mishkan* from then on. Aaron, not Moses, lit the *menorah* every day. Aaron, not Moses, offered the sacrifices on the altar every day. As Rabbi Rodman puts it: "We too have to learn to let go of what we have created, to recognize the boundaries that we once could cross, but that now can no longer cross. We too have to learn to respect the integrity and the independence of the other, even if that other is one that we ourselves brought into being." This is the insight that David Ben-Gurion taught, when he accepted the right of the guards at the door of the Provisional Council that he had created to check his credentials, as they did everyone else's. This is the lesson that Moses learned at the end of the book of Exodus when he drew back and allowed others to take his place in the Tabernacle that he had built. He learned that day, and he taught us, we who are his descendants, on that day that no one is above the law, not even those who created the law.

What can I add to this story about Ben-Gurion and this insight into the meaning of this chapter of the Torah, and these applications of this insight into our lives that I have learned from Rabbi Rodman? Not much, for his insights are very clear, and their implications for our own lives – as builders of businesses or as authors of literature or as creators of children are very apt. All I can add is the greatest example of letting go that exists, and then one personal experience, which I think supports what Rabbi Rodman has taught me.

The supreme exemplar of letting go of what one has created is God. According to the Jewish mystical tradition, all that is, was originally part of God. If so, how could there be creation? The Kabbalists say that God performed an act of *Tsimtsum*. God withdrew in order to make room for the world. And ever since, God stands outside the world, and lets its creatures do as they see fit, instead of controlling them. Can you imagine how hard it must sometimes be for God to let the creatures that He has made do things their way, and sometimes harm each other and harm the planet? But that is what God must do, if human beings are to be free. Like all parents, God must let go of those He has created.

And now, my personal experience:

Some years ago, I was invited to speak on the meaning of the stories of Elie Wiesel at the 92nd St Y. I received a very gracious introduction from the chairman, and I began my talk. I took one of my favorite Wiesel stories, and I started to analyze it. And then – much to my shock – Elie Wiesel walked in!

Can you imagine how intimidated I felt? If I could have found an opening in the floor, I would have crawled into it. How could I presume to talk about what a story meant in the presence of its creator? I wanted to stop, but he graciously insisted that I go on with my talk. And so I limped through my talk, as best I could.

And then, much to my amazement, halfway through the talk, I saw him reach into his pocket and take out a pen and a notebook and start to take notes!

After the talk, I spoke to him and thanked him for his kindness, and then I asked him what he had written down. He said to me: "I wrote down your explanation of what this story means – because I had never thought about the story that way before – and you may be right."

What Elie Weisel taught me that day is something that every storyteller learns, which is that once you have published a story – it no longer belongs to you. The reader is allowed to see in the story whatever he sees, and you, who are its author, have no right to deny him the right to understand your story from where he is.

And as it is with stories, so it is with those whose children take over the business that they have created and want to run it their way; and so it is with the children whom we have created who choose to live their lives their way; and so it is with the institutions that we have created that choose to grow and change and develop in ways that we could never have imagined . . . and so it was with Moses, who built the *Mishkan*, and then let go and made room for Aaron and his sons to serve the Lord within it without him.

When you are next in Jerusalem, let me suggest that you give Rabbi Rodman a call, and tell him that his Torah was heard today, many, many miles from where he lives. I think it will give him great pleasure to know that. And then tell him that I developed his thought by telling about an experience of my own. I suspect that he will probably say: "It is no longer my Torah. From the moment that I taught it to your rabbi, it became his, and from the moment that your rabbi taught it to you, it became yours, and so it is now your right and your task to apply this insight to the world in which you live."

For that is the way it is with a living Torah: from the day you teach it, it no longer belongs to you.

Fly Now – Pay Later

VAYIKRA

I WANT TO SHARE TWO DOCUMENTS with you today. One comes from the Middle Ages; the other comes from our own time.

I want to share these two documents with you today because I believe that, taken together, they provide a very important lesson in how to live, and in how not to live, that all of us – including me – need to learn.

First, the medieval document. It comes from a book called the Sefer HaChinuch by Rabbi Aharon Halevi of Barcelona.

In this week's Torah reading, the Torah says that a person who sins has to bring a sin-offering in order to win atonement. And then it provides a sliding scale of sacrifices that can be brought. On principle, one who sins should bring a sheep or a goat. But, *im eyn yado masseget*, "if the person is poor" and if he cannot afford to bring a sheep or a goat, then he may bring two doves or two pigeons instead. And then it says that if he cannot afford to bring two doves or two pigeons he may bring a tenth of an ephah of flour instead.

So far, the Text is clear. If you have a lot, then you are required to give a lot in order to atone for your sin. But if you are poor, and you only have a little, then you only need to give a little in order to atone for your sin.

Now listen to what Rabbi Aharon Halevi says on this passage:

"If a poor man decides to give more than he can afford in order to atone, if he decides to give more than the Law requires him to, if he decides to bring a sheep or a goat instead of a pigeon or a dove or an ephah of flour, and if he goes into debt in order to buy these animals or these birds, he does not fulfill his obligation. In fact," says Rabbi Aharon of Barcelona, "he sins!"

For if God showed compassion on him by allowing him to bring a sacrifice that is within his means, then it is not right for him to reject the favor and to incur an expense that will put him into debt.

And then Rabbi Aharon goes on to say one more thing, something that I find very impressive. He says: "If, in order to win atonement for sin, a person is not allowed to spend more than he can afford, then surely for no other purpose should a person spend beyond his means, for once a person becomes caught up in spending beyond his means, he may be driven to doing unethical things in order to sustain his habit of borrowing."

I find that a very powerful statement. If not even for a sacred purpose are we allowed to spend beyond our means, then surely for no lower purpose are we allowed to live beyond our means.

The reason why I find this a powerful statement is because we live in a culture that is constantly tempting us to live beyond our means. We are constantly being bombarded by ads that make us feel the need for luxuries that we could actually live very well without. We all walk around carrying plastic credit cards, whose purpose it is to tempt us to buy things that we may or may not be able to afford. And we are all caught up in a frantic, never-ending chase to keep up with our neighbors and to get ahead of our neighbors. And we feel like failures if we don't have as much or if we don't spend as much as they do.

We live in a credit culture. And the psychic and the economic cost of living beyond our means is something that we can all testify to from our own personal experience. And so the point of view expressed by Rabbi Aharon Halevi stands in complete and utter contrast to the way in which we live. If even for atonement purposes we are not allowed to spend beyond our means, then surely we are not allowed to do so for luxuries.

Let me teach you a law that may surprise you.

Do you know that according to Jewish Law, there is a limit to the amount of charity that you are allowed to give? I know lots of people who observe this law, even though they don't know that it is a law. I know some people who observe this law, even though they don't observe any other Jewish law. But there is a law that there is a limit to how much you are allowed to spend for charity.

What is the reason for this law?

The reasoning is that if you give away too much, you may end up in debt, or you may end up becoming dependent on charity yourself.

Now, if a religion that reveres *tzedakah* as much as ours does, nevertheless sets a limit on how much you are allowed to give, in order to prevent you from spending beyond your means, then surely we ought not to spend more than we have in order to acquire things that we don't really need.

I wish that this comment of Aharon Halevi's could be posted in our homes, and in the loan offices of our banks, and in the offices of the people who write the ads that entice us to spend more than we should. It might serve as an antidote to the addiction to acquire that possesses us all. It might serve as an answer to the slogan of the airplane companies and the tourist agencies that I sometimes see in the papers: FLY NOW, PAY LATER.

It might serve to remind us that living beyond our means is not only bad economics, but that it is also a violation of the Torah.

The second document that I want to share with you today is a brochure that I picked up in Los Angeles recently. I was in Los Angeles with my family on vacation, and we happened to drive up Wilshire Blvd. in Beverly Hills, and as we did, we passed the canyon of condominiums that were being built there at the time. And just for the fun of it, we decided to stop and look at one of these new buildings – which, by the way, is something that you are not allowed to do according to Jewish Law. You are not allowed to ask a salesman the price of an object if you have no intention of buying it, for you are stealing his time, and you are getting up his hopes and you are only going to disappoint him in the end. But I confess that that is what we did. We picked up a couple of brochures that describe these new and elegant high-rises, and I still have one as a souvenir of the trip. And we spoke for a few minutes to the person who was in charge of marketing these condos.

I remember that he was a well-dressed man, who spoke with a

British accent, and had a flower in the lapel of his dark suit. He looked like the kind of person who would be comfortable discussing a million-dollar apartment.

Nevertheless, I asked him: How much does a one-bedroom condo in this building cost? The person in charge of marketing answered: One-bedroom condos in this building start at seven hundred and fifty thousand dollars. He said that without blinking.

I grew up in Pittsburgh, where, when I was a child, you could buy a whole plantation – WITH SLAVES – for that kind of money! But I gulped, and then I continued the conversation. I asked: How much does the deluxe penthouse cost?

The gentleman answered: It sells for fifteen million dollars, but I am sorry to tell you that it is no longer available. It was sold this morning.

When I heard that, I felt sorry that I had arrived just a few hours too late. If I had come just a little bit sooner, I could have bought it. So I asked: How much does the next most expensive condo cost? And he told me that that one was only fourteen million dollars.

And then the salesman said something that made me feel a little bit better. He said: The credit terms on these condos are very reasonable, and that makes them a bargain.

Oh, I thought to myself: Thank you for explaining that. Because if you hadn't said that, I would not have known that a fourteen million dollar condo was a bargain.

And then I asked the salesman: Can you please tell me why this place is so expensive?

The salesmen said: "Because of its location. It is within walking distance of Tiffany's and all the other stores on Rodeo Drive. And besides, the views from here are glorious."

I don't know about you but it seems to me that if you can afford to buy a condo that costs fourteen million dollars, you can probably afford to take a bus, or maybe even a cab to Rodeo Drive. But evidently, one of the pitches that the salesmen make for these apartments is that they are within walking distance of Rodeo Drive.

It seems to me that you would have to walk to Rodeo Drive an awful lot of times to save enough money to buy a condo for fourteen million dollars – but what do I know?

I walked out that day without buying a condo, and as I did, I wondered to myself: What really counts the most when you are buying a house? Is it the view from the window – or is it the point of view of the people who live inside?

If you have a certain point of view on life, on love, and on family, than a house can be a very happy place. If not, then it isn't, regardless of the view outside.

The brochure that they gave me that day says that each condo has golden door knobs! That is a nice accessory, I must admit, but what does it mean to a person who comes home from work at night and dreads having to open the door, because of the anger and the bickering that awaits him inside?

The brochure that they gave me says that the living room has four distinct areas for conversation. That's nice, but what does that mean if the people who live in this apartment have nothing to say to each other?

If you stand in the lobby of this building, or, if you go around the corner to Rodeo Drive, you will undoubtedly see people who are elegantly dressed and who are bedecked in glittering jewelry. But what does that mean if some of these people have souls that are in rags, and spirits that are tarnished?

What good does it do, I wonder, to build or to buy the house of your dreams if you can't sleep in it at night without nightmares?

This brings me to telling you about the most *shabbasdik* community that I have ever visited. It was not in Jerusalem. It was not in Williamsburg and it was not in Boro Park. It was in Prestwick, Scotland, where as far as I know, there are very few Jews.

I remember once spending a Shabbat in Prestwick, which is near the airport, in Scotland. I had been to Iceland for a week, as a civilian guest of the army, conducting Pesach services for the soldiers. And now that Pesach was over, I was hitchhiking from Iceland to London, with the air force, and so I flew to Prestwick. I was supposed to transfer planes in Prestwick, but by the time I landed there, it was too late to take a flight to London before Shabbat. And so I was stuck in Prestwick for the day. And I knew no one there. I had dinner at the hotel, and then I wandered the streets of Prestwick. And I still remember what I saw. As I walked the streets that night, I looked into the windows of the houses that I passed by. I don't know if there were any Jews in Prestwick or not. My guess is probably not. But it was one of the most *shabbesdik* scenes that I have ever seen in my whole life. In each and every home that I passed and looked into, the family was sitting together at the table and I could hear them singing and talking and laughing and celebrating. And I have never gotten over that sight. It was one of the most tranquil, one of the most serene, scenes that I have ever seen. I don't know if these people had golden door knobs – I kind of doubt it. And I don't know if they had four different conversation corners in their living rooms or not – I kind of doubt that too. But my guess is that they were at least as happy as the people who live in those fancy condos near Rodeo Drive, and maybe even more so. The view from the houses I saw in Prestwick may not have been as fancy, but the point of view inside those houses seemed wonderful.

I share these two documents with you today, one from the Sefer HaChinuch, the other from the brochure that I picked up on Wilshire Blvd. in Los Angeles, because I think that they both make the same point, that they both teach the same lesson, which is that to put yourself in debt in order to have "the best things in life" is to lose one of the best things in life – which is: peace of mind.

"Fly now – pay later" is one way to live.

But I think that Rabbi Aharon Halevi's way is wiser. He teaches us to live within our means and to know what our goals are. He teaches us: Live now, love now, serve God now, and pay attention to your family now, so that you won't have to pay later.

What Should You Say
When You Don't Know What to Say?

SHEMINI

HAVE YOU EVER HAD the experience of standing outside the door of a *shiva* house, and trying to gather up your courage before you walk in?

I have—more than once.

What do you say when you don't know what to say? What do you say when everything that you can think of saying feels so glib, so insufficient, and so inadequate?

More than once, I have been tempted not to pay a *shiva* call out of fear that I won't know what to say or what to do when I get there. Have you had that experience too?

Sometimes, we say the wrong things – out of nervousness, or out of stupidity. I have a friend who kept a notebook during *shiva* in which she wrote down all the stupid and insensitive things people said to her. What else can you do, when you have to sit there and listen to people saying stupid things? So she gritted her teeth and listened politely, and after they left, she wrote down in her notebook these stupid things that they had said, and when she was in a better mood she would take them out, and reread them, and smile instead of feeling angry.

I have my own collection of bloopers that I have heard at a house of *shiva*, or that people have told me were said to them.

Here are some of my favorites – and honestly, believe me – I have not made these up:

"At least you were prepared." Isn't that a nice thing to say to somebody whose spouse was ill for a long time? – "At least you were prepared?"

Or: "At least she went quickly." Isn't that a stupid thing to say to someone who is in shock at the sudden loss of someone whom he loved? "At least she went quickly?"

Or: "I know how you feel." Really? Do you? Have you gone through what I am going through? And if you have, are you now going to tell me in gory detail what you experienced? Am I supposed to comfort you? I thought that I was the one who was supposed to be comforted here?

Or: "You're young and pretty. You'll find someone else." That gets my vote for the dumbest thing that I have ever heard anyone say at a house of *shiva*. "You're young and pretty, and you will find someone else?" Is that what someone wants to hear at a time like this? I have actually heard someone say that to a mourner just an hour after they had come back from the cemetery – believe it or not!

And there is one more example of what not to say at a *shiva* house that I want to share with you today. I was present when someone said to the mourner: "Are you planning to sell your house now, and if so, how much do you think you will be asking for it?" As if that was what was on the mind of a mourner during *shiva*? I did not make that up. Honest.

What then should you say at a time when you don't know what to say?

I think that we can learn what to say from the example of Aaron in today's *sedra*. At the moment of his greatest glory, at the climax of his installation ceremony as High Priest, after a whole week of pomp and circumstance and celebration – two of Aaron's sons, Nadav and Avihu, die. There are all kinds of theories as to why they died: the bottom line is that to a parent it doesn't really matter how or why they died. The bottom line is that they died, and that, in one fell swoop, Aaron's day of glory turned to dust and ashes.

What does Aaron say?

Vayidom Aharon. "Aaron was silent." He gritted his teeth and said nothing. And when his brother, Moses, tried to comfort him by uttering some kind of a cliché, Aaron puts him in his place.

Aaron kept silent.

What were his choices? He could have blasphemed, if he wanted to. I am sure he must have been tempted to. Who wouldn't be at such a time? But if he had, what would he have done for an encore? And who would he have hurt by blaspheming: God? Or himself?

He could have carried on just as he had before. He could have continued doing the work of the Tabernacle, as if nothing had happened. But if he had, would his service have been sincere? Would the words that he recited have come from the heart or would he have just been reciting the words that he was supposed to say, even though he did not mean them?

And is God so desperate that he needs the praises of people who do not mean what they say?

There is a strange law in the Jewish tradition – one that you may not know about. The law is that from the time you experience the loss of a loved one until the time of the burial, a mourner is not supposed to *daven*. In fact, a mourner is not allowed to *daven*. If there are nine people present plus the mourner, there is no *minyan*, because the mourner does not count towards the quorum that is needed for a *minyan*. I know some people who observe this rule of not *davening* many times during the year, but this is the law of the mourner. From the time of the loss until the time of the burial, the mourner is not allowed to pray.

Why?

The assumption is that the mourner's mind is on other things. The assumption is that he is in no mood to pray or to praise. And so, the law says: Let him attend to the arrangements instead. If there are nine people present and the mourner, there is no *minyan*. At the time of his loss until the burial the mourner is excused from *davening*, and is in fact barred from *davening*. This is the rule: a mourner should not, and cannot, pray. A mourner is not counted as a member of the *minyan*, from the time of his loss until the time of the burial. Then, starting with the burial, starting with the *Kaddish* that he or she recites at the graveside, the mourner is snapped back into the order of Jewish life again. But for that one day, the mourner does not, and should not, pray, because God does not need the prayers of one who has no heart to pray or praise.

Perhaps that is why Aaron withdrew and did not officiate at the services as if nothing had happened on the day when his children died. Instead, Aaron withdrew into himself. He nursed his wounds. And then, when he was able to, he came back and officiated at the service once again.

And I have no proof, but I imagine that his service after this experience must have been different than his service had been before. Perhaps his faith was deeper. Perhaps his grief had changed him, for better or for worse. But at the time of his calamity, Aaron said nothing. He did not recite clichés that he did not mean. He did not blaspheme or vent his anger at God. Instead: *Vayidom Aharon* – "Aaron was silent."

And from this, the Sages derive a rule about the etiquette of a *shiva* call. They say that the comforter should take his cue from the one who is in mourning. If the mourner wants to speak – you should listen. If the mourner wants to listen – you should speak. And if the mourner wants to be silent, then you should be silent too. Better to share in the silence than to prattle and say words that are inadequate or inappropriate at a time like this.

I think of two experiences from which I learned how to pay, and how not to pay, a *shiva* call; two experiences from which I learned what to say and what not to say.

The first occurred in my former congregation. A young man died suddenly – with no warning. He died of a heart attack while helping to clean the synagogue building after a water main had broken and the floor had been flooded.

This man left a wife and two teenage girls behind. For a week, the house was mobbed. And when *shiva* was finally over, the girls asked me a very strange question. They said to me: "Rabbi, why are you not allowed to talk to the mourners during *shiva*?"

I didn't know what they meant until they explained. The house had been full of people all week, but most of the visitors did not know what to say to these young kids who had just lost their father, and so they avoided them. They spoke to each other instead of speaking to the mourners. And they talked about everything under the sun except the reason why they were there. They spoke about sports, and about business, and about politics, and about movies they had seen, and they avoided the real reason why they were there. And so, at the end of the *shiva*, the girls thought that you are not allowed to talk to the mourners, for no one had talked to them, and so they asked me: Why are you not allowed to talk to the mourners during *shiva*?

That is my first word of advice to you today. If you come to make a *shiva* call, don't ignore the mourners. Listen to them, talk to them, hug them, sit with them, be silent with them – but be with them! For they are the reason why you have come.

My second story is a beautiful one. It comes from Deborah Lipstadt, who is now a professor of Jewish Studies at Emory University in Atlanta. She writes that she lost her father when she was a college student. People came to the house, and during the course of their visits, many people told her stories about her father, and what he had meant in their lives.

One person told her this story. Her father had to go for radiation and chemotherapy, which, as many of you know, is not a very pleasant experience. The doctors wanted him to go on *Shabbat*, but he asked if he could go on another day instead, because he was an observant Jew. They said that he could go on another day if he wanted to, but they warned him that the day he chose was the day when some of the most severely ill patients came for treatment.

He went in, and there was a room full of people waiting to be called. There were people – and there were shards of people – sitting there in the waiting room. There were people who were hoping that treatment would help them, and there were people who knew that treatment would not help them. And they all sat there waiting their turn. They sat there silently, grimly, each one wrapped up in his or her own thoughts.

Mr. Lipstadt came in and sat down, and quickly sized up the situation. And so he quietly began to hum a *niggun* to himself. And one by one, these people sat up and began to listen, and then some of them eventually joined in with them. By the time he was called by the nurse to go inside, he had the whole group singing along with them. As he got up to go inside, he turned and said to them: "Would you like to know the meaning of the words to this song? It is a song from the Psalms, set to music by Shlomo Carlebach, and it means; "I will lift up my eyes to the mountains. From whence shall my help come? My help will come from the Lord, the Creator of the heavens and the earth."

And then, like a conductor bidding farewell to his choir, he bowed, and wished them well, and told them to keep singing the song as he went in to have his treatment.

Deborah Lipstadt had never heard this story before, and she might never have heard it if it were not for the thoughtfulness of this person who told it to her during *shiva*. What a comforting story that must have been!

If you can do that, if you can share with the mourners a beautiful memory of what this person meant to you and what he taught you, your *shiva* call will be a blessing indeed.

So this is my advice to you on what to say when you don't know what to say:

First: know that it is alright to be silent, and to share in the pain that the family is feeling without words. You need not be a philosopher or a poet at a time like this. It is enough to be a friend, and you can be a friend by your silence as well as by your words.

Second: know that if you feel that you must speak, try not to be glib, and try not to say clichés. You need not defend God, nor do you need to deny the pain. It is enough to say that you care about them, and that you wish you knew what to say, but that you don't.

And one thing more you should do. The house is full to overflowing during the week of mourning. The real test of a friend is if you come back the week after, when the house is empty, and the rooms are so terribly quiet. Lots of people say as they leave the house of *shiva*: "Call me if you need anything." That does not cost anything to say. The real test of a friend is if you say: "Can I take the kids to my house for a while?" Or: "What would you like me to bring you for lunch?" Or: "Do you need someone to do the laundry, or to take someone to the airport?" Or: "Can I help you with the thank you cards?"

Don't just say: "Call me if you need anything." Be specific. Say: "Can I do this for you?" Or "can I do that for you?"

Let us learn from Aaron in this week's Torah reading that there are times for silence. Let us learn from Job that there are times when the mourner wishes to speak, and when he or she does, we have the duty to listen. And let us learn from Job that there are times when the mourner wishes to listen, and when he or she does, we have the duty to speak. And let us learn from the person who came to Deborah Lipstadt's house and brought the family so much comfort by telling them a story that described to them what the one they had lost was really like.

And let us try, when sorrow comes to those whom we care about, to bring them a measure of comfort – either by our words or by our silence. And may God help us in this task.

"These You May Eat" – Sometimes

SHEMINI

L ET ME BEGIN by asking you a question:

There is a basic principle in Jewish Ethics that *Ezehu chacham? Halomed mikol adam* – "Who is truly wise? The person who is willing to learn from everyone."

My question is: Which group in Jewish life do you think needs to hear this teaching the most nowadays? Which group in Jewish life today do you think needs to be reminded that you can and should learn from every group and not lock yourself up within your own group and ignore the wisdom that can be found elsewhere?

Anyone?

My guess is that most of you would answer: the *Haredim*, or as the media sometimes calls them the Ultra-Orthodox. We think of these people as insular, as parochial, as locked up within their own society, as people who know nothing and care nothing and learn nothing from the people in the world outside. Is that who you were thinking of when I asked this question?

If so, you were wrong. For the truth is that many of us are just as isolated and just as provincial and just as parochial as we think they are. Many of us know even less about them than they know about us. And the truth is that there is much that we can and should learn from them, just as there is much that they can and should learn from us.

Let me give you just one example of what I mean today. Rabbi Avi Shafran is the spokesman for the Agudath Yisrael organization in the United States. Agudath Yisrael is the organization of the

Haredi Jews, and so you would expect him to write with no interest and no knowledge of the secular world. And you would be wrong. I read him whenever I can because he writes clearly and wisely about the world in which we live – from the perspective of the Jewish tradition.

For instance, this is the Shabbat on which we read from the Torah the laws about which foods we may eat and which foods we may not eat. And so I want to share with you a brief essay on this topic that Rabbi Shafran has written. It is about a page and a quarter long, and yet it includes insights that come from the world of sociology, from the world of psychology, and from the world of ancient history. And it makes a suggestion at the end that I believe we should consider.

Rabbi Shafran begins by making this observation about food that I had never thought about before.

He says that that unless you live in a third-world country, you have more choices about what to eat than 99.99% of the people who have ever lived before. Even if someone who only lived a hundred years ago were to come back today and were to take a trip through a typical supermarket, or if that person were to go to a typical restaurant and look at the menu, he would be simply overwhelmed by the amount and the variety of food that would be available for him to choose from.

How do you choose between six different kinds of soup or between five different brands of tuna fish that are for sale side by side on the shelves of a typical supermarket? And how do you choose between the seven different entrees that are offered at the average restaurant?

Our visitor from the last century would probably walk out of the supermarket or the restaurant bewildered and simply unable to choose between so many different choices.

And yet we moderns are not as impressed as he would be. We take the variety of foods that we can buy at the store and the variety of foods that we can eat when we go out to a restaurant for granted. And therefore, we are constantly on the lookout for some new delicacy that we can eat, for some new restaurant that we can try. By the third time we go to the same restaurant or by the third time that we try the latest delicacy that is for sale in the supermarket, we are jaded. The visitor from a hundred years ago would be ecstatic the first time he tasted a hamburger or savored a cheesecake, but for us, who have eaten these things all our lives, they are experiences that we take for granted and that bore us.

And that brings me to the second lesson that I learned from Rabbi Shafran. He writes about a scientific experiment that was carried out last year which was described in an article that appeared in the *Journal of Social Psychology.*

The people in one group were allowed to eat as much chocolate as they wanted whenever they wanted. The people in the second group were allowed to eat only one piece of chocolate a week.

Can you guess the results?

Those who could eat chocolate whenever they wanted to reported that after a while it was not a particular pleasure to eat. Those in the group that were only allowed to eat one piece of chocolate a week reported that it was a real delight whenever they ate it. From which we learn, he says, that what we eat is important, but when we eat and how much we eat is also important. If you only eat a delicacy once in a while, it tastes much better when you finally eat it than it does if you eat it every day.

And now, to the lesson from ancient history. When we think of having a meal, we think of meat, or perhaps of fish, as the main course. Isn't that so? But it was not like that in the ancient world. In the ancient world, the term for having a meal was "breaking bread together." And here is the proof: When we begin a meal, what blessing do we recite? We say the *motsi* in which we thank God for bringing BREAD forth from the earth. We don't begin the meal by thanking God for the meat or for the fish we are about to eat. We thank God for the bread we are about to eat. Because the average meal in antiquity consisted essentially of bread, perhaps with some salad on the side, perhaps with relish of some kind, but essentially a meal consisted of bread. That is why if you eat a five-course meal but you do not have any bread with it, you are not supposed to say the *birkat hamazon*, because technically what you ate was not a meal.

Meat was eaten on occasion. The Sages of the Talmud were not vegetarians, although there is a vegetarian stream in the Bible and in the Talmud. But meat was a delicacy, an expensive delicacy, and so it was usually eaten on the Sabbath or on the Holy Days. The

Talmud tells of how the great sage Shamai, when he went to the marketplace, if he found some delicacy he would buy it, and say that he was buying this special food for the Sabbath. And then, if he found another delicacy even tastier than this one was, he would declare the second one earmarked for the Sabbath, and he would eat the first one during the week.

That was the classic Jewish view of meat. Both because it was expensive, and because it was so good, meat was reserved for the Sabbath. During the week, people ate other, more available, and less expensive foods.

Which leads Rabbi Shafran to raise the question that I want you to consider with me today on the Sabbath when we read the laws of permitted and forbidden foods:

What would it be like if we took meat off the menu for weekdays and made it part of the way in which we honor the Sabbath instead?

I think that at least three things would happen, and all of them would be good.

First, if the study that was published in the *Journal of Social Psychology* is right, the study that said that chocolate tasted better to those who ate it only once a week than it did to those who ate it every day, then our Sabbath meals would taste better. If meat were a treat, we would enjoy it more than we would if we ate it all the time.

Second, obesity is one of the major problems facing people today. The people of Central Africa may be coping with starvation, but the people of this country are struggling with the problem of obesity. Study after study shows that obesity is endangering the lives of millions of people in America. This is why Michelle Obama has chosen to devote her efforts to fighting obesity, both in children and in adults. She is on a campaign to persuade the public schools to provide more whole grains and more vegetables and more fruits in their cafeterias, and to offer less sweets and fats. She is also campaigning for people to exercise more, but that is a subject that I do not want to get into today, for, as you know, I am not a great *chassid* of exercise. I believe that exercise may prolong your life, but not by as much time as you waste exercising. But imagine how different our lives would be, and imagine how different our health would be, if we only ate meat once a week.

And third, imagine how much more festive our Sabbath tables would be if we only ate meat once a week, if we only ate meat *l'kavod shabbas*?

For all three of these reasons, so that the meat we eat will taste better, as every delicacy does when it is eaten rarely, so that our health will be better, and so that our Sabbath will be a day of delight, let us consider making meat a once-a-week delicacy, shall we?

And let this be the Sabbath on which we begin.

Sweat

EMOR

HAVE YOU EVER BEEN in an argument, and then, when it was over, you think of what you should have said? That is what happened to me last *Shabbat*. I had a disagreement here. It involved one of our retired rabbis. I won't tell you who it was, but I will tell you that it was not Rabbi Miller, and it was not Rabbi Herring, and it was not Rabbi Routtenberg. And if you guess who it was, I will deny it. This is what happened:

The day was a real scorcher. The temperature was at least 95 – maybe more – and the humidity was unbearable. And so, one of our retired rabbis – who lives about three-quarters of a mile from here, and who walks to *shul* on *Shabbat*, came to *shul* that day without a tie, and without a jacket. Evidently, this rabbi feels that *kavanah* is more important in prayer than what you wear, and evidently he feels that it is hard to have *kavanah* when you are sweating and overheated.

Someone came up to me after the services, and said: "Do you see what this rabbi is wearing – or to be exact – do you see what this rabbi is not wearing today?

"Isn't that terrible? Would you please speak to him and tell him that coming to *shul* without a tie and without a jacket is disrespectful, and that he should not do it again."

My first reaction was to say: "What do you want from me? I am not the rabbi of this congregation. I am just the interim rabbi. And so I don't want to get involved in this matter. If you don't like the way this man is dressed, go tell him so yourself."

My second reaction was to say to this man: "Haven't you ever been on a religious *kibbutz* in Israel on a *Shabbat*? If you have, you have seen men come to *shul* in their white shirts – without a tie, without a jacket – put their rifles in the closet, and take out their *tallesim*, and begin to *daven*. If they can do that there, then why can't we do that here?"

That was what I said, but it was only afterwards that I realized what I should have said. I should have realized that you can argue with the customs of the religious *kibbutzim* in Israel, but you can't argue with the Bible, and there is a passage in today's *haftorah* which clearly states that my rabbi friend is permitted to come to shul without a tie and without a jacket if he wants to. It is right here in today's *haftorah*.

The Prophet Ezekiel describes the way in which the *Kohanim* and the *Leviim* will officiate at the Holy Temple when it is rebuilt. He says that when they enter the gates of the inner court, they shall have nothing woolen upon themselves. And then, in verse 18, it gives the reason for this law:

It says: *Pa-arei fishtim yihiyu al rosham, umichnisei fishtim yihiyu al matneihem; lo yachgeru ba'yaza.* "They shall wear linen turbans on their heads, and they shall wear linen breeches on their loins, they shall not wear anything that causes sweat."

So there you have it: If the *Kohanim* and the *Leviim*, who did the holiest work in the *Bet Hamikdash*, were commanded to wear only linen and not wool, so that they would not sweat, then surely my rabbi friend is allowed to wear no tie and no jacket when he has to walk nearly a mile or so to *shul* in hot weather so that he does not sweat.

I think that my friend, and the farmers who live on these *kibbutzim*, are both right. God cares much more about the spirit and the integrity with which we pray than about the clothes that we wear. I have seen people come to the synagogue dressed to the nines who never even open a *siddur*, much less pray a word. God surely prefers the prayers of someone who prays sincerely than the prayers of someone who comes to the synagogue dressed like a fashion plate but whose heart is not in the words that he or she recites.

But when I was confronted with the question about my friend

who comes to services without a jacket or a tie, and when I noticed what it says in today's *haftorah* about how the *Kohanim* and the *Leviim* were commanded to wear linen, not wool, so that they would not sweat, it led me to think about the place of sweat in our lives.

There was a psychologist some years ago who made a fortune by writing a book called: "Don't Sweat the Small Stuff – And It's All Small Stuff." Do you remember that book?

The book was an instant best-seller, and there were all kinds of spin-offs. You could buy pins to wear on your lapel with the words of this title on them, and you could buy signs with these words to keep on your desk at work. There were sequels to this book that dealt with how to be a parent without sweating it, and how to run your office without sweating it, etc., etc. The author of these books made a fortune. In the first year after the book came out, he made thirty-five million dollars. The only thing wrong was that the following year, at the height of his popularity, he had a heart attack and died at the age of forty-five! Who knows? Perhaps he sweated too much and died from not being able to handle the stress that comes with great success. I don't know if that is true or not, but I wonder. I am sure that if I were to make thirty-five million dollars in one year, that I would probably find that very stressful, wouldn't you?

I must tell you that, when that book came out and everybody was buying it, I was a little bit skeptical. I think that the title is a half-truth. He was right: We should not sweat the small stuff, no doubt about it. The executive who has to make sure that the pens and the paper clips in his office are arranged just right is being overly concerned about something trivial, and that will do him no good. The parent who has to be asked for permission for everything that his child wants to do is making too much of small things. That person is heading for trouble – for himself and for his child. The board member who makes a do-or-die issue about every single small item on the agenda needs to be reminded that a hundred years from now, this matter will not really be so important, and therefore that he should not treat it as if it is a matter of life or death. And so the title of the book is right: a person should not sweat the small stuff. It is not a healthy way to live.

But I question the validity of the second half of the title of that book: "And It's All Small Stuff." Is that really true? Is everything really small stuff? Are there not some things that are worth sweating over? What kind of children I am raising? Who I will marry, and how I will treat my spouse? Whether my boss treats me with dignity and with respect or not? Whether I am making a living, and whether I will have enough to retire on? What are my values and am I living by them? Are these not ultimately important matters, and are they not well worth sweating over?

I want to tell you two stories this morning. One is a story about when not to sweat; the other is a story about when it is right and good to sweat. One is a story against sweating, and one is a story in favor of sweating. Listen to them both:

The first story I heard from a rabbi who is a chaplain in the United States Army, whom I met some time ago. This man had recently come home from a tour of duty with the American Army in Afghanistan. He was in Dallas on some kind of a military assignment, and he was on the way home from there, looking forward to being with his family for *Shabbat*.

When he got to the airport, he learned that his plane was delayed by an hour, for some reason. There was nothing he could do about it, so he shrugged and sat down to wait in a seat near the gate.

From where he was sitting, he could not help but overhear the commotion that was going on at the ticket counter. There was a man there who was going ballistic over the fact that the plane was late, and he was taking it out on the poor woman who was working at the counter. He told her that it was an outrage that the plane was late. He told her that he would never fly this airline again. He told her that he was going to write a letter of protest to the company. He told her that he wanted a refund because of this delay. And he said all this at the top of his voice, just in case the woman at the counter was hard of hearing.

The plane finally came in, and after a few moments, they were able to board. The chaplain struck up a conversation with the person who was sitting next to him, and they were so engrossed in their conversation that they simply did not notice when the airline stewardess went by their aisle, offering drinks. When they realized that she had passed them by, the chaplain got up and went to the back of the plane, where the stewardesses were sitting, and asked if they could still have something to drink. The stewardesses said that they would be happy to accommodate them, just as soon as the pilot took off the "Fasten Your Seat Belt" sign. When the sign went off, she brought them their drinks, and some snacks as well.

The chaplain – who by the way was a rabbi – did not think much about the incident, but the passenger in the row behind him was very upset. He said, in a very loud voice, that the stewardess had probably passed him by on purpose, because he was wearing a *kipa*, and that this was a clear case of anti-Semitism. The man – who turned out to be the same person who had caused such a commotion over the fact that the plane was late taking off – was furious now over how the rabbi was being treated. He urged him to get a lawyer and sue the airline, just as soon as the plane landed.

The rabbi thought about how this man was behaving, and he wondered to himself: "How come I am not upset over these incidents, and this man is so angry about them?" And then he figured out what it was. He said to the man, "You have to understand why I am not as angry as you seem to be."

"Really? How come you aren't as mad as I am? I thought people in the military were supposed to have some guts," said the man.

"It's not a matter of guts," said the rabbi. "It's a matter of perspective."

"What do you mean – perspective?" said the man with suspicion.

Well, I must tell you that, compared to the last flight that I took, this one is pure pleasure. You see, my last plane trip was on a C-130 in Afghanistan. This plane may seem crowded to you, but that one was a lot more crowded, believe me. We were jammed in together like sardines, and we had no place in which to store our luggage or our guns. So we had to hold them on our laps all during the flight. And the air conditioning on this plane may not be working perfectly; on that flight there was no air conditioning and the temperature on board was over a hundred degrees. But I guess the main difference between that flight and this one is that when we come in for a landing in Pittsburgh, no one will be shooting at us. On that flight, we had to come in close and quick in order to avoid the missiles that were being shot at us. So, when you look at things in that perspective, this is really not such a bad flight after all. After you have flown on a C-130 under fire in Afghanistan, you learn not to sweat the small stuff, and you don't get upset if the stewardess forgets to bring you a cup of coffee."

The man calmed down and did not utter a single word of complaint for the rest of the flight.

The point of this story is that there is a time not to sweat. When little things go wrong – remember that that is just what they are: little things. And don't let them aggravate you to the point where you lose sight of all the good things that are going on in your life. Don't be like that traveler who kept losing his cool over every thing that went wrong on his flight, and forgot to focus on the main thing: which is that he was on the way home to his family, and that the plane was bringing him there in safety.

And don't be like those people in this synagogue, who get all worked up over whether someone wears a jacket or a tie, instead of staying focused on what really counts the most – the opportunity to pray and to study Torah which are the real reasons for coming to the synagogue on *Shabbat*.

And now, let me tell you a story that makes the opposite point, the point that sometimes it is a *mitzvah* to sweat, and to care, and to be aggravated. I do so, because, as so often happens in life, opposites can both be true.

A certain rabbi was once hospitalized. In the morning, the rabbi did what he did every day of his life. He took out his *tallit* and *tefillin* and *davened* in his hospital room. And when he came to the passage in which we pray that God will help those who are poor, he sighed with empathy. And when he came to the passage in which we pray that God will provide for those who have no clothing, he groaned with sympathy. And when he came to the passage about how God should be good to those who are homeless, he groaned again with sympathy.

A doctor came in and asked him to please stop making so much noise. He told him that he was disturbing the other patients with his groans and his sighs. Just at that moment, a patient down the hall let loose with a terrible scream of pain.

The rabbi asked the doctor: *Far vos lost du eym shrein?* "Why do you let him scream?"

The doctor said: Because *eym tut vey* – "he is in pain."

Mer tut oich vey, said the rabbi. "I am in pain too."

The point of this story is that a good human being is, and ought to be, in pain, not only when his own body is suffering, but when he thinks of all the other people in the world who are suffering. He should feel for, and with, those who are poor, those who are hungry, and those who are homeless. And if he doesn't, if he is oblivious to or not bothered by the suffering of others, then there is something wrong with his piety.

A truly pious person sweats and suffers, worries and loses sleep, over the state of the world, and not just over the state of his own self. A truly pious person is offended by the idea that "it is all small stuff." The Buddhists believe that. Buddhists believe that anything and everything that happens in this world is trivial, compared to the cosmos itself. But Jews don't believe that. We believe that hunger and injustice, poverty and homelessness are real and serious, and that it is our duty to care about them and to do what we can to alleviate them. I believe that any religion that teaches us to ignore these things and to focus on spiritual things instead, is a distortion of how God wants us to live.

And so I have two lessons to share with you today, and I am not sure which is the more important. The first lesson is that we should not sweat the small stuff. If the *Kohanim* and the *Leviim* in today's *haftorah* were told to dress in a way that would be most comfortable, then so can we. The synagogue is not a place devoted to high fashion, and so it is permitted and perhaps praiseworthy to dress in a way that will avoid sweating. That is why we have air conditioning here. Perhaps my friend, and those who live on the religious *kibbutzim*, could leave their jackets and ties in shul so that they would have them there when they arrived, and not have to wear them in the summer heat. That might be a fair compromise. But those who make a big deal out of what they wear or do not wear during services are wrong. They are sweating the small stuff instead of paying attention to the big stuff which ought to occupy us in the synagogue. And so, to these people, let me say: please don't sweat the small stuff. It really is not worth it.

But the second lesson I have for you today is the opposite: sweat the small stuff. By the small stuff, I mean the pain and the suffering of others. Know that their pain has to be ours too. The suffering of the hungry and the homeless has to be our responsibility, and no one dare be indifferent to it. Sweat the small stuff – for this kind of stuff is worth getting aggravated about; it is worth getting involved in dealing with; it is worth fighting to overcome and to correct. To a callous person, the pain of others may be small stuff. To a righteous Jew, the pain of others is no small thing. It is the meaning and the measure of our own humanity.

So if someone asks you: what did the rabbi say today? You can tell him that he said two opposite things, not to sweat the small stuff, and to know that there are many things in life, especially the pain of our fellow and sister human beings which are not small stuff, not at all, and that we should sweat to overcome them.

And if that person says to you: how can this rabbi say two opposite things to you in the same sermon? Tell him that Judaism is often not an "either-or" but instead is a "both-and" religion. And if he does not understand that, will you stand up for me, and defend me, will you please?

Don't let me sweat this alone.

Some of My Favorite Curses

TWO THINGS HAPPENED during the Torah reading today that were very strange.

Did you notice them?

The first was that the Torah reader got the sixth *aliyah*. That does not usually happen.

And the second thing that happened this morning that was strange was the way in which the Torah reader read this *aliyah*. Usually, the Torah reader reads the Torah slowly and carefully, making sure that we can hear every word. But when it came to this *aliyah*, he read it as fast as he could, and he read it in a whisper, and therefore, unless you were paying very careful attention, you were probably not able to keep up with him.

Who knows why the Torah reader got this *aliyah*?

And who knows why he read it in such a strange way?

Anyone?

The answer is that this *aliyah* has a special name in the Jewish tradition. It is called *The Tochechah* which means: "The Warning" or "The Threat." It is called that because the *aliyah* begins with a short list of blessings that will come to the Israelites if they keep the covenant, and then it goes on to list all the curses that will befall the Israelites if they do not keep the commandments of the Lord.

It says: If you are not loyal to the covenant, then you will be defeated by your enemies. And then it says that if you still do not listen to the Lord, your God, you will suffer famine and thirst. And then it says that if you still do not obey the Lord your God, you will undergo consumption and fever and misery. And then it goes on to say that if you still do not obey the commandments, that which you will plant, your enemies will harvest. And then it says that if you still do not obey the commandments of the Lord your God, that you will flee, even when no one pursues you.

And if that is not enough, it goes on to say:

Then I will make your skies like iron,
And your earth like copper,
So that your land will not yield its produce,
And your trees will not yield their fruit.
And if that is not enough:
I will unleash wild beasts against you,
And they will bereave you of your children,
And they will kill your cattle.
And then it says: If that is not enough,
I will bring a sword against you,
And I will send pestilence amongst you,
And you will eat the flesh of your own children,
And I will destroy your altars,
And I will cut down your incense stands.
And if that is not enough,
I will destroy your cities,
And I will make your sanctuaries into ruins.
And if that is not enough,
I will make your land desolate,
And I will scatter you among the nations,
And I will make your cities into rubble.
And you will flee at the sound of a driven leaf,
And you will not be able to stand your ground before your enemies.

Wave after wave after wave, this *aliyah* goes on with ever-increasingly vivid and gory descriptions of the horrors that will befall you if you are not loyal to the covenant.

Is it any wonder that people were afraid to take this terrifying *aliyah* with its awesome list of curses?

Is it any wonder that it became the custom that the Torah reader had to take this *aliyah* for himself, because everyone else was afraid to take it?

There are very few places in the Torah or in all of human literature that contain as terrifying a collection of curses as the ones that are found in today's Torah reading.

And the reason we treat this passage the way we do, the reason we read it as fast as we can, and the reason why we are reluctant to take this *aliyah*, is because, even today, all of us are uneasy receiving curses.

And even today, all of us get a little bit of satisfaction out of uttering curses.

If you are in a fight with someone who is bigger than you, and you can't beat them physically, at least you can curse them – under your breath if he is listening, or out loud, if he is not.

Curses are still the weapon of choice that many of us use when we are angry.

And therefore, it is about curses that I want to talk to you today.

What I want to do today, if I can, in honor of the *Shabbat* when we read the *Tochechah*, is share with you some of my favorite curses.

The reason I do so is because I recently discovered a wonderful book that was published by the Hebrew University in Jerusalem. It is a book called: *Lomer Heren Gitte Bisores – May We Hear Good Tidings.* It was written by Professor Chaim Guri, who teaches Yiddish at the Hebrew University. And what this book does is collect and organize dozens of Yiddish blessings, and hundreds of Yiddish curses, so that a new generation of Jews can learn them.

Just as in our *sedra*, the blessings in this book are a much shorter list than the curses. I am not sure why. Perhaps it is because the promises of reward don't convince us to behave as well as the threats of punishment do. Or perhaps it is because the human imagination is better at inventing curses than it is at inventing blessings.

At any rate, I found this book fascinating. And so I want to share some of the blessings and some of the curses that I found in it.

The blessings and the curses in this book are arranged in alphabetical order. And next to each one, there are three translations: one into Hebrew, one into English, and one into Russian.

What does that tell you? It tells you that the editor of this book understood that we now live at a time when Hebrew-speaking Jews, and English-speaking Jews, and even Russian-speaking Jews no longer know Yiddish. And so, if we want them to understand the world of Yiddish literature, we have to translate its insights into a language that they understand.

So let me share with you today a few of my favorite blessings, and then some of my favorite curses.

First the blessings:

Let me begin with one that every one of you knows:

A brocho oif dein keppele: "a blessing on your head." Did anyone ever say that to you when you were a child?

You usually say this to a child who is precocious, and who comes up with the right answer. You know the story of the child who climbs up on Santa Claus's knee in the department store. Santa says: What do you want for Christmas, little boy? And the child says: I don't want anything for Christmas! We're Jewish, and we keep Chanukah! And Santa Claus pats the child on the head and says: *a brocho oif dein keppele.*

Or: who knows this one? *B'sha-ah tovah* – which literally means "at a good time." Who knows when you say this blessing?

You say it when you are told that someone is pregnant. *B'sha-ah tovah* means: may the baby come at a good time – not too early for that would be dangerous, and not too late, for that would be uncomfortable, but at the right time.

This one everyone knows: *zei gezint.* Which means: "be healthy." And perhaps you know its cousin: *abi gezint* which means: "as long as you have your health, nothing else matters."

I must tell you that, when I was young, I didn't understand this *bracha*, because when you are young, you take your health for granted. You feel that you are entitled to it. But when you get older, you know better, and you appreciate this *bracha* – *zei gezint.* Isn't that so?

And then there is the *bracha: abi mir zeitsich* – "at least we see each other," which means: at least we are still alive, at least we are still able to see each other. And then there is the Florida version of this *bracha*, which is: *abi mir DEKENTSICH*, which means: "at least we can still recognize each other" – which is a comment on the rise of Alzheimer's.

Then there is this one: *Gott zol ints hiten fun fayer un fun vaser – un fun mentschen's mol.* "God should protect us both from fire and from water – and from people's mouths." I like this one because it expresses the truth that people's mouths can be as dangerous and as harmful to us as fire and floods are.

Zol kein mul nisht zain erger, "it should never be any worse." Remember that one? I like this blessing, because it expresses gratitude and contentment with what we have. It only asks that things should never be any worse than they are today. A person who makes this wish is safe from envy, and is also a person who understands how fragile and how insecure our lives are. May it never be worse – is a reminder that it can easily become worse, and it is a reminder to be grateful for the way things are.

Rabbi Lehrman of Miami used to tell a wonderful story. When he was a child, a famous Chassidic rebbe came to America, and so his mother took him for a blessing. For hours they stood outside in line in the heat, waiting their turn. When they finally got to the head of the line, the rebbe asked his mother:

How is your family's health?

She answered: *Baruch Hashem.* "Thank God."

The Rebbe asked her: And how is your family's *parnosseh*?

She answered: *Baruch Hashem.* "Thank God."

The Rebbe asked her: How is your son doing in learning?

She answered: *Baruch Hashem.*

At this point, the Rebbe was puzzled. He said: If your family's health is good, and if your *parnosseh* is good, and if your son is doing well in learning, then what *bracha* do you want from me?

And his mother answered: *zol kein mul nisht zain erger.* "It should never be worse." That is a wise request. It means that you are grateful for what you have, and that all you want is that it should not get spoiled.

And one last blessing let me tell you: "May you live to be 120."

Who knows the origin of that blessing?

It comes from the Torah. Moshe Rabbeinu lived to be 120. Surely it would be greedy to ask for more years than he got, and so we only ask that we may live as long as he did.

Enough blessings?

Now, let me share with you some of my favorite curses:

Let me begin with a long one. I think that it sounds much better in Yiddish than it does in English, but I hope that, even in translation, you will get the general idea:

> May you break your head.
> May your eyes drop out,
> May your mouth twist sideways,
> May your tongue drop out,
> May your legs be chopped from under you,
> May your liver come out of your nostrils – piece by piece.
> May your innards come out,
> May your guts be pulled out of you,
> May your bones rot in Hell.

And then comes the climax:

Un nochten, zolts de hoben emesdike tsores. . . . "and after all these things happen to you, THEN you should have real trouble!"

Isn't that last line lovely? After all these things, after your tongue drops out, after your liver comes out, after your eyes drop out, and after you break your head, etc., etc., etc. THEN you should have real trouble.

Now let me share with you some shorter curses:

"May the third plague of Egypt come upon you."

That takes some Jewish literacy to appreciate. You have to open your Bible and look up the ten plagues in order to understand this one. Who knows which was the third plague that befell Egypt? Anyone?

It was lice.

Here's another one: "May a young child soon bear your name." It sounds like a blessing, but it is not. Jews, or at least Ashkenazic Jews, are named after dead relatives. So: "May a young child soon bear your name" means: may you soon be dead.

Here is another one that I like. I like this one for its vividness.

"May worms hold a wedding in your stomach, and may they invite all their relatives and friends to the *simcha*, and may they all dance with enthusiasm." I ask you: isn't that a charming wish?

This one is more familiar. You may have heard it: "May you be like a lamp – that is: may you hang by day, burn by night, and be snuffed out in the morning."

And see what you think of this one: "May you become so rich that your widow's husband should never have to work in order to make a living." Ouch! This one hits you in the *kishkes*, doesn't it? Or to be more formal and more elegant, this one hits you in the solar plexus, doesn't it?

And how is this one for someone who is about to go into business and become your competitor: "May your store be full of merchandise, and may your customers never ask for what you have, but only for what you don't have."

Isn't that a nice curse?

And I like this one: "May you have Haman's *kavod* and Korach's *nisim*" – may you have Haman's glory – *och im vey* – he had only disgrace. Remember? He had to go through the streets of Shushan saying: So shall be done for the one whom the king wants to honor – for Mordechai! That by you is *kavod*?

And Korach's miracle? That refers to the miracle that was done TO HIM, NOT FOR HIM. The earth opened up and swallowed him. That was the miracle. But notice how literate you have to be, notice that you have to know both the Torah and the *Megillah* in order to understand this curse. Otherwise, if you are an *am ha'aretz*, you might think it is a *bracha*.

And this one you probably know: "May you have a hundred homes, and may you have a hundred rooms in every home, and may you have twenty beds in every room, and may you wander from room to room with fever that keeps you from sleeping." The point of that curse is to remind you that wealth by itself is nothing, that, even if you have everything you can imagine, you can still suffer immeasurably.

A similar curse is this one: May you have twenty safes full of gold, and may you spend it all on doctors."

And then there is this one: "May your luck shine upon you as brightly as the moon does at the end of the month." Is that clear? What does the moon look like at the end of the month? The answer is that it is invisible. And how much light does it give at the end of the month? None.

And one more: "May your stomach make as much noise as a greggar does on Purim." I like that one because it shows how the Jewish tradition permeated the language, even the curses.

One last one – and this one is serious. It comes out of the Holocaust. It comes from a book called *Min Hameytsar*, which is a collection of songs and stories and poems from the concentration camps. I don't know who wrote it, but it surely expresses the anger that all human beings must have felt during those dark days and in those dark places. This one, too, loses much in translation from the Yiddish original, but I hope that some of its power comes through:

"I call down a curse from the *Tochechah* section
  to strike you, Hitler, the bloodsucker,
  In the same way that you have stripped us of our lives,
  So may the skin be stripped from you with knives.
  Upon you and yours in your land,
  May there come down a burning brand.
  May your cities be destroyed, and each of them become a burnt heap,
  And may not a single path remain that memory can keep."

Who cannot feel the pain, and the anger, the deserved anger, that fills the heart of the poet – whoever he was – who wrote this curse? And who, who was alive in those years, and who went through what he went through, would not have said amen to this curse?

And now one last word. Why have I recited some of my favorite curses today? And why does the Jewish tradition contain these curses? Are we not a spiritual people? And should not a spiritual people refrain from cursing? Don't we tell our children that it is not nice to curse?

My answer, very simply, is that a curse can be a great cathartic. When you have no power, and you have no weapons, and you have no army – at least you have words, and you can hurl these words at your enemy as if they were weapons, and you can derive some psychological fulfillment from doing that. Curses, I would suggest, have a therapeutic value. They have no power to change reality, and the Jewish people knew that. They learned that from the story of Bilaam, the pagan prophet, who tried to defeat Israel with curses, and was taught a lesson by God, who turned his curses into blessings. The curse – like the blessing – is simply a wish. It is a prayer to God that there should be some justice in the world, that evil not tramp over good forever, that there be some retribution for those who hurt us – not only for our sakes, but for the sake of God's good name.

And there is a touch of humor, of whimsy, a touch of satire in some of these curses, is there not? Many of them are genuinely funny in the way they twist language. "May you have someone named for you soon" sounds like a blessing. The hearer, if he is stupid enough, may even think it is – until he thinks for a minute and realizes what it means. "May you suffer the third plague that befell Egypt" is a line that will go over the head of an *am-ha'aretz*, and can only be understood by a Jew who is literate. And so the curses are not only a way to relieve anger. They are not only the way in which a helpless and unarmed people fought back with the only weapon they possessed – which was words. They are a way in which a people who lived in the midst of an insane world kept their sanity. They are the way in which a people who lived in the midst of a cruel and wicked world expressed their faith that justice would yet triumph, that good would yet prevail, and that right would somehow, someday, someway, overcome evil.

The curses that I have shared with you today are the curses of a powerless people, of a people that had no other weapons but words. The curses that you hear in Israel today are very different. They express the sentiments of a people that no longer feels helpless. The spiritual situation of the Jews in Israel is very different from that of the Jews who lived in Eastern Europe. And yet I think we ought to keep alive and remember the curses of the Eastern European Jews, and not forget them, for they contained important spiritual truths.

These are the truths by which our people lived for centuries. And so, on this, the *Shabbat* of Bechukotai, the *Shabbat* on which we read the awesome list of blessings and curses that appears in the Torah, I have shared some of my favorite blessings and some of my favorite curses with you, so that you may appreciate the kind of people from whom we come.

Other people express their response to cruel behavior with foul language, with curses that pollute the world and poison human speech. Our people expressed their response to cruel behavior with subtle curses, with curses that are puns that tickle the imagination, curses that are based on stories in the Torah, curses that express anger, but that do not desecrate or denigrate human dignity. Our people express their resentment at the cruelty that they have had to endure for so long in ways that tickle the funny bone, and that touch the heart, and that move the soul. And so, for this reason as well as for so many more, we can say in truth, and with much pride: *mi k'amcha Yisrael* – "who is like Your people Israel, O God!"

May we learn from the blessings, and even from the curses that we have inherited, and may we use them carefully and cautiously, but may we know how to use them when they are justified and when they are required.

A Moment of Truth and Reconciliation

L ET ME BEGIN by asking you a personal question, a question
that you do not have to answer if you do not want to.

Is there anyone here who, for at least a brief moment
or maybe even more, lost interest during today's Torah
reading?

Is there anyone here who, when we were reading the details of
the census, the report on exactly how many people belonged to each
tribe, or when we were reading the description of which tribes were
stationed where when the Israelites marched through the wilderness, nodded off?

If you did, I don't blame you.

For the truth is that the *sedra* of Bamidbar is, to put it mildly, not
very exciting.

It contains such topics as which tribe marched where, and exactly
how many men were in each tribe. And I think that you have to
admit that who marched first and who marched last, who marched
on the eastern flank and who marched on the western flank many
centuries ago are not exactly fascinating topics.

And how many men were in each of the tribes? That, too, is not
a topic that is very interesting. We understand that the Israelites
had to know precisely how many men they had in each tribe for
military purposes. And we understand that knowing that they were
a numerous people was good for their morale, that it gave them a
sense of confidence as they marched through the wilderness. But

do we really need to know the exact number of men in each tribe centuries ago? That is surely not a matter that interests us today.

And therefore, I think that the *sedra* of Bamidbar ranks high on the list of *sedras* that are low in drama in the Torah. If I dare say so, I believe that the *sedra* of Bamidbar competes with some of the *sedras* in Vayikra for the title of "The Least Interesting *Sedra* in the Whole Torah."

In the same way, we in America hold a census every ten years. And when it comes out, the one number that captures our interest is the total: how many people are there in this country? But the details? Exactly how many people live in each state, exactly how many people are native-born, and exactly how many people are immigrants, exactly how many people own their own homes, and exactly how many people are college-educated – these are matters that may interest the demographers or that may interest the politicians, but do the rest of us really need to know these details? It is enough for us to know the totals. And that is the way we feel about the census in this week's *sedra*. Do we really need to know exactly how many men were in each of the tribes? And do we really need to know which tribe marched where? I don't think so.

And so the *sedra* of Bamidbar, when you first read it, with its description of who marched where, and with its report on the census, seems irrelevant to our lives.

And yet?

Let me give you a rule that I think works in almost every case: the more boring, the more irrelevant, the more technical a passage in the Torah seems to be, the more insightful, the more exciting, and the more relevant the Midrash on that passage usually is.

And therefore, never underestimate the power of a passage in the Torah. *Davke*, in the passages that seem least meaningful there are important moral lessons to be found – if only we look carefully. *Davke* the passages that seem least relevant on the surface are the ones that are most fascinating when you read them through the eyes of the commentators. And this is what I learned this week from studying this *sedra* of Bamidbar.

Let me share with you today three important moral lessons that are found in this week's *sedra*, three lessons that I believe are relevant to the world in which we live today, three lessons that are not obvious in the Text, three lessons that you probably could not find if you looked at the Text a hundred times, but which are to be found in the commentaries.

I learned all three of these lessons from an essay on this *sedra* by Rabbi David Greenstein, who is the rabbi of Congregation Shomrei Emunah in Montclair, New Jersey.

The first concerns the order in which the tribes marched.

The Torah says: "On the north: the standard of the tribe of Dan, troop by troop."

That seems clear enough. The tribe of Dan camped on the north. But then, look what it says just a few lines further on in the chapter:

L'achrona yis'oo lidigleyhem – "they shall march last, with their standards."

What does it mean: "to march last"?

It means to march on the west or on the south. For the Israelites marched southeast to northwest when they journeyed from Egypt towards Canaan. And so, the tribe of Dan may have been stationed on the northern side of the camp, but every time the people broke camp and began to journey, the tribe of Dan evidently had to move from the northern side of the camp to the southwestern side.

Why?

According to the Midrash, the reason the tribe of Dan marched behind the rest of the camp was so that, if anyone fell by the wayside, the tribe of Dan would be there to gather them in, to give them water, and time to rest, and to see to it that they did not get lost.

And if so, why did they camp on the north if they were going to march from the southeast?

So that the other tribes in their area would see them swinging around to occupy the rear and would learn from them. The other tribes, or at least the ones on the northern side, would see them change positions every time the people broke camp and began to march, and they would learn from them how important it is to bring up the rear in order to care for the weak and the stragglers. They would learn that to march last is not a disgrace, as it is in our competitive culture. They would learn from them that to march last is a *mitzvah*, because if you march last you can gather in the weak and the weary who have fallen by the wayside, and you can save them. And the fact that they knew that someone was there behind them, waiting to help them if they fell by the wayside, must have given the other tribes much confidence as they journeyed.

Do you remember: There was a recent administration in Washington that came up with the slogan: "No Child Left Behind"? The tribe of Dan taught a different slogan: "No Person Left Behind." And thanks to them, the people marched with confidence because they knew that if they fell by the wayside, if they ran out of strength and simply could not go another step, the tribe of Dan would be there to gather them in, and rescue them. And the tribes would see them moving into position every time they marched so that they too would learn the lesson that caring for the weak and the weary is a great *mitzvah*.

Is that not a lesson that all of us need to pay attention to today? We live in an age when many people are falling by the wayside. We live at a time when thousands of Americans have lost their jobs. We live at a time when tens of thousands of people have lost their homes. And these people need to know that there is somebody – whether it is the government or whether it is good people or whether it is both, who will help them. They need to know that there are some people who bring up the rear purposely in order to pick them up when they fall, in order to give them strength when they feel that they can go no further, in order to gather them in when they feel that they are exhausted.

On the surface, this listing of who marched where seems technical and of little consequence. But if we understand it through the eyes of the Midrash, this idea that one tribe was designated to bring up the rear in order to rescue those who fell out along the way, and that this tribe had to move into this position each and every time the people started out, so that what they were doing would be seen and appreciated, is an idea that speaks to our time as much as it did to theirs.

You might never see this insight if you only looked at the Text itself. But if you look at the Text through the eyes of the Midrash, is this not an important moral lesson?

And now, let us turn to the census.

Why do we have a census – then and now?

The easy answer for then is that the Israelites needed to know exactly how many men they had who were available to fight, in case of attack. This is why only men were counted in this census, and only men twenty years old and above. And the easy answer for now is that we take a census so that we will know exactly how many people we have in this country in order to enhance our self-confidence. We want to know exactly how many people we have so that we can feel good about our strength and our size.

But Rabbi Greenstein suggests that there was a different, deeper, reason for the census, both then and now.

Notice that the Text says: "Take a census" – literally: "Lift up the heads of the whole Israelite community by their clans, listing the names of every male, head by head."

What does that mean?

The census gave every single soldier a moment of recognition. It gave every single male a moment in which they were called upon to stand and be recognized, one at a time, by their own individual names, as well as by the name of the tribe to which they belonged.

Slaves are called by their numbers or by demeaning nicknames. Free men are called by their names. And so the census was a very special moment – a moment in which every single person announced his name.

Andy Warhol once said that in the messianic age, every human being will be entitled to fifteen minutes of fame. In a sense, the *sedra* did that for every Israelite male. He received, if not fifteen minutes, then at least a minute or so when he was able to announce who he was, and which group he belonged to, and that he was reporting for duty. We think of the census as a time when people are treated as numbers, and that is true. But it is also a moment when each and every person is treated as an individual. It is a moment when each and every individual comes forward and announces who he is. And if you think of it that way, says Rabbi Greenberg, then the census is more than a boring exercise in bureaucracy. It is a moment of individual recognition. It is a moment in which each and every person literally counts.

And that is the spiritual meaning of the census. Its practical purpose was to tell the generals precisely how many soldiers they had. Its spiritual purpose was to tell each individual that he counted. And that is a lesson that the Israelites needed to learn then and that we need to learn today. We live in an age in which we are treated more and more as numbers. The bank does not want my name; it only wants to know my I.D. number. The people who take my credit card do not want to know my name; they only want to know my number. The computer does not want to know my name; it only wants to know my password.

And in the midst of all this "numberization," it is good to remember that the Israelite soldiers came forward one by one, and declared who they were by their names, as well as by the tribe to which they belonged.

Perhaps that is why the biblical term for making a census is *se'oo et rosh* – which means: "lift up the heads of the people." When you call someone by his name, you give that person confidence and dignity. When you call an ex-slave by his name, you demonstrate that he is truly free. And that was the spiritual purpose of the census!

And now, let me show you one more insight into the census, one that I find very exciting. Rabbi Greenstein finds this insight in a little known commentary on the Torah called the Yalkut Reuveni. The Yalkut Reuveni is a seventeenth-century compilation of kabbalistic commentaries on the Torah. And in its commentary on the census, the Yalkut Reuveni focuses on one detail of the law that we would probably never notice.

Remember the rule I mentioned – the more boring the *sedra*, the more exciting the Midrash? Here is a perfect example.

The Torah says that when Moses and Aaron stood to count the people, *itchem yeheyu ish ish lemateh, ish ish leveyt avotav* – "With you shall be one person from each tribe, one person who is the head of his ancestral home."

Who were these people who were to stand with Moses and Aaron during the census?

The Yalkut Reuveni says that these people who were to stand with Moses and Aaron during the census were the very same people who had been appointed by the Egyptian taskmasters to supervise the Israelite slaves.

The Egyptians were fiendish in the way they treated the Israelite slaves. They appointed Israelites to supervise them, and, if the Israelites did not produce enough, the Israelite supervisors were the ones who beat them.

Can you imagine a more tragic role than the role that these people had? They were caught between the Egyptians, who ruled over them, and their fellow Israelites, whom they had to rule over. Can you imagine the guilt that these people must have felt? Can you imagine the contempt they must have endured from those above them, and the hatred they must have endured from those below them?

And so the Yalkut Reuveni says that they did *teshuvah* for the sin they had committed by supervising the slavery of their fellow Israelites, by supervising the census of their fellow Israelites.

How was helping in the census an act of *teshuvah* for mistreating their fellow Israelites?

The answer is: when you enslave someone, you dehumanize them. You treat them as if they have no names. When you count them one by one, when you hear them proclaim their names, as well as the names of their families, you atone for dehumanizing them by affirming their humanity. By looking at them, and by listening to them as they declared their names, the ex-masters atoned for having treated them as nameless. By being present at this sacred moment when they declare who they are, their presence made for a moment of mutual recognition.

Rabbi Greenstein pictures it this way: As each ex-slave, who had once been abused by these very officials, passed by one by one, for one brief moment, their eyes met. Those who were doing the counting were also recognized for who they were and what they had done. By facing their brothers, whom they had helped to oppress just a short time ago, the chieftains and their victims were both pushed into a moment of "truth and reconciliation."

Do you remember that phrase – truth and reconciliation? It was the process through which the people of South Africa brought an end to the period of apartheid. They knew that they could not wipe out the ex-ruling class. And they also knew that they could not rebuild their society without first coming to terms with what they had done. And so they arranged for a Truth and Reconciliation Commission, to which all those who had committed acts of brutality could come and confess and ask forgiveness. And when they did, when they asked forgiveness from those whom they had mistreated, when they admitted the evil that they had done, they brought closure to the past and enabled a new society to begin.

And so it was here. When the ex-slaves came forward, and looked into the eyes of their ex-oppressors, there was a moment of recognition. The ex-slaves understood that these people had only done what they had to do, at the orders of their supervisors. And the ex-supervisors understood that those whom they had supervised were human beings, people with names and identities, and not just objects to be ordered about. The census may have seemed like a boring bureaucratic business to those who watched it from the outside. It may seem that way to us, who read about it centuries later. To us it may seem like a hodge-podge of names and numbers. But to those who participated in it, to those ex-slaves and ex-masters whose eyes met at that moment, it must have been a holy and a healing moment.

Imagine how the ex-slave must have felt when he looked his ex-master in the eye, and compelled him to count him, to recognize him as a brother. It must have been a moment of redemption for the ex-slave and it must have been a moment of repentance for the ex-oppressor, and it must have been a holy moment for them both.

And what about us? Who will we count as a brother or a sister in our community? Who will we take in, whom we have once driven out or made to feel unwelcome in our midst? Who will we count as a valid member of our people from now on, even though we used to look down upon them in the past and call them names? Who will we do *teshuvah* to, and how will we atone for the way we excluded them and demeaned them in the past?

The mentally and physically handicapped – who frighten us by their appearance, and whom we would rather shut out of our community than confront the fear that we may someday be like them?

The gays and the lesbians – whom we have for so long made to feel unwelcome in our midst?

The poor – whom we have made to feel like second-class citizens in our congregations?

The ex-criminals – who have paid the price for their crimes and who seek employment and the chance to begin over again?

These are just a few random examples. Each one of us can make his or her own list of people who have been made to feel unwelcome in our midst, whom we need to confront and to do *teshuvah* to, and whom we need to welcome back into the community.

And depending on how we answer these questions will determine the openness and the moral integrity of our community. And so this Midrash about the ex-oppressors doing *teshuvah* by being the ones who were chosen to help in the census and by facing those whom they had mistreated, takes on powerful meaning in our time and in our lives.

Here we have three passages in the Torah, which, if we read them superficially, seem boring and irrelevant. And yet, look how much wisdom they have to teach us if we only look beneath the surface, and read them through the eyes of the Midrash and the commentators.

And therefore, may I suggest that, when this *sedra* of Bamidbar is read aloud next year, that you do not close your eyes – and surely that you do not close your ears – but instead, that you listen, that you listen well, and that you listen closely. I suggest that you listen to the words that are being chanted aloud, and that you think about the Midrashim that take these words and make them come alive.

For if we do, then the *sedra* of Bamidbar will speak to us with power, and will teach us much, not only about how our ancestors lived long ago, but also about how we should live today.

And that, after all, is the reason why we study the Torah, is it not?

I was Wrong, and I Owe the Torah an Apology

LET ME BEGIN by making an apology today.

I was wrong, and I owe the Torah an apology.

For many years now, I have read the story of the *Sotah*, which appears in this week's *sedra*, with a certain sense of smugness and superiority. I thought that it was a primitive and an outdated story that had no meaning in our time, and that we moderns have no need and no interest in such a story, but now I realize that I was wrong.

Do you remember the story? If a man suspects his wife of having committed adultery, he must bring her to the *Kohen*, and make her go through a strange, mysterious ritual. The *Kohen* prepares a drink of some kind. One of the ingredients in this drink is a piece of parchment on which was written the name of God. The woman had to drink this concoction, and then, one of two things would happen: If she was guilty of having committed adultery, her stomach would sag, and her belly would distend. If she was not guilty of having committed adultery, nothing would happen and she would be proven innocent.

That is the law as it is found in today's *sedra*. I must tell you that, every year when I read this passage, I am offended. What became of the law in the Torah that you have to have a trial, and you have to have two witnesses in order to convict someone of a crime? What became of the idea that trial by ordeal was a pagan practice, and not something that could be found in Jewish law?

And then I read Dr. Jacob Milgrom's commentary on this *sedra*, and he answered all these questions for me.

Dr. Jacob Milgrom gives a very simple and a very logical explanation for why in this case – and only in this case – do you not require witnesses. He says that in his experience, most people who commit adultery do not do so in front of witnesses.

But still, I was bothered by the law of the *Sotah*. And when I read in the Mishna that the law of the *Sotah* had been in effect abolished by the Sages, when I learned that the Sages said that the law of the *Sotah* can no longer be applied, because it only works when we are sure that the husband has not sinned as well as the wife, and it only works in the time when the Temple stood, and not in our time, when I read that, I was pleased and I felt relieved. Good for them – I said to myself. Now this ancient law may still be on the books but it can never be applied anymore.

And then, I read a commentary this year by Rabbi Anne Brener that made me see this law of the *Sotah* in a whole new light. Rabbi Brener is a social worker as well as a rabbi, and one of her jobs over the years has been working with victims of domestic violence.

I learned from her that domestic violence is much more common than we realize. In fact, she says that there are shelters, in Los Angeles which is where she lives, and in many other cities as well, which have been set up so that victims of domestic violence can take refuge from abusive husbands who beat them up. And she says that many of the women who come to these shelters come with terrible stories of insanely jealous husbands, who follow them to the grocery store because they think that they are having an affair with the grocer, or who make them account for every moment that they are out of the house, or who accuse them of having a secret relationship with the mailman or someone in their office. She says that some of these women come to the shelter bruised and battered. She says that some of them come to the shelter with black eyes and even with broken bones, because they have been beaten up by their husbands. And some of them say that their husbands are peaceful and gentle and loving until they get drunk, and then they become violent and abusive. And she says that some of these abusers come from upstanding homes and not just from the slums, as we might think.

And when she said that, one verse in the *Sotah* story suddenly stood out and caught my attention. It says right at the very beginning of the story: *v'avar alav ruach kin'ah* – "if a fit of jealousy comes over the husband," *v'hee lo nitma-ah* – "and she has not defiled herself," i.e. she is not guilty, he shall take her to the *Kohen*, and he shall arrange for the trial by ordeal to be carried out.

What does this passage mean?

I think it means that we are dealing with an insanely jealous husband, one who does not trust his wife, who does not believe his wife, and who will not accept her protestations of innocence. In such a case, in order to protect the woman from the anger of her husband, especially if he is drunk, we take the power to punish her away from him and give it to this ritual. If she is guilty, the ritual will prove it. If she is innocent, the ritual will prove it. But in either case, the judgment will come from the ritual, and not from the husband.

Read it this way, and the ordeal of the *Sotah* can be understood, not as a put-down of the woman, which is the way I always thought of it, but instead as a way of protecting the woman from the anger of an insanely jealous husband.

If that is the way this passage is to be understood, then I owe the Torah an apology for having misjudged it. I really do.

And how do you do *teshuvah* for a mistake that you have made, according to the Jewish tradition? You do so by admitting that you were wrong, which is what I have just done. And you do so by atoning for your sin with a concrete action to make sure that you have learned your lesson and will not do this sin again.

And therefore, I want to make an announcement this morning. We have created a new ritual object in the synagogue this week. I believe that it is a very, very important ritual object. I believe it is a ritual object that has the power to save lives. And let me tell you what it is:

We have put a notice up in the women's bathrooms of our synagogue. It is a very simple statement. It says: If you are being abused, and if you are in danger of being hurt by an abusive husband, this is the address, and this is the phone number, and this is the website of the nearest domestic shelter. We have put this poster in the women's bathrooms out of respect for privacy, so that no one will see if a woman takes this poster and puts it in her purse, or if she copies down the information on it.

I confess that when I went to rabbinical school, nobody ever talked about domestic violence. If it existed, we didn't know much about it. But now we do. Now we know that it is a real problem in our society. Now we know that it occurs among Jews as well as among other people. And therefore, now we know that it is the synagogue's task to do whatever it can to meet the needs of those whose lives are in danger because of it.

Now I understand that the story of the *Sotah* is not as naïve and not as outdated as I used to think it was. Now I understand that it is a warning in our time, and in all times, against the danger of abusive husbands who do violence to their mates, when *ruach kin'ah* – when a fit of jealousy – takes hold of them. Perhaps that is why the Talmud in *Masechet Sotah* says that "whoever sees a suspected wife in her disgrace should refrain from drinking liquor."

I was wrong. I underestimated the relevance and the meaning of the story of the *Sotah*, and so I apologize. And I pray that the action that our congregation has taken this week on behalf of those who are in danger will be a token of our repentance, and a statement of our concern. May this new object that we have placed in our building save lives.

How Tall Are You? and How Old Are You?

THIS IS IT.

I am coming into the home stretch of my stay as the interim rabbi of this congregation, and therefore, I am going to give two sermons this morning.

And I don't want to hear any complaints about it.

I am going to give two sermons instead of one today, because what are you going to do to me, if you don't like it? Fire me?

The first sermon, for reasons which will become clear in a few moments, is dedicated to my wife, and to all the other people in the room today, who – how shall I say this politely – who are not exactly very tall.

And my second sermon, for reasons, which will become clear in a few moments, is dedicated to George Herbert Walker Bush, not because I agree or disagree with his politics – as you know by now, I never talk about politics from the *bimah*. My sermon is dedicated to George Herbert Walker Bush, not because of his politics, but because of the way in which he celebrated his birthday five years ago and the way that he celebrated his ninetieth birthday as well.

My two sermons are going to deal with these two questions:

The first one is: How tall are you?

And the second one is: How old are you?

Let me begin by telling you about a new organization that was formed this year which I am happy to endorse.

It is the N Double A SP . . . the National Association for the Advancement of Short People.

They held their first meeting on December 21st. Why? Because that is the shortest day of the year. They held their founding meeting in Little Neck, N.Y. And the main course at the meeting was shrimp, which was served together with shortnin' bread. And for dessert they served strawberry shortcake.

The reason they have created this group is in order to fight against the discrimination against short people that is found in this country.

The Jews have the Anti-Defamation League, the blacks have the National Association for the Advancement of Colored People. I think it is time, and more than time, for short people to have an organization that is dedicated to protecting their rights, because they need one.

Studies have shown that short people earn less money than tall people do. You can actually chart it. The sociologists say that the difference in salary can be as much as several thousand dollars a year per inch.

Politicians will tell you that short candidates have a much harder time winning elections than tall candidates too.

A man like Abraham Lincoln who was six-foot-three had an easy time running for president. People looked at him, and said: that is the way a president should look. Whereas a man like Thomas Dewey, who was only five-foot-two, or a man like John McCain who is only five-foot-three, have a much, much harder time looking presidential.

And it is the same in the rabbinate.

I have a friend who is a rabbi who told me that he once tried out for a position in Northern California, and he thought that he had it. The sermons went well, the interview went well, the search committee seemed satisfied, they even arranged for him to meet with a real estate agent and look into possible housing for himself and his family.

And then, much to his surprise, he got a letter from the search committee, telling him that the board of directors had decided on somebody else.

My friend was hurt, and he was surprised, and so he called up the chairman of the search committee and asked what happened.

The chairman was embarrassed, but he told him. He said:

I was for you, rabbi, I really was, but when we came before the board, people felt that we couldn't hire a rabbi who was so short. They felt that a rabbi who was only five-foot-three was not the kind of rabbi who could represent our *shul* to the community. And so they hired someone else instead. They hired a rabbi who was six-feet tall instead.

Where did this feeling that small people are not as good as tall people come from?

It doesn't come from our *shul* – in our *shul*, Sue Kirschner and Harriet De Costa run this place with an iron hand. Everybody in the congregation is afraid of them. Isn't that so?

You are either nice to them or you don't get an *aliyah*. That is just the way it is.

It doesn't come from my house . . . where my wife is barely five feet, and yet she is the boss in our house, and I do whatever she says – without question.

So if it does not come from our synagogue, and if it does not come from my home, where does this idea that small people are weak people come from?

I think it comes from today's *sedra*, where the ten scouts come back from their mission to spy the land of Israel, and they say that the people there are giants.

And they say that when we looked at them, we felt like GRASSHOPPERS in our own sight.

The people hear that – and they panic, and they want to go back to Egypt.

Notice that they didn't say we felt like little lambs, or that we felt like little puppies; they said: we felt like grasshoppers.

Think of it. Do you realize how small grasshoppers are????

And God hears that, and says: if you feel that you are THAT small, if you feel that you are no bigger than grasshoppers, if you have so little self-confidence, and so little self-esteem as to think that, then there is no way you can conquer the land.

And so God decrees that the people must wander around in the desert for forty years, until a new generation arises that feels more confident about itself.

For that is the whole point: IT IS NOT HOW TALL OR HOW SHORT YOU ARE THAT MATTERS. WHAT MATTERS IS HOW TALL OR HOW SHORT YOU FEEL.

If you feel you are a midget, if you feel you are a grasshopper, then there is no way you can ever accomplish anything. Whereas if you have a deep sense of inner worth, and you have a deep sense of self-confidence, then there is no limit to what you can do.

Let me finish this first sermon by telling you about two rabbis whom I knew. I think that the rabbis who are here today knew them too.

The first was Rabbi Harry Halpern of the East Midwood Jewish Center in Brooklyn. He was barely five-feet tall – and that was only if he stood on his toes. And yet, he was elected president of the New York Board of Rabbis and then of the Rabbinical Assembly.

And I remember how, when he was elected president of the Rabbinical Assembly, I asked him: How do you feel being the rabbi of so many great rabbis? Don't you feel intimidated?

And his answer was: How do I feel? Like a dime among nickels.

My second story is about Rabbi David Aronson, who was the rabbi of Congregation Beth El in Minneapolis for forty years. I think that if you looked at him, you would have voted him the rabbi least likely to succeed. He was about four-foot-eleven, MAYBE a bit more. He had a sallow complexion. He had a lisp. And he had an accent.

And yet he ruled – not only Beth El, but all of Minneapolis – with an iron hand for more than forty years. He would go to the Budget Committee of the Federation every year and he would say in that quiet but firm voice of his: This is how much you are going to give to the Talmud Torah this year. And that was how much they gave to the Talmud Torah that year.

And I always wondered: how did he do it?

And then I found out.

Rabbi Aronson's wife, Bertha, had a niece, who was married to Rabbi Merle Singer, who was the rabbi of the large Reform synagogue in Boca, Temple Beth El. And Rabbi Singer told me that one year he invited his uncle to speak at his Temple on a Friday night.

Rabbi Aronson walked in, and noticed that the gift shop was

open. Very quietly, he said to his nephew – close the gift shop. And so Rabbi Singer ran and closed the gift shop.

When he told me that, I said to Rabbi Singer: I don't understand it. You're almost six feet tall, he is barely five feet tall. And it is your synagogue, not his. When he asked you to close the gift shop, why didn't you say "no"?

And his answer was: In my whole life, I never once thought of saying no to David Aronson.

And that was the key to Rabbi Aronson's success. He was so sure that he was right; he had such inner confidence, and such certainty, that no one dared question him. Ever.

And that is the lesson of the *sedra* today. If you think that you are no bigger than a grasshopper, then you are. But if you think, as many short people do, that people should listen to you, then people WILL listen to you.

And so the question of how tall are you – is not a question that can be determined simply by using a ruler or a measuring rod. How tall or how short you are depends partly on what the ruler says – and partly on what YOU say, and on how YOU feel about yourself.

And so, that is the first sermon that I want to give today. Never, never believe that you are as weak and as helpless as a grasshopper, for, if you believe that, there is nothing you can accomplish, nothing at all.

And now, my second sermon, which deals with the question of how old are you?

I want to introduce you to two biblical figures who give two different answers to this question.

The first is a man named Barzilai.

In the book of Samuel, the story is told of how King David was nearly overthrown by his son, Absalom, who tried to stage a coup and seize his throne. David retreats from Jerusalem, but eventually he is saved, thanks to Joab and the army, and thanks to a wise man named Barzilai, who gives him good advice. And so, when David regains his throne, he feels grateful to Barzilai, and he says to him – would you please come back to Jerusalem with me. If you do, I will provide for you there, and you will eat at my table, and you will be my advisor.

Think about that for a minute. If the president of the United States said to you: Come to Washington, and I will provide for you there, and you will be my advisor. Wouldn't you be tempted to say yes? I would.

But Barzilai says: Thank you, but no thank you. You go back to Jerusalem, and I will stay here.

And then he explains why:

He says: How many years do I have left that I should go up to Jerusalem with you? Behold, I am now EIGHTY-FIVE YEARS OLD. Can I tell the difference between good and bad? Can I taste what I eat and drink? Can I still enjoy the singing of men or women? Why then should I be a burden to my lord, the king?

Let me stay here, and die in my own hometown, and let me be buried near the graves of my parents. Let someone else go with you, instead of me, for I am too old.

David has no choice. And so reluctantly he permits Barzilai to stay in his village, and to live out his years there. But he says to him: If there is ever anything you want me to do for you, let me know, and I will be glad to do it.

The two men bid farewell on the banks of the Jordan. David goes back to Jerusalem; Barzilai stays and lives out his remaining years in his village.

Did you notice how old Barzilai was at this time, when he turned the king down, and said that he was too old to go to Jerusalem and be his advisor???

He was eighty-five years old.

Now turn with me to the book of Joshua, and let me introduce you there to another man, a man whom you know already, a man whom you met in today's *sedra* – Calev ben Yifuneh.

Remember him? He was the one who, together with Joshua, brought back a good report of the land. But unfortunately, the people did not listen to him, and therefore they had to stay in the wilderness for forty more years, until all that generation died out, all except Joshua and Calev ben Yifuneh.

Now look with me at chapter 14 of the book of Joshua. It is one generation later. It has taken five years to conquer the land, and Joshua is now dividing the land between the tribes.

The tribe of Judah approaches Joshua at Gilgal. And Calev ben Yifuneh, who was the head of the tribe of Judah, says to Joshua:

You know how we served the Lord forty years ago. You know how you and I brought back an honest report unlike the other spies. It is now forty-five years since the Lord sent us on that mission. Here I am today EIGHTY-FIVE YEARS OLD, and I am still as strong as I was on the day that Moses sent us.

So will you please give to me and to my tribe the hill country, for that is the section that I want. And if there are giants there, I can dispossess them, as the Lord promised.

And so Joshua blessed Calev and he gave him and his tribe the hill country as his portion.

Look at the difference between how Barzilai feels at the age of 85 and the way Calev feels at the age of 85. One is tired and old and weary. The other is eager to face new challenges.

I am sure that part of the difference lay in their different physical conditions. If your body is weak, there is no way you can undertake new and difficult challenges. I know that. But I think there is a deeper difference between these two men.

Barzilai FEELS OLD. He says in effect – been there, done that, I don't want any more new challenges. He has done enough, seen enough, and achieved enough, in his lifetime; now all he wants to do is rest.

Whereas Calev, who is the same age as Barzilai, still wants to achieve and to conquer. He could have asked for land in the plain or in the valley. He could have asked for land that was easier to farm, but he didn't do that. He asked for the hill country, because he wanted to face new challenges.

And so I ask you the question; HOW OLD ARE YOU? Are you like Barzilai, or are you like Calev? Do you still have a goal in front of you, do you still have a task that you want to achieve, do you still have a place that you want to visit, before you go?

Or are you bored and blasé, are you worn out and weary? If so, then you are old, regardless of what your birth certificate says.

I remember how it was with my parents when they got old. We used to get two newspapers delivered to the house everyday: a Yiddish newspaper and an English newspaper. And I remember when they grew old, when I came home to visit; I would see a pile of newspapers piled up – unread. They had lost interest in the outside world. They no longer cared what was happening in the outside world. And that is when I knew that they had become old.

In a very real sense, each one of us determines how old we are by the way in which we live. If you are willing to do something that you have never done before, then you are young – regardless of what the calendar says. If you are sated and disinterested in life, if you fold up into yourself and live in isolation, then you are old, regardless of what the calendar says.

And that is the reason why I dedicate this sermon today to George Herbert Walker Bush.

Do you know what he did for his 85th birthday?

He celebrated it by parachuting from an airplane, in honor of the day. And five years later, when he celebrated his 90th birthday, President Bush did it again.

To be fair, he piggybacked on the back of someone else, but still I am impressed. And I am thinking – I have not decided yet, but I am thinking – of celebrating my 90th birthday, when it comes, the same way that he celebrated his, by parachuting from an airplane.

I think that I will work up to it gradually.

This year, on my birthday, I think I will climb up on a little stool and jump down from there.

And then, next year on my birthday, I think that maybe I will climb up on a regular chair and jump down from there.

And then, when my 90th birthday comes – provided my wife gives me permission, otherwise, I won't do it – but if she gives me permission, maybe I will parachute down from an airplane.

And if you think that that is a good idea,

And if you think that I should do it,

Then, will you please give me your support and your encouragement, by saying amen.

The Abilene Paradox

SHELACH

OW MANY OF YOU know what the Abilene Paradox is? It is an expression that sociologists use in order to describe the way in which people sometimes make their decisions.

It takes its name from the Texas town of Abilene. This is the story that led to the expression.

One summer afternoon, four members of one family were sitting on the porch in hundred-degree weather, wondering what to do. One of them suggested that they drive to Abilene, which was fifty some miles away, for dinner. Despite the fact that their car had no air-conditioning, the second one said: "Great idea." The third one said: "It's fine with me." And the fourth one said: "Sure, let's do it." So they took the long hot ride to Abilene for what turned out to be a lousy meal, and they returned home four hours later, completely exhausted. And only then did they discover that none of them had really wanted to go. The first one suggested it because he thought that the others were bored and wanted to go somewhere, and the others went along because each one thought that this was what everyone else wanted to do.

The Abilene Paradox is a form of groupthink in which people go along with what others seem to be thinking rather than using their own minds to arrive at the right decision.

There is a famous case in recent American history in which the Abilene Paradox may have been operative. Back in 1987, NASA had to decide whether to launch the Space Shuttle Challenger or not.

They decided to launch it, and seventy-three seconds into flight, the Challenger broke up and crashed into the Atlantic, killing all the members of its crew. Upon investigation, it was discovered that all thirty-one of the engineers who worked on this project opposed the launch, and yet somehow the launch was approved unanimously, because each one went along with the others, and no one voiced his doubts.

When I heard this story of how thirty-one engineers kept their doubts to themselves, and allowed a launch to take place that they did not believe was safe, and when I heard the story of how four people schlepped 100 miles for a dinner that none of them really wanted, I wondered: Is there anything like the Abilene Paradox to be found in the Torah?

And then I realized where the biblical parallel to the Abilene Paradox is to be found. It is found right here in today's Torah reading.

Remember the scene? Moses sends twelve scouts to look over the land of Israel and to report back on what kind of a land it is, and what kind of people live there. I picture the twelve going through the land, and taking notes on how fertile it is, and on how strong the people who live there seem to be. And then I picture them travelling back together to report on what they have seen. I imagine them talking to each other on the way back, and sharing with each other their impressions of the land and the people that they have studied. All twelve agreed that it is a good land. On this, they were unanimous. But they disagreed on whether the Israelites were capable of conquering this land or not. Ten said that the land was beautiful, but that the people who lived there were tough. They said that these people were giants, and that they would destroy anybody who tried to invade their land. Two of them disagreed. Calev and Joshua said that, with God's help, the Israelites were capable of conquering this land, and of defeating its inhabitants.

The Torah does not say, but I wonder: Who spoke first, and who spoke second, when the twelve scouts exchanged impressions of the land and its people with each other? My hunch – and I admit that I can't prove it – my hunch is that one of the ten who believed that the enemy was too strong, and that there was no way they could overcome them, spoke first. And because he spoke with such certainty, and with such conviction, a second one of the spies spoke up next and agreed with him. And then a third, seeing that the first two were so sure, spoke up and agreed with them. And so it went. Ten of the twelve scouts spoke one after the other, and they all said the same thing. Only Calev ben Yifuneh and Joshua bin Nun, had the courage to stand up and disagree with the ten, and report what they had seen and what they believed instead of just going along with what the others said.

I believe that the ten scouts who brought back a negative report were the first examples in history of people who fell for the Abilene Paradox. I believe that they were the first ones who went along with what those who spoke before them said instead of speaking their own minds.

And what was the result of these two conflicting and contradictory reports?

Calev inherited a prime piece of property in the land of Israel for himself and for his tribe. And Joshua was given the honor of leading the Jewish people in the next generation, and he succeeded in conquering the land. And the ten scouts who parroted what each other had said? They and the people who believed them all died in the wilderness.

So I guess the lesson of this *sedra* is that a person should not be afraid to believe in himself, and should not be afraid of taking a stand against what the others around him say.

Following your own conscience and risking standing out from the crowd is not easy for any of us to do. It is especially hard for young people to do, because young people want to be liked, and therefore they find it very difficult to stand up to peer pressure. If everyone wants to do something – even it is something stupid or dangerous – it is hard for young people to say "no." They don't want to stand out for fear that they will be ostracized or made fun of by the rest of the group if they do.

And yet, it is the claim of the two scouts in this *sedra* that a person should think for himself or herself. We Jews have been non-conformists ever since we came onto the stage of world history.

We began with Abraham who smashed his father's idols. Why is Abraham called *Ha-ivri*? Says the Midrash: because the entire world was on one side, and he was not afraid to take his stand and be on the other side. And that has been the way that Jews have lived ever since. When all the world worshipped Caesar, or Mars, or Mammon, Jews were not afraid to say "No." That is what has made us a special people down through the centuries.

I know it is not easy to tell a teenager not to be afraid to be different. I know that it is not easy to tell a teenager that, even if everyone else wears their hair one way or that if everyone else dresses one way, they do not have to. I know that it is hard for young people to stand up to the pressures of their peers.

But I ask you: What would have happened if one of those thirty-one engineers had said: "I don't believe that the Challenger is ready to be launched yet!" What if just one of those thirty-one had said "no"? Those seven astronauts who perished when the Challenger blew up might still be alive today!

And so what should we say to our teenagers?

Even though we know in advance that they will probably not listen to us, even though we know in advance that they would rather go along with the crowd than stand up for what they believe is right, I think we should say to them what Calev ben Yifuneh and Joshua bin Nun would say to them if they could speak to them today.

I think we should say to them:

God gave you a brain, a brain that is as good as any of your friends have. Use it!

We should say to them: If you have a Porsche, would you let it stand idle in the driveway, and travel in a friend's old and beat-up car instead? If not, then why would you use his mind instead of your own, which is just as good as his or maybe even better?

I think we should say to our young people: Realize that at the end of the day you will be the one who will pay the price for the decisions that you make. Do you really want to let your friends make the decisions for you, when you will have to pay the price if these decisions turn out to be wrong? Would you like to be like those thirty-one engineers who will have to live for the rest of their lives with the knowledge that by going along with the crowd, they did so much damage, and they cost so many lives?

And we should say to our young people: Believe it or not, people will respect you more if you stand up for your beliefs instead of just copying what others say and do. The whole Jewish world reveres Calev and Joshua. The ten who copied each other and parroted the same report have long been forgotten. Calev and Joshua will be remembered for as long as people read the Bible.

The Abilene Paradox was not too expensive. All the people who were involved in it, only lost a few hours of time, and some gas. The thirty-one engineers who went through their version of the Abilene Pardox lost much more. They lost seven lives, and they set back the course of NASA for many years. We need to tell our young people not to commit the same mistake that they did. We need to tell them to stand up for what they believe is right, whether or not anyone else stands with them or not.

For if they do, then Calev and Joshua will be proud of them. And so will we!

Too Much Rightness Can Kill You

I WANT TO STUDY WITH YOU today one aspect of the story of Korach and Moses which I must tell you I never really appreciated until now. Two people enabled me to see this old story in a way that I never really understood before. One was the great Israeli poet, Yehuda Amichai, and the other was my mentor and friend, Rabbi Wolfe Kelman.

Amichai has a poem called: *Hamakom Shebo Anu Tzodkim*, "From the Place Where We Are Right," and this is what it says:

> From the place where we are right
> Flowers will never grow
> In the spring.
> The place where we are right
> Is hard and trampled
> Like a yard.
> But doubts and loves
> Dig up the world
> Like a mole, a plow,
> And a whisper will be heard in the place
> Where the ruined
> House once stood.

Do you understand what the poet is saying here?

"From the place where we are right, flowers will never grow."

The land of those who are sure that they are right is hard and unyielding. It is more like a stony courtyard than it is like a fertile field. There is no doubt in the hearts and minds of those who are certain that they are always right. And there is no love in the hearts of those who are sure that they are completely right and that those who disagree with them are completely wrong. But things only grow where there are doubts. Doubts enable us to see what we believe from a different perspective, and sometimes the interchange between what I believe and what you believe leads to the birth of a new idea that is better than either my original idea or your original idea. And if there is love between two people who disagree, that love enables them to listen to each other's ideas and to grow from the interchange.

That is what I think the poet means when he says: "From the place where we are right, flowers will never grow." The place where we are sure that we are right, and that only we are right, is a cold and stony ground, a ground on which nothing can ever grow.

Rabbi Wolfe Kelman, *zichrono livracha*, expressed the same truth, not in poetry, but in this story, which his daughter, Rabbi Naamah Kelman, recalled to me recently.

"There was once a young disciple of a great rabbinic master who wanted to marry the daughter of a very wealthy businessman. The businessman agreed to the match, and he agreed to support the young man for a certain number of years while he studied, but he set down one condition. The young man must study on his own, and not spend any time studying with his former teacher. The reason the father-in-law set this condition was that he wanted his son-in-law to be an original scholar and not just a disciple of somebody else.

The young man accepted the condition, but over time, he found that he could not abide by it. He missed his old teacher. He yearned to be with him and to learn from his wisdom. And so, every so often, when his father-in-law was not around, he would slip off to study with his former teacher.

When his father-in-law found out what his son-in-law was doing, he was furious. He said to him: "You made an agreement! You signed a contract that you would not do this! It was on this condition that I let you marry my daughter, and it was on this condition that I have supported you all these years. You broke your word! And therefore, I am no longer going to support you!"

Rabbi Kelman said: The father-in-law was right. The young man had broken his word. And therefore, the father-in-law was legally allowed to cancel his agreement to support him. There is no doubt about it. Any court that read the agreement would have found for him.

But the son-in-law was also right. He yearned to have the benefit of his teacher's wisdom, and so he slipped away in secret in order to study with him. Can you blame anyone for wanting to study Torah? He too was right to do what he did.

And what about the young man's former teacher? Can you blame him for wanting to teach his disciple? Can you blame him for wanting to help this young man deepen his knowledge of Torah? Can you blame him for wanting to teach his favorite student, even if it had to be in secret? Was he not right too?

Rabbi Kelman used to say: the father-in-law was right. There is no question about that. A deal is a deal. And the son-in-law was right too. How can you not admire him for wanting to study Torah with his favorite teacher? And the teacher was right too. How can you blame him for not turning down a student who wanted to study with him?

But do you know what? Rabbi Kelman said: "The father-in-law was right, and the son-in-law was right, and the teacher was right. There is no question about that. But the Mashiach will only come for those who are not right."

I love that answer, don't you? Because, like Yehudah Amichai's poem, it warns against the danger of always being right. It teaches us that there is a value in being open to the possibility that the other person may also be right, or at least partly right, and that, if you want to grow in understanding and wisdom, you have to be open to the possibility that you are only partly right, and that your opponent may also be partly right.

I must tell you that I never understood one dimension of the story of Korach and Moses until I read this poem and this story. So, let me go over the story again, even though we are all familiar with it, and think that we understand it, and let me read it again, this time as a quarrel between two people: one of whom is absolutely certain that he is completely right, and one of whom is open to the possibility that he just might not be entirely right.

The story begins with Korach making an accusation. He says that all the people are equally holy, and that therefore Moses has no right to rule over them. He accuses Moses of arrogance in setting himself up above the people. And even though the traditional commentators all agree that this was just demagoguery, and that he did not mean what he was saying – that it was just a way to fire up the people and get them to be on his side – let us grant for a moment that Korach just might have been sincere, and that he might have meant what he was saying.

What is Moses's reaction to this accusation? The Torah says: *Vayishma Moshe, vayipol al panav* – "when Moses heard this accusation, he fell upon his face."

What does that mean?

I used to think that Moses fell upon his face in exhaustion or in disappointment. After all he has done for this people – this is the way they treat him? I always thought that he fell upon his face in exhaustion and in despair. That is what I thought the passage meant.

But one of the commentators – forgive me but at the moment I don't remember which one – one of the commentators says that "Moses fell upon his face" means that Moses went into himself. He closed his eyes to what was going on around him for a few moments, and looked back over his life to see if there was any truth to this accusation. Had he perhaps lorded it over the people more than he should have? Had he perhaps raised himself over the people improperly? And only then, only after he had examined his conscience, and convinced himself that he had not done any of the things of which he was being accused, only then did he stand up and answer the accusations of Korach.

Korach may have been sure that he was right. Moses was not sure.

Moses invites Korach and his cohorts to come forward and join in a test. He says: "You each take pans and put fire and incense in them, and Aaron will do the same thing, and let us see which pan God will respond to."

I always assumed that Moses was sure that God would respond to Aaron's pan, and that is why he offered this test. But the story does not necessarily have to be read that way. Perhaps what it means is that Moses meant it to be a real test, that Moses was content to let God decide who the rightful leader should be, and that if the test had come out in favor of Korach and his cohorts, he would have been able to accept that.

And then, further on in the story, Moses sends a message to the rebels who have risen up against him. He says to them: "Come up and let us talk. Perhaps we can arrive at some kind of a compromise." And they answer: "We will not go up! We have nothing to say to you. We are right and you are wrong. That's it. Settled."

Rashi puts it very well. He says that because they would not go up, therefore they went down. Their sin was not so much rebelling against Moses. Their sin was refusing to even talk to him to see if their dispute could somehow be resolved. And it was for this – for their certainty that they, and only they, were right – that Korach and his allies were destroyed. Rightness can kill you, if you think it is all on your side.

Let me spell this lesson out – first as it applies to the people who live in Israel, and then as it applies to each one of us who are here today.

Israel is terribly divided. And the division is between people on both sides who are sure that all the right is on their side.

The secular Jews are right; they really are, when they say that the Haredim should carry their fair share of the burdens of citizenship. They are right when they say that our blood is not cheaper than yours, and that if you are citizens, you must bear the burdens of citizenship, just as we do. They are right. There is no question about that.

But they are not entirely right. They need to realize that if it were not for those who studied the Torah down through the centuries, there would be no state of Israel today. They need to realize that if it were not for the pious people who wrote their questions in Hebrew and who received their answers in Hebrew, there would be no Hebrew for the modern Jews to revive. They need to know that they are right – but not the only ones who are right.

And the Haredim must feel the same way. In what other state in the world could they feel free to picket and to protest on behalf of their right to observe the Torah as they understand it, as they do in Israel? In what other state in the world could they demand and receive the kind of support that their schools and their students receive in Israel? Should not a measure of gratitude come with this support that they receive? And do they not have an obligation to respect the rights and the needs of those who do not see things the way they do?

They may be right – but as Wolfe Kelman said: The Mashiach will only come for the sake of those who are not right, or at least for the sake of those who do not claim that all the right is on their side, and none is on the side of the other. For nothing grows in a society that thinks that way.

And so it is with the hawks in Israel who sincerely believe that the doves are endangering the security of the state, and so it is with the doves in Israel who sincerely believe that the hawks are endangering the security of the state. Both sides need to listen to the partial truth of the other side, and both sides need to grant the partial truth of the other side, for if they cannot listen to each other, the state will be undermined more by that than by their different points of view!

Listen to how the Women of the Wall fight for their right to pray their way at the Wall and how they call those who object names, and listen to how those who have always prayed at the wall their way and who are offended by these women call them names. If you do, you will understand why one wise Haredi rabbi whom I know says that the God who dwells on the other side of the Wall, must be weeping at the bad behavior of them both.

Let us move from talking about Israel, for I never feel very comfortable judging Israel from here. Let us move from judging Israel and let us look at ourselves. Listen to the fierce debate that goes on within our own community. Listen to the name calling that goes on between the groups in Jewish life. Listen to how one side says that J Street is a traitorous organization and should not be allowed to speak to our young people, and listen to how the other side says that AIPAC is a puppet of the Israeli government that should not be allowed to speak to our youth. Listen to how both groups on so many issues insist that all the right is on their side, and that their opponents are completely wrong. And remember Yehudah Amichai's warning: Nothing grows in soil like this. Nothing grows in a place where we are completely right and our opponents are completely wrong.

It is easy to criticize the name calling and the divisiveness that goes on in Israel. It is easy to denounce the ways in which the doves and the hawks, the secularists and the Haredim, the liberals and the conservatives treat each other there. But that is a cheap shot, for those of us who do not live there. Instead of doing that, let us look into our own behavior here at home. How many of us live in families in which parents and children dismiss each other, or denigrate each other, or call each other names, instead of listening to each other and learning from each other? How many of us belong to organizations that duplicate each other and that ought to merge with each other, but are unable to do so, because each believes that all the right is with them, and none is with the other side?

The story of Korach versus Moses is a story that is all too relevant, that is painfully relevant, in our time. I give Korach the benefit of the doubt and believe that he really believed he was right. But I hold him responsible for believing that only he was right. That was his sin, and it is often ours.

So let us learn today the art of compromise. Let us learn today the art of listening to those with whom we disagree to see if we can find the kernel of truth within their arguments. For if we can learn to do that, our arguments with each other will be more persuasive, and the results of our disputes will be more productive.

Let me tell you one more word which I learned from Rabbi Wolfe Kelman. I remember how once he was arguing on behalf of the concepts of pluralism and mutual respect, and someone challenged him. Someone stood up and said: "Can you please tell me where the idea of pluralism is found in the classic Jewish sources? Where does it say that we should be respectful to those who are against the values that we believe in?"

You and I could have answered that question with half a dozen sources, and I am sure that Wolfe Kelman could have too. But this is what he said:

"The fact that you can stand up and ask that question, and that nobody here says: Who are you to be so presumptuous as to speak in the name of the tradition? And the fact that I can answer this question and nobody here says: Who are you to be so presumptuous as to answer in the name of the tradition – that in itself is the answer to your question."

And he was right. It is good to travel through life in the company of those who seek the truth, for you can learn from being with them. It is hard to travel through life in the company of those who possess – or who think that they possess – all the truth, for they are not open to learning and therefore they cannot teach.

Let me remind you of what we say and what we do every time we finish a book of the Torah. We stand for the last words, and we wish each other well. We say to each other: *Hazak, hazak, v'nitchazek.* And this is what I believe that blessing really means. It means "May you be strong, and may I be strong, and may we strengthen each other."

That is true pluralism.

And therefore, this is my prayer on the Sabbath when we read the archetypal story of what happens when people fight over who is right in the Torah: the story of Korach and Moses. May the blessing that we say each time we finish a book of the Torah come true in our organizations, in our synagogues, in our homes, and in our lives. May we not be so sure that we, and only we, possess all the right and that those we disagree with possess none of the right, for as Korach and his cohorts learned: being too right can be lethal.

A Story That Comes from Another World

I WANT TO TELL YOU a story today that comes from another world.

It comes from another world – not only geographically, but spiritually.

But before I tell you this story, I want to share with you the opening words of today's Torah reading, and then I want to make a couple of comments about the world we live in today.

The *sedra* begins:

Ish ki yidor neder l'Adonai, o hishova shvua l'esor isar al nafsho, lo yachel divaro, kichol hayotsei mipiv ya-a-seh – "If a man makes an oath, imposing an obligation on himself, he shall not break his word. That which comes out of his mouth – that he shall do."

The statement is clear and blunt: that which you promise – that you shall do.

Compare that statement with the world in which we live today.

Do you know that every single candidate for the presidency in the last forty years has promised that, as soon as he is elected, he will move the United States Embassy from Tel Aviv to Jerusalem?

And do you know that no person who has been elected to the presidency in the last forty years has done so?

I am not sure whether the embassy ought to be moved or not. I am no expert. Perhaps these people know something that I don't know. Perhaps there is a good reason not to move the American Embassy from Tel Aviv to Jerusalem. But one thing I do know: That a candidate should not make promises like this, and then break them. That is not right. A person's word ought to mean something, shouldn't it?

Many years ago, I heard Rabbi Harry Halpern, of blessed memory, say: "A political platform is like a train platform. It is meant to help you get on board; not to stand on once you are on board."

Politicians spend a lot of time at their national conventions working on their platforms, and then, once they get elected, you never hear a word about their platforms again.

And politicians are not alone in ignoring the promises and the statements that they make. An athlete comes before Congress, and says that he never took performance-enhancing drugs, and later on we find out that he did. And no one is surprised. We have become accustomed to people lying, even under oath.

What's the old joke? How can you tell if a person is lying under oath?

If his lips move.

It is against this background that I want to tell you this story, which I learned from Gary Rosenblatt, who is the editor of the *Jewish Week* in New York City.

About a century ago, his grandfather, Louis Feldman, made a vow that changed his life. He was barely a teenager at the time. His parents told him that they had decided to move from Poland to America, and that his older brothers and sisters were going to go with them. They were tired of the poverty and the anti-Semitism in Poland, and they believed that they could have a better life in America, and so they were going to go.

The young man had a different opinion. He had heard that America was a *treife medinah*, that America was a country in which you could enjoy a better way of life economically, but that it was a land in which it was very difficult to live a Jewish life – certainly more difficult than it was in Poland. And he was a yeshiva *bochur* in Poland, who had a promising future as a scholar.

And so this thirteen-year-old took a *neder* that he would never go to America.

His parents and his siblings were upset, but what could they do? A *neder* is a *neder*. And so they left without him.

Can you imagine the strength and the will power that it must have taken for a thirteen-year-old boy to take such an oath? Can you imagine how he must have felt, and how his parents must have felt, when he stood on a street corner, and waved goodbye to their carriage, as they left for the new world without him?

The years passed. The family arrived in America. They settled in Baltimore, and lived out their years there. The young boy whom they left behind in Poland grew up to become a young Talmudic scholar. He married and had a child. And then, one day he received a letter from America, telling him that his mother was dying, and that her wish was for him to come to America, so that she could see him one last time before she died.

The young man was torn between his commitment to his family and his commitment to his faith. He wanted to go, but he had taken an oath – and how can you break an oath?

He decided to ask the advice of the Chofetz Chaim, who was one of the leading rabbinic authorities of his generation. And so, he traveled all the way from the small town in Poland where he lived to Radun, which is in Belarus, where the Chofetz Chaim lived. It was not a small trip to make, in those days in which there were no planes. He had to hitch a ride with a wagon driver, and then transfer to another one several times along the way until he got there.

He arrived late at night, and went straight to the home of the Chofetz Chaim. The Rabbi saw how exhausted he was, and so he told him that it was better not to make a decision in haste, and sent him off to an inn to rest. He promised that they would listen to his case the next day.

The next morning, Gary Rosenblatt's grandfather came to the home of the Chofetz Chaim and tried to present his case. The Rabbi said: If this is a case that involves a *neder*, I cannot hear it by myself. A *neder* case requires a rabbinic court of no less than three judges. And so the Chofetz Chaim sent him back to his hotel room while he gathered three judges to hear the case, and then he summoned him back.

Gary Rosenblatt's grandfather met with the Bet Din, and explained his problem. He explained that, on the one hand, he knew that the *mitzvah* of honoring parents is very great, and therefore, he felt an obligation to go see his mother before she died. But on the other hand, he knew that an oath is a very serious thing, and that one cannot simply disregard it. After all, the Torah says in this week's *sedra*: *kol hayotsei mipiv ya-aseh* — "whatever you promise, you must keep." So he asked the court to advise him: which has priority — *kibud av v'em* — "honoring a request from a parent" — or keeping your word?

The Beth Din questioned Gary Rosenblatt's grandfather for hours. It asked him to tell them in detail about the circumstances in which he had made the oath. It asked him to tell them in detail about what kind of medical situation his mother was in, and it asked him to tell them in detail about what kind of Jewish life they were living in Baltimore. And then, they asked him to leave, while they examined the Torah, and the Talmud, and the Responsa literature on this question.

Finally, they reached a decision. The Beth Din said that because of the sacred obligation to honor your parents, which is one of the Ten Basic Statements in the Torah, that he could annul his oath and go to America. But on one condition: He could go to America, but only on condition that he would do all that he could while he was there to put out the fires of assimilation and to lead people back to Torah while he was there.

Mr. Feldman thanked the court for the permission to rejoin his family, and went to America. There he became a highly respected Torah scholar who, throughout the rest of his long life, devoted himself to studying and teaching Torah. And he fulfilled the second oath that he had taken by bringing many people closer to the Jewish way of life.

Why do I tell you this story today?

I tell it to you in order to show you how far we have traveled, not only geographically, but spiritually, from the world in which this story took place.

Can you imagine someone traveling hundreds of miles today in order to consult a rabbi on whether to annul a promise that he had made years before?

Could a story like this be told about any of the candidates running for office today, or about any of the athletes who have testified before Congress about whether they have used steroids to advance their careers or not? Could a story like this be told about any of the officials of Wall Street or any of the officers of British Petroleum who have testified under oath in Congress regarding what they have done? Could a story like this be told about any of the people who work for the tabloids in England or in America, who have been accused of hacking into people's e-mails, or eavesdropping on their phone calls, in order to find out private information which is not their concern?

And most important, could a story like this be told about us?

We live in a world very, very different from the world of Gary Rosenblatt's grandfather's in Poland, just a century or so ago. I don't mean to glorify or to exaggerate their piety or their way of life, but they lived in a world where words were sacred, and we live in a world where words have become cheap.

They lived in a world in which, when they made an appointment, they said: "I will see you at four o'clock on Tuesday afternoon *bli neder*," which means: don't consider this an oath, for if something happens and I am not able to meet you on time, I don't want to be considered as having broken my oath. They lived in a world in which, if you made a promise, you would say: I will keep it *im yirtse Hashem* – God willing, because they did not want to be counted as having broken their word if something came up and they could not fulfill what they had promised to do.

There is a story that is told about a *meshulach*, a collector for charity, who went from Poland to America to raise money for some charity. When he came back, the people asked him: "Did you learn any English?" He said: "A little."

They pressed him to tell them one example of the English that he had learned.

He said; "I learned that, when I ask someone for a donation, and he says: Maybe — Maybe means 'no.'"

The *meshulach* was right. He and we speak different languages. When we read in the papers an ad that says: "This is the world's greatest product," that means it is probably fairly good. When we buy a box of soap suds or cereal that says: "Giant size," that means it is probably medium size. When we see a movie advertised as "riveting" or "spell binding" or "unforgettable," that means it is average. We speak one language and they spoke another. They spoke a language that was based on the opening words of today's Torah reading: lo yachel divaro, kol hayotsei mipiv ya-aseh – which means: "Do not desecrate your word. Whatever comes out of your mouth, that you shall do."

I will not tell you who to vote for today. I have no right to do so from this pulpit. But this I will tell you: Listen to what the candidates say. Listen carefully. And if you believe that they are only promising, and that they will not keep their word once they get elected, then do not vote for them.

For we are a people that takes the holiness of words seriously. We are a people that begin our prayers on the holiest night of the year by reciting Kol Nidre, and by asking God to forgive us if we have made promises and then have not been able to keep them.

And let us not just point a finger at the politicians and the athletes and the advertisers. Let us remember that whenever you point a finger at someone else, three fingers point back at you. And let us ask ourselves:

That each time we say the Amidah, we begin by asking God to open our mouths, because we understand how sacred words are.

That each time we finish the Amidah, we end by asking God to guard our tongues from speaking evil and our lips from saying guile.

And therefore, may we make no rash promises that we will not keep.

May we make no oaths that we will be sorry for afterwards.

May we keep our word.

For this is what the Torah asks of us in the opening words of today's sedra, and this is what God wants of us every single day.

Yihiyu liratson imrey fi – "May the words of our mouths be pleasing to God."

What Will I Do When I Finish with this Job?

I HAVE AN ANNOUNCEMENT TO MAKE this morning. People here have been asking me for some time now: what will I do when I finish my job and retire as the Interim Rabbi of Anshe Shalom? And I have been telling them that I am exploring a number of different options but that I am not sure yet what I will do. Today I want to tell you that I have made up my mind.

And since you are my good friends, I want you to be the first to hear what I am going to do. I have decided that I am going to open up a Jewish driving school. I know that there are many other driving schools available, but my school is going to be different from all the other schools in that MINE is going to be a JEWISH DRIVING SCHOOL. That means that I will teach driving from the point of view of the Torah and the Jewish tradition.

To the best of my knowledge, there is no other school anywhere in the world that teaches driving from the point of view of Judaism. And so, I figure that if I open up a Jewish School of Driving, people will come from all over the world in order to study driving from the point of view of the Torah. Therefore, I believe that I will make a fortune.

Seriously, do you know why am I thinking of opening up a driving school? I am thinking of opening up a driving school for three reasons:

The first reason is because of what happened to our son, Steve, recently. He was driving along on Highway 75, minding his own business, when someone, who later told the police that he had fallen asleep at the wheel, plowed into him, and as a result, Steve injured his neck. Steve now has to go for therapy three times a week. I know that we Jews are supposed to be a stiff-necked people, but still. . . .

And so, I would like to open up a driving school in order to teach that person who said that he was driving while he was half asleep what the Jewish religion has to say about sleeping while driving.

Do you know what the Jewish tradition says about that? According to the Jewish tradition, you are supposed to save your sleeping for when you are in shul, you are supposed to save your sleeping for during the rabbi's sermon, and you are not supposed to sleep while you are driving. That is what Judaism says, and that is what my Jewish driving school will teach this man, who caused this accident.

I want to teach this man what it says in the Psalms: *Shomer yisrael lo yanum v'lo yishan*, "The guardian of Israel does not slumber nor does He sleep." And I want to teach him that when you are driving, you are the guardian, not only of Israel but of all those who are on the road, and therefore, you should save your sleeping for when you are in shul, and not fall asleep on the highway.

The second reason why I am planning to open up a Jewish driving school is because, as some of you may know, my wife was in an automobile accident some time ago as well. The case has still not been settled. The reason it has not been settled is that we still have one unresolved issue. The insurance company is willing to pay for the cost of our car which was totaled – without question. They are willing to pay the cost of the other car that was involved – without question. The insurance company is willing to pay for the time that my wife spent in the hospital and in the rehab center – without question. And they are willing to pay for her pain and suffering.

Do you know what is holding up the case? They are not willing to pay for my pain and suffering. After all, I suffered too? I will let you know how the case comes out.

By the way, I want you to know that the rehab center that she went to is a wonderful place. It has a lovely garden. It has a devoted staff. It has fine food. They have better food there than I get at home. And so do you know what I do? If you promise that you will not tell anybody – this is what I do. Three times a week, I put on my pajamas, and I put on a bathrobe and I put on my slippers and I pretend to be a patient, and I go there for lunch. That is how good the food in this rehab place is.

It is such a lovely rehab center that I recommend it to every one of you, should you ever need one – or even if you don't need one. It is called the Regents Park Rehab Center, and the director of nursing services is a woman named Tova, and she is good just like her name. One of the best things about this accident is that we have gotten to know her, and she is a real treasure. And she says that if I bring in any people, that she will pay me a commission, so I am happy to recommend the Regents Park Rehab to you today. If you go there, just ask for Tova, and mention my name.

But meantime, the second reason I want to open up a driving school is because of the woman who caused my wife's accident. I won't tell you who it was – but this woman was going down the ramp onto Highway 95, when she suddenly realized that she had made a mistake. She meant to go onto the south lane of Highway 95, and by mistake she went down the ramp that leads to the northern lane of Highway 95. Now what would you do if you made a mistake like that? You would probably continue driving north until you got to the next exit, and turn around there. Right?

But this woman figured: If I do that, do you realize how much gas I will waste??? This woman evidently knew that wasting is considered a big sin in Judaism. It is called: *ba'al tashchis*. So do you know what she did instead? She made a U-turn. . . right in the middle of the ramp that led down to 95 North. . . she made a U-turn right in the middle of the ramp and she tried to go up the down ramp. And that is what caused the accident.

And so, I am hoping that this woman will come to my Jewish driving school so that I can teach her what the Torah says about what she did. Does everyone here know what the Torah says about making a U-turn in the middle of Highway 95? The Torah says that when you are doing a *mitzvah*, and you encounter an obstacle – you are not supposed to turn back.

If she came to my Torah school of driving, I would teach her the book of Bamidbar which we have been reading these last few weeks. And I would teach her not to be like those Jews in the wilderness who every time they ran out of water, or every time they got tired of the manna, or every time they ran into an enemy, came running to Moses and said: let us turn around and go back to Egypt.

I will teach this woman, if she comes to my Torah Centered Driving School, that the moral of the book of Bamidbar is that if you are on the way to doing a *mitzvah* you should never turn around and go back, but that instead you should go forward, despite all obstacles, and that, if you do, you will eventually arrive at the Promised Land. That is the second reason why I want to open up a driving school that will teach you how to drive according to Jewish values.

By the way, in case you are wondering, my driving school is going to teach Conservative Judaism. What do I mean by that? Some schools teach you to drive on the right side of the road. Some schools, especially in Europe, teach you to drive on the left side of the read. But my school believes in Conservative Judaism, and therefore, we will teach you to drive in the middle of the road.

The third reason I want to open up a Torah centered driving school is because of a law that appears in today's Torah reading, and because of a case that was tried in the courts of California this year – the case of George Weller.

You should know that if a law appears, not once and not twice but three times in the Torah, it is probably an important law. And yet I confess that until this year I never really understood or appreciated the importance and the relevance of the law of the City of Refuge, which we read about in the Torah reading for today.

Three times, first in Mishpatim, and then in Massei, and then in Va'etchanan, the Israelites are told that when they come into the land, they should establish Cities of Refuge so that anyone who kills someone without intending to, can go there and take shelter from the anger of the family of the one whom he has accidentally killed. The Torah ordains that these people must stay in the City of Refuge for the rest of their lives or until the *Kohen Gadol* dies.

I must tell you that until recently I did not take this law very seriously. Because the Torah's example of a person who commits an accidental killing is someone who is chopping wood in the forest and the head of his axe accidentally flies off and hits someone else who happens to be standing nearby. Now I ask you: How many people in this synagogue are wood choppers? If you are, please raise your hands. No one. And even if you were, I don't know if there are any forests left here in Delray Beach. They have all been cut down to make room for condos or for shopping malls. So what are the odds that if you or I were chopping wood in a forest here in Delray Beach that the head of the axe we were using would fly off and kill someone? The only person that I can think of who chopped wood in recent years was Ronald Reagan, and to the best of my knowledge he never killed anybody while chopping. I don't know of anybody who has ever killed somebody by accident while chopping wood. Do you?

And so this law, even though it is repeated three times in the Torah, seemed to me to be outdated, and irrelevant to the world in which we live. That is what I thought until something happened this year that made me realize how wrong I was. And that was the case of George Weller.

There was a man whose name was George Weller who was driving in Santa Monica, California. He was not a very old man. He was only 91 years old, which does not seem as old to me now as it used to. George Weller was driving along the street in Santa Monica, minding his own business . . . and there happened to be a street fair going on that day and so the police had blocked off the main street. George Weller did not notice the wooden horse that the police had put up to keep traffic out and so he drove right through it. When he saw people strolling on the street, he realized that he had made a mistake, and so he tried to stop, but in his confusion, he stepped on the gas pedal instead of the brake by mistake. I can understand that happening. If you look, you will see that the gas pedal and the brake are located very close to each other . . . and so I can understand somebody hitting one when he meant to hit the other. George Weller stepped on the gas pedal instead of the brake that day, and as a result, he killed ten people and injured more than sixty people before he was able to stop the car. And so, George Weller was put on trial by the city of Santa Monica, and he was charged with ten counts of vehicular manslaughter and sixty counts of gross negligence.

Let me ask you: If you were on the jury, how would you have voted in this case? Would you send a man who was ninety-one years old to jail and give him a long-term sentence? Or would you say that a man who killed ten people and who injured sixty people should go free?

I confess that I don't know how I would vote if I were on that jury. Sending a man that age to jail does not make much sense to me. But letting a man who has killed ten people, go free, even if he did it accidentally, does not make much sense to me either.

You know the story of the jury that comes in after many days of deliberation? The judge says: Ladies and gentlemen of the jury have you reached a verdict? And the foreman says: Yes, your honor. We have examined all the facts in this case, we have listened to both sides, and we have decided that we would rather not get involved.

I must tell you that I feel a little bit like the members of that jury when I think about this case. At the very least, and I think there is no question about this: they should take this man's driver's license away. Anyone who is so old and so confused that he can step on the gas pedal instead of the brake should never be allowed to drive again. And I think we ought to take away his keys as well, for there are many people who continue to drive, even after their license has been taken away from them. And we should make sure that that does not happen in this case.

And if he has any money, I think that some of it should be distributed amongst the families of his victims. I realize that all the money in the world will not heal the pain that these people must feel over the loss of their loved ones, but still, it would be a gesture of restitution. And if he owns a house or a car or has any other assets, let them be sold to pay at least some part of the damage that he caused.

But I think that a case can be made that he is not the only one at fault in this case. Do the police not bear some measure of responsibility for having put up just one wooden barrier to keep out cars? Shouldn't they have put up a bigger blockade? And does not part of the blame for what happened go to them for not having done so?

And are the city of Santa Monica and the county of Los Angeles not partly at fault as well? They have created a city that has a terribly inadequate bus system and no subways, and so anyone who wishes to travel, whatever their age and whatever their driving ability, has to drive in order to get anywhere. Is that right?

But there is one question more that is in my mind when I think of this case – and this is the question that I want to talk to you about today. Whether he goes to jail or not, whether his license is taken away from him or not, whether his car is taken away from him or not, I wonder: How will this man live with himself for the rest of his life, knowing that he killed ten people and injured sixty people?

George Weller is not the only person who will have to live for the rest of his life with this kind of guilt on his mind. He is a member of a large club, composed of people who have done the same thing. Do you know that Laura Bush, the wife of George W. Bush, for example, once killed someone in a driving accident many years ago? And do you know that Mathew Broderick, the actor, did that too? And there are many others who have at some time in their lives killed someone in a vehicular accident. You should know that a car can be not just a means of transportation. A car can be a lethal weapon.

Sometimes it was their fault, and sometimes it was not. Perhaps someone darted out into the street whom they were unable to see or someone did it so quickly that they did not have time to hit the brakes? If so, what they did was surely not murder. It may not even have been involuntary manslaughter. It may have been through no fault of their own. And yet, these people will have to live for the rest of their lives with the knowledge that they killed another human being.

Can you imagine the trauma that these people must feel? Unless they are made of stone, can you imagine the weight of guilt that they must carry inside them for the rest of their lives? What should they do? And what can we do to help these people live with the burden of guilt that they carry?

Well-meaning friends may tell them to put the experience behind them and move on with their lives. But can they? Could you? Could I? Lawyers will tell them that they should never apologize, because to do so is to admit liability. But what should we tell them, and what should we do for them, if something like this ever happens, God forbid, God forbid, to one of our friends.

Could you or I ever get behind the wheel of a car again without remembering what we had done? I don't think I could, and I doubt if you could either. An experience like this, taking the life of an adult or, God forbid, taking the life of a child – has to have an effect upon the soul of the person who does it that is not easy to get over.

What should we do for these people who will be in pain for the rest of their lives? These people live with their traumas – alone, isolated, hurting on the inside, and feeling responsible in their consciences, even if they are not found liable by the courts.

And NOW DO YOU SEE why the idea of a City of Refuge makes sense? It is not such an outmoded, irrelevant concept as we thought it was at first. These people are deeply wounded, and they need spiritual counseling and therapy. And therefore the idea of the City of Refuge makes sense in our time just as it did in days of old. It makes sense, not only and not primarily, because we are afraid that the families of the victims will go after them and seek revenge, though that is always a possibility. It makes sense because the people that are involved in such accidents are spiritually wounded people and they need spiritual help. The accidental killer in the time of the Torah was not absolved of all responsibility for what he or she did. They had to go into exile because, even though they did not intend to do harm, nevertheless they did take a life, and that is no small thing. They were required to stay in the City of Refuge until the death of the High Priest, which meant that they were forced to live in a place where they had a spiritual mentor, either a *Kohen* or a *Levy*, with whom they could meditate on the meaning and the sanctity of life. And the community, by establishing and maintaining these cities, showed that they too had a share of responsibility for what happened. If the community had put up better blockades instead of wooden horses at the Santa Monica street fair, this accident might not have taken place. And if the community had educated people to be more careful and more respectful of life, there might not have been such accidents.

And so I wish there was a City of Refuge to which George Weller and people like him could be sent today. I wish he could be sentenced to live with a *Kohen Gadol*, or with some other spiritual teacher who could bring him a measure of comfort and healing after the trauma that he has gone through. And I wish that the members of the town council of Santa Monica could go to a City of Refuge too, so that they could meditate there on their failures as a community, such as their failure to provide some transportation alternatives to having to drive, for the elderly who live there.

Can we have Cities of Refuge today? I don't know. Maybe we should. But until the state gets around to building one, I believe that you and I ought to become Cities of Refuge to those whom we know who have to go through this trauma.

I want to suggest that if we give a hug, or if we write an encouraging note, or if we lend a sympathetic ear, even when the person repeats the same story over and over again, as traumatized people always do, or if we host an informal get-together for these people, a get-together in which there is no excusing and no accusing, but only caring – if we do any of these things, then we can be Cities of Refuge to those people whom we know who are going through this dreadful experience.

And so let me say it clearly. I was wrong all these years when I thought, naively, that the law of the City of Refuge was antiquated and irrelevant in our time, even though it is found in the Torah three times. Now I understand that the way in which we treat accidental killers says something about our own values and our own humanity. If we say to them: forget about it, as if nothing has happened, we demonstrate our own insensitivity to the sacredness of human life, and to the pain that these people are living with. And if we turn away from them and leave them to live with their pain and their shame and their guilt, we demonstrate our own callousness and self-righteousness and our own lack of awareness that what happened in their cars could, God forbid, God forbid, God forbid, happen in ours too.

And therefore, what we should do if anyone we know is in this situation, is hear them and heal them, and support them, in their time of pain, and guilt, while they struggle to find some way of atoning and some way of living with what they have done.

And so this is my suggestion to you today. If you or I ever have a friend who has done what George Weller, *nebech*, did, don't leave him to the courts, and don't abandon him to the police, but reach out and help him, reach out and heal him, reach out and be a City of Refuge to him.

And may all our friends know that we are there for them if they should ever need us in their time of trouble and distress.

When Plowshares Are Turned Into Swords
(Reflections of a Wounded Dove)

DEVARIM

SOMETHING AWFUL OCCURRED in the streets of Jerusalem at the beginning of July.

It was on the front page of every single newspaper in the world on the day it happened. And then it faded from our consciousness. Except for the families of the three people who died on that day, except for the sixty-seven people who were injured on that day and those who care about them, and except for the people of Israel, the incident was soon forgotten. Something else happened someplace else the next day that took our minds off this gruesome incident.

And yet – for some reason – I am not sure why, this awful incident has stayed in my mind. And so, I want to think about it with you today.

I am referring to the incident in which an Arab construction worker named Husam Tsayir Dwayat of the East Jerusalem neighborhood of Sur Bahir, took his bulldozer, and drove it down *Rechov Yaffo* in Jerusalem, smashing cars and overturning buses as he went, chasing and killing pedestrians who tried to get out of his way, and shouting *"Allah Akbar!"* Finally, finally, a soldier who happened to be standing nearby, grabbed his gun, climbed onto the bulldozer, and shot him dead, but not before he had murdered three people and injured sixty-seven.

I have been thinking about this awful incident for several reasons. One is because of Batsheva Unterman. Batsheva Unterman was a thirty-one year old kindergarten teacher whose *mazel* was that she happened to be on *Rechov* Yaffo that day. She had a six-month-old child sitting next to her in the car. With remarkable presence of mind, she took the child out of her carseat, opened the window, and handed the child to a pedestrian who happened to be standing there. A few seconds later, the bulldozer crashed into her car, and she died.

I can't help but think of Batsheva Unterman, and about her six-month-old child. I can't imagine how hard it must have been for the principal of her school in Har Homa to break the news to the children in her kindergarten class that *Morah* Batsheva is dead.

And I can't imagine what will happen to her six-month-old child, who lost her mother that day. And I can't stop thinking about that pedestrian, whose name was Jeremy Aronson, who was walking down the street minding his own business one minute, and who was standing there holding a baby in his arms, a baby whose mother was murdered a half moment later. What did he do with that child? What did he say to that child's father when they met? And will he ever forget that bloody day on *Rechov* Yaffo?

And I think of Lilly Gordon-Friedman, age 54, who died that day. She was a mother of three, and a teacher of the blind in Jerusalem. The doctors tried to save her, but she died on the operating table at Shaarei Tzedek Hospital, and she was buried that night in the Givat Shaul Cemetery.

Hundreds of people came to her funeral, for she was evidently a very special person. Who else but a special person becomes a teacher of the blind? And I wonder: Who will care for her two teenage sons and her young daughter now? And what will become of her students?

I think of the construction worker who did this dreadful deed. His picture was in the newspapers, and I must tell you that, when you look at this picture, you would never know that this young man was capable of what he did. He looks like any other normal human being. By the looks of him, he could be your son or mine. And you have to wonder: what makes a normal-looking man, a man who is the father of two young children, go off on this kind of a rampage? Was it insanity, or was it zealousness, or was it that he was brainwashed from childhood to hate, or was it the vision of inheriting the world to come? What was it that made this man take a bulldozer and go roaring down *Rechov* Yaffo killing anyone and everyone on his path?

Understand, this was not a military area, and this was not a West Bank settlement. This was *Rechov* Yaffo! Jews have lived and worked in this neighborhood for more than a century. Shaarei Tzedek Hospital was originally on this street, and Jewish doctors and nurses have treated Jewish and Arab patients alike here since 1902.

And yet, on a quiet, peaceful morning, this man took it upon himself to kill Jews – any Jews – not soldiers, not Israeli security forces, but any Jews he could find – even women and children, even the elderly and the infirm. He set out to kill Jews – Jews who may be in favor of two states or who may be against two states, Jews who hate Arabs or Jews who have nothing against Arabs. He set out to kill Jews.

And to make it worse, within just a few hours of this incident, THREE DIFFERENT ARAB GROUPS claimed credit for what he did!

Credit??? As if the murder of innocent people was something to take credit for? As if the murder of innocent people was something to brag about?

Hamas issued a statement that said: "We consider it a natural reaction to the daily aggression and crimes that are being committed against our people."

"Natural?" Can someone please explain to me what is natural about killing women and children?

Bradley Burston of *Ha-aretz* pointed out that just a few days before this incident, people in the United States – some of them Muslims, some of them Christians, some of them Jews – lobbied certain Protestant churches and certain universities to divest themselves from the Caterpillar Company, because it manufactures bulldozers, and the Israeli army uses bulldozers in order to demolish the homes of terrorists.

And yet, when this happened, when a Caterpillar bulldozer was used in order to crush and kill Jews – not to demolish houses but to demolish human beings – I did not hear anyone complain about it.

I did not hear anyone say: Let's divest from the Caterpillar Company because of this act of terrorism. I did not hear anyone call this what it was: intentional, brutal, premeditated, immoral murder.

What are we to think when something like this happens? What is it that we are supposed to think that these people want? Is it only a state of their own? Or is it to see our people dead? Is it the thrill of vengeance? Is it nothing more than the pleasure of seeing dead Jews?

And what should Israel do in response?

The first reaction in Israel was anger – more than anger – fury. People called for tearing down this man's family's house in order to teach the Arabs a lesson. The Labor Minister, Eli Yishai, said legislation should be passed to restrict the movement of East Jerusalem Arabs from now on. Haim Ramon, the vice prime minister, said that "one of the reasons for the ease with which this attack was perpetrated is the fact that he came from one of those Palestinian villages, that for some reason are technically called 'Jerusalem.' No Jews live there, and they were never considered part of Jerusalem until the city was annexed in 1967. And therefore, they should be treated as if they were Ramallah, or Jenin, or Bethlehem, and not considered a part of Jerusalem any longer."

"The people who live in Sur Bahir should not have Jerusalem identity cards," Ramon said. "How many more Israelis have to die before this is understood?"

On the other hand, people like Jeremy Milgrom wrote that harsh collective punishment won't work, that it will only increase hatred. He wrote that, whenever he goes to Sur Bahir, he sees a great many construction vehicles parked there, a reminder of how mutually dependent the Jews and Arabs of Jerusalem are on each other. He said: "There is no way that we can condone what this man did. There is no excuse for the murder of a kindergarten teacher and the murder of someone who dedicated her life to working with the blind. But will collective punishment really persuade anyone to live peacefully? Or will it only increase their desire for revenge?"

Who is right – Haim Ramon who wants to see the Arabs of Sur Bahir punished for what this man did, or Jeremy Milgrom who wants to see them treated better in the hope that that will persuade them to live differently?

I don't know. As the old Yiddish proverb puts it: *Vi mir likt dem kranken iz nisht gut* – "Wherever you put the sick person, it is not good." Harsh punishment has not worked very well. Tearing down houses has only made more terrorists. But giving them jobs has not worked very well either. And so I am not sure whether Israel should go the way that Haim Ramon advocated after this incident or the way that Jeremy Milgrom advocates. Neither one seems to work very well. What do you do with people who are raised from childhood to be mass murderers and child killers? Does anyone have an answer to this question? I don't.

Perhaps there is no answer – except to reconcile ourselves to a never-ending state of hostilities. That could very well be the reality. But if so, what will that kind of life do – not only to the Arabs – but to the Jews of Israel as well? What will it do to the morale and to the morals of young Israelis who will have to spend three years of their youth on guard duty – with no sign of peace on the horizon?

These were some of my reflections on the day when this awful incident occurred. And then I found one sentence in the news coverage of this story that caught my attention. A man whose name is David Booth – I have no idea who he is – was quoted in the newspapers. And this is what he said:

"This was a case of someone turning a plowshare into a sword."

He was right. The bulldozer that this murderer used in his rampage was meant to be an instrument of peace. It was being used that day in order to clear the ground for the construction of the Jerusalem light rail project, which the city of Jerusalem is eagerly awaiting. And yet it was turned from an instrument of peace into a weapon of war by this mad murderer.

When I read that line, I thought of the vision of Isaiah. The *Haftorah* for today is Isaiah's passionate and powerful condemnation of the evils of Judean society. But unfortunately – at least in my opinion – the *Haftorah* ends a little bit too soon. It contains almost all of chapter one, but if I had my way, it would continue on through the first part of chapter two as well. Because chapter two of Isaiah is the great vision that the day will come when the nations of the world will assemble and say: Come, let us go up to the Mount of the Lord, and let us learn to walk in His ways, *ki mitsiyon teytsei Torah, u'dvar Adonai miYerushalayim* — "for out of Zion shall come forth Torah, and the word of the Lord from Jerusalem."

And then comes the line that I love: *v'chititu charvotam l'itim, v'chanitoteyhem limazmeyrot* — "they shall beat their swords into plowshares, and their spears into pruning hooks."

That is the line that David Booth was alluding to when he said that this murderer had beaten his plowshare into a sword. The vision of Isaiah is that someday, someday, someway — the nations will beat their swords into plowshares. And somehow, somehow, I don't know how, but somehow — we must hold on to that vision, despite all that the world does to make it seem naïve. If not today, if not tomorrow, if not tomorrow, then in the foreseeable future, if not in the foreseeable future, then in the unforeseeable future, we have to believe that there will come a time when people will beat their swords into plowshares. If we think that dream is achievable now, we are insanely naïve, and we open ourselves up to the attacks of the wicked and the bloodthirsty and the dangerous people around us. But if we believe that that dream is never achievable, then we doom ourselves to a life of despair and that is not a way to live.

Let me finish with a brief and a simple poem that comes from Yehudah Amichai, who is one of Israel's most beloved poets. He served in the Israeli army when he had to, but he held on to the dream of eventual peace even while he did. And there are many soldiers today who carry Amichai's poetry books with them in their knapsacks, when they go off to fight.

And this is one of their favorite poems. It is a kind of a postscript to Isaiah, chapter two:

> Don't stop after beating the swords
> Into plowshares. Don't stop! Go on beating,
> And make musical instruments out of them.
> Then, whoever wants to make war again,
> Will have to turn them into plowshares first.

Let that dream be! Let it be!

Let the vicious murderer who stepped on the gas as he shouted "*Allah Akbar!*" rot in Hell as he deserves, for he blasphemed against

Allah by using God's name to justify killing women and children. But let the dream continue. Let us live and someday, somehow, someway – let it come true.

Till then, *Adonai oz l'amo yitain; Adonai yevarech et amo bashalom.* "May God bless Israel with the physical strength that it so much needs to have, and at the same time, may God bless Israel with the ability to hold on to the vision that peace will someday come."

For we need both: the strength to fight and the courage to hope. We need them both so very much.

Who was Right – The Father or the Teacher?

I WANT TO TELL YOU today about a dispute that took place recently at a certain day school. There was a disagreement between a teacher and a parent. When I first heard the story, my sympathies were with the parent, because I am a parent, but then, as I began to think about the matter more closely, I switched sides and I think that I now agree with the teacher.

Let me tell you the story first, and then you tell me which side you are on. Tell me whether you agree with the parent or with the teacher in this case. Alright?

I learned about this case from Rabbi Joel Wolowelsky, who is an educator at the Yeshivah of Flatbush. Let me tell it to you precisely as I learned it from him.

There was a child in the fourth grade of a certain day school who took a test in math. Somehow – I don't know how it happened – but somehow – the teacher made a mistake in grading her paper. I guess she must have marked one section of the test twice or made some other mistake. At any rate, she gave the child an 85 instead of the 75 that the child had actually earned on the test.

The child noticed the mistake, and so she went up and showed it to the teacher. The teacher said: "Thank you very much," and deducted ten points from the child's score. The child ended up the year with a C instead of a B.

When he heard what had happened, the father of this child was furious. He said: "Can you imagine that! The teacher taught my child a terrible lesson. The teacher taught my child that it does not pay to be honest."

Rabbi Wolowelsky says that he has told this story to a number of people since he heard it. He has told it to both parents and children. And he has asked them: "Do you agree with the father or with the teacher? Did the teacher do right in deducting the ten points, or did the teacher do wrong in teaching the child that it does not pay to be honest?" And much to his surprise, he says that he has found that most people agree with the father and not with the teacher.

So let me ask you: How many of you agree with the father?

And how many of you agree with the teacher?

Rabbi Wolowelsky says that he votes with the teacher, and, after thinking about it, I think that I do too. For if the teacher had rewarded the child for being honest and had given the child ten extra points on the test that she did not deserve, she would have sent her the message that honesty pays – and the truth is that it doesn't. Sometimes honesty pays, and sometimes, in case you don't know this yet, sometimes honesty does not pay.

Whoever thought up that slogan that we were brought up on – "crime does not pay" – was not telling the truth. The truth is that sometimes crime pays. You and I probably know some people who have become very rich by doing immoral and even illegal things. Not every crook gets caught. Some crooks live in fancy houses. Some kids cheat on exams and don't get caught, and some of these kids end up with higher grades than the ones who study and do their homework. And so the teacher would have been misleading this child if she taught her that honesty always pays. Sometimes it does and sometimes it doesn't.

And one thing more the teacher would have been doing if she had given this child ten extra points for being honest. She would have been lying. She would have been saying that this child earned an 85, when in fact she didn't, when all she earned was a 75. And she would have been cheating the rest of the members of the class of the rank that they deserved.

If this had been a test in honesty – if the teacher had purposely upgraded the students in order to see how they would react – then there is no question in my mind that this child would have deserved an A. But this was not a test in honesty. It was a test in math, and so the teacher would have been lying if she gave this student a higher grade than she deserved, just for being honest. It would have been no different than if the teacher gave those students whom she liked higher marks than she gave those students whom she did not like. Everyone would have been robbed of the recognition that a true grade represents. And so I agree with Rabbi Wolowelsky, and not with the parent. I think that the teacher did right in deducting the ten points that the child had received by mistake.

Do you agree?

Not if it is your child – but otherwise, I think you might agree.

I think that the teacher should have praised the student to the class for her honesty. I think that the teacher should have called the parents and complimented them on raising a child with such good character. But I think that the teacher should not have changed the grade, just because the child was honest. That, I think, would have been a mistake. It would have been a disservice to the child, to the class, and to the grading system.

But if this is so, then the question is: if there is no reward in being honest, and if there is sometimes a reward in cheating, then why not cheat?

That is a valid question, isn't it? If there is no reward in being honest, and if there is sometimes great reward in cheating, then why be honest? Why not cheat?

It was in light of this question that I noticed something that I don't think I had ever really noticed before.

Where does the commandment that we should not cheat appear in the Torah?

Who knows?

It appears twice in the Torah – in the *Aseret HaDvarim,* in the Ten Fundamental Statements. It is found in the *sedra* of Yitro, which describes the Moment at Sinai, and then again in the *sedra* of Va'etchanan, where Moses recalls that moment and remembers the ten basic statements on which all of human civilization depend, that are found there.

And what is the argument that the Torah uses in these two places for not cheating?

Who remembers?

What argument does the Torah use in the *Aseret HaDvarim* for not stealing and not cheating? Who knows?

The answer is: it offers no reason. It offers no argument. It offers no promise of reward for being honest and it offers no threat of punishment for being dishonest. All it says is two words, two clear and blunt words: *LO TIGNOV.* "Thou shalt not steal" – period – or rather, exclamation point. The Torah gives no reason to be honest. It promises no reward for being honest. It provides no threat to those who are dishonest. It simply says: lo tignov – thou shalt not steal.

Compare this commandment to the other commandments on the list. It says: "You shall worship the Lord because . . . ." It says: "You shall not worship false gods because . . . ." It says: you shall guard the Sabbath because . . . ." It says: "You shall honor your parents because . . . ." But here there is no because. Here – and in the other five commandments of which it is a part – here it simply says: "Thou shalt not . . . ." No reason is given. No "because" is stated. No promise of reward is made. No threat of punishment is offered. All it says is: "Thou shalt not steal" – period.

According to the Torah, being honest is what the philosophers call a categorical imperative. It is something that we should do because it is the right thing to do. Sometimes it will pay off. Sometimes it will not pay off. But either way, we should be honest!

And therefore, what I think the teacher should have done is explain to the class what she was doing and why. She should have told the children that it would not have been right to give this child extra points in math for being honest, that that would have been a disservice to her and to the rest of the class. She should have used this as a teaching moment, and helped the children to understand that honesty is the gold standard by which a student in a day school ought to live; that, more important than whether you get a B or a C, is whether you are honest or not, and that changing this grade would have been a lie that would have harmed the whole class. That is what it means to study math in a Jewish school, in a school in which all subjects are taught with values and with ethics.

Most of our schools today suffer from the terrible disease of competitiveness. Kids will do anything and everything in order to get a high grade because which college they get into will depend, in good measure, on what grades they get. And this is why cheating is so rampant even in many of our best schools. Even in schools that are attended by children from well-off families, even in schools that are attended by kids who would never think of shoplifting or of stealing merchandise from a store, kids will cheat on exams. That is how powerful the addiction to good grades has become. In many of our schools, grades conquer all. But in a Jewish school, in a school that stands for Torah values, there should be some things that are above good grades. And one of those things is honesty. And so the teacher was right, at least in my opinion, in not lying and in not giving this child a grade she did not deserve, for that would go against the teachings of the Torah.

If a child graduates one of our Jewish schools with a perfect 4.0 average, and if that child gets into an Ivy League school, but has not learned that honesty trumps grades, then that school has failed – at least by Jewish standards. Honesty is central, and therefore you do not reward honesty with a lie. If you do, you undermine everything that the school is really all about. And so I would have thanked and praised this child, but I would not have changed her grade. To say that she knew more math than she actually did, just because she was honest, would have been a lie – to her, to her classmates, and to the grading system.

Nechama Leibowitz, who was one of the great Jewish educators of our time, tells a story about honesty that I want to share with you today. Nechama Leibowitz says that when she started out teaching, she was assigned to a small high school in the Galil. And one day, a student reported a purse missing. The next day a student reported a necklace missing. And the third day a student reported her wallet and all the money in it was missing.

What should they do? Reluctantly, they called in the police. The policeman met with the students and this is what he said to them:

"I am an experienced policeman. I have been doing this work for many years. And so I can tell you from experience that not all criminals are caught. We have lots of open cases in our files, and I can tell you that many crooks get away with stealing. That is a fact.

"Let me tell you, whoever you are, that if you have succeeded in stealing three times and gotten away with it three times, you will probably continue, and let me tell you that you will probably not get caught.

"You will see that it is not so difficult to steal, and so you will probably continue. Eventually, you will be rich. You will have money and jewelry and watches and other nice things that other people do not have. And you will become wealthy, respected, and a person of prominence. But – you will be a thief all your life. You will never be able to cleanse yourself of that fact.

"Now I am going to make a suggestion. It is now 12:30. We are all going to go home, because it is *erev shabbat*. Between one and two o'clock at the latest, will whoever took these things put them back. Put them in some open place where they can be found. And if you do, you will be absolved. You will no longer be a thief."

The policeman took his briefcase, put on his coat, said "*Shabbat Shalom*," and left the room. The students were in shock. Nobody spoke. They had all expected to be searched, and to be cross-examined. Instead, this was all that the policeman did.

An hour later, Nechama got a call from the principal. The things that were taken had all been found.

The student had decided that, even though crime sometimes pays, it is still crime, and it has an effect on its perpetrator as well as on its victims.

So this is why I vote for the teacher in the story that I told you, and I hope that you do too. Crime does sometimes pay, and honesty does not always pay. That is true. But crime takes its toll on the soul of the one who does it, and honesty has its effect on the one who lives by it. And therefore, I believe that this teacher did right, and that she taught her students a lesson, not only in math, but in *mentshlickeit* as well.

May we and our children learn this lesson as well.

Keeping Down with the Joneses

I WANT TO PROPOSE a new phrase today that I believe should be added to the language.

Everyone knows the phrase: "keeping up with the Joneses." It means that if your neighbor buys his wife a mink coat, then you have to buy your wife a mink coat too. It means that if your neighbor buys a Mercedes or a Cadillac, then you have to buy one too. It means that if your neighbor joins an expensive country club, then you have to join too. Otherwise, you will be looked down upon as someone who has less than he does. It means that if his child gets three A's, then your child has to get at least four A's. It means that if your neighbor's child gets into an Ivy League college, then yours also has to, no matter what.

"Keeping up with the Joneses" can be an all-consuming task. It can drive you into spending more than you should, more than you have. It can make you obsessed with having everything and doing everything that he has and that he does, or else feeling that if you can't, you are somehow inferior to him. Trying to keep up with the Joneses can drive you into unending envy and even into financial bankruptcy.

And therefore, I want to propose a new phrase which I would like to see enter the language. It is a phrase that I learned from Dr. Asher Meir, who is the head of the Business Ethics Center of Jerusalem. The phrase is: "Keeping DOWN with the Joneses." What it means is giving up this endless rat-race of trying to keep up with your neighbors and spend as much as they do, and instead, adopting a simpler way of life, and challenging them to match you – not in ostentatiousness but in modesty.

I believe that "keeping down with the Joneses" is a much more Jewish way to live than "keeping up with the Joneses." And I want to prove that to you by studying with you three remarkable passages in the Mishna. One has to do with literacy. One has to do with dating. And one has to do with how to mourn in a proper way.

Let me begin with the Mishna that deals with literacy, because it is related to this week's Torah reading. This week's Torah reading begins with a clear commandment. It says: "When you come into the land and you settle down in it, you shall take some of the first fruits that you harvest, put them in a basket, and go to the place where the Lord your God will choose to establish His name. You shall go to the *Kohen* AND YOU SHALL SAY TO HIM: "I hereby acknowledge before the Lord my God that I have entered the land that the Lord swore to our ancestors to give to us. And the Kohen shall take the basket from your hand and set it down in front of the altar of the Lord your God."

According to this passage: WHO is supposed to make this declaration?

The person who brings the first fruits. It is clear, isn't it? The Torah says that when you come into the land, you shall take some of the first fruits of your harvest, put them in a basket, take them to the place that the Lord shall designate, and you shall say these words.

Could it be any clearer than that?

And yet, that is not the way they did it.

Look with me at the Mishna, Mishna *Bikkurim*, Chapter three, Mishna seven and see what it says:

"Originally, whoever could recite the prescribed words recited them, and those who could not recite them repeated them, a phrase at a time, after the *Kohen*. But when those who could not recite the words by themselves refrained from bringing their first-fruits out of embarrassment, it was ordained that everyone, both those who could read and those who could not, were to recite the words of the declaration, a phrase at a time, after the *Kohen*."

Understand what happens in this Mishna. Originally, every farmer recited the declaration by himself. But in the course of time, it became clear that not all farmers, then as now, could read. The Mishna could have ruled that those who could read the declaration should do so, and that those who could not read should repeat the words after the *Kohen*, but that would have embarrassed the illiterate. And so the Mishna ruled that everyone, whether they could read or not, should recite the words of the declaration after the *Kohen* – out of concern for the dignity of those who were illiterate.

By the way, that was the origin of the *Baal Koreh*, whom we now have in every synagogue. Originally, every person who was called to the Torah read his portion for himself. But then there were some who could not read the Torah, and so a reader was appointed to read for them. And then the Sages ordained that the Reader should read for everyone so as not to embarrass those who could not read.

I love this Mishna for the sensitivity that it shows to people who are unable to read. Instead of allowing the presentation of the *bikkurim* to become a contest, in which some people would show off how well they could read and others would be embarrassed at how poorly they could read, the Mishna provides that everyone shall be made to recite the words after the *Kohen*. It is a wonderful example of "Keeping Down With the Joneses."

The second example comes from the laws of mourning. When people lose a loved one, they are in great emotional turmoil. And they are vulnerable. And so the morticians sometimes take advantage of them. If they choose to purchase a plain, simple casket, the morticians may not say anything, but they give them a look, a look that says: "What's the matter? You didn't love your mother?" And who can withstand the pressure of that kind of a look?

And the same thing happens at *shiva* houses. The idea of *shiva* is for the community to come together to comfort the mourner. The *shiva* is not supposed to be a party, and the bereaved are not supposed to be hosts. And yet it often happens that the mourners, misunderstanding what *shiva* is really all about, think that it is their obligation to make a royal feast for those who come to visit. And when they do, that puts pressure on other people, when they have a loss, to do the same thing.

That same problem of peer pressure, of the need to keep up with the Joneses in the kind of casket you choose, and in the kind of meals you serve during *shiva*, existed in the time of the Mishna as well. And look at how the Sages, led by Rabban Gamliel, dealt with it.

The Mishna in *Moed Katan* says that originally, the expense of a funeral was harder on a family than death. It reached a point where some of the relatives would simply abandon the body and run away, in order to avoid having to pay the costs of a fancy funeral. Then came Rabban Gamliel who ordained that he should be buried in simple garments, and from then on, all people accustomed themselves to being buried in plain, simple garments, like him.

In order to appreciate this Mishna, you have to know that Rabban Gamliel was a very, very wealthy man. He owned property all over the country. If HE could be buried in plain, simple garments, then surely everyone else could too. Rabban Gamliel is the father of the simple funeral – and he deserves our eternal admiration for that good deed. His is a perfect example of "Keeping Down With the Joneses."

And then the Mishna tells us of a second change which the Sages brought about:

> At first, when people brought portions to the house of mourning, the rich would bring their gifts in trays of silver and gold, and the poor would bring their gifts in baskets of woven reeds. The poor were ashamed, and so the Sages decreed that everyone should bring their gifts in baskets of woven reeds, so as not to embarrass the poor.

And then the Mishna goes on to say:

At first, they would pour drinks in the house of mourning, the rich in fancy white glasses, and the poor in inexpensive, colored glass, and the poor were embarrassed. And so the Sages decreed that everyone should use inexpensive colored glass, out of respect for the poor.

I must tell you that these are statements that are not behind the times, not at all. The idea that funerals should be simple needs to be affirmed and reaffirmed in our time. I have seen people pressured to buy caskets of mahogany and bronze in order to keep up with their neighbors, and every time I see that happen, I wince. It is putting good money into the grave, for the dead do not need fancy coffins, and it is not the Jewish way. This is a free country, and so the synagogue cannot tell anyone how to spend their money, but I know of at least one congregation that has done something to take some of the pressure of keeping up with the Joneses out of funerals. What this synagogue has done is create a cover – a simple black cover – which is put over every single coffin that is buried in their cemetery. No one who comes to the funeral can tell what is under this cover. No one knows whether there is a mahogany or a bronze coffin, an air conditioned coffin or an elegantly decorated coffin or a plain simple coffin underneath the cover. And that takes some of the pressure off the mourners to buy a fancier coffin than they can afford in order to keep up with the Joneses.

And now, let me show you the third area of our lives in which people then and people now are driven to keep up with the Joneses and in which the Sages of the Mishna took a stand.

Is there any area of our lives in which we are tempted to show off, and to try to be more impressive, than in our dating? I know young men who own a Chevrolet, but borrow a Mercedes when they go out on a first date. And I know some young women who spend fortunes on a dress and jewelry so that they can impress a guy on a first date. And I think that that is a mistake – for two reasons. One is: what do you do for an encore? If you spend a fortune on clothing or on a car for the first date, what will you do on the second? And second, I don't think it is wise to deceive someone, to pretend to be wealthier than you are, when you are dating, because deception, it seems to me, is a terrible way to begin a relationship.

The Sages of the Mishna dealt with this challenge in a remarkable way.

The Mishna in *Masechet Taanit* describes the holiday of Tu B'av. Tu B'av was a kind of Sadie Hawkins Day in antiquity. It was the day when all the single women in Jerusalem would invite the single men to come join them in the vineyards to sing and dance.

Rabban Shimon ben Gamliel says: "There was no happier day in Israel than the 15th of Av, for on this day, the maidens of Jerusalem used to go out, all of them dressed in white garments, to dance in the vineyards.

And what would they say to the boys who came out to dance with them on this day?

They would say: "Young men, lift up your eyes and see who you would like to choose as a mate. And do not set your eyes only on physical beauty, for is it not written in the book of Proverbs "Charm is deceitful and beauty is brief."

And how did they make sure that the young men would judge them, not only by external beauty but by more important things?

They made sure that this would happen by doing something very bold and very simple. They all borrowed dresses. No one came in her own dress. Every single woman came in a dress that she borrowed from someone else. So that no one could tell by looking at them who was rich and who was not.

Wasn't that a remarkable thing that they did?

Can you imagine what it would be like if we had a custom something like that in our culture?

Can you imagine what it would be like if every single girl who came to the prom had to come in a borrowed dress? Can you imagine what it would be like if every single guy could ignore such things as: what is she wearing? And every single girl could ignore such things as: what is he driving? And if they could both focus instead on what kind of a person is this? Is this the kind of person who I might want to have a serious relationship with?

I think that we have much to learn from these three mishnayot: the one that says that when the farmer brought his *bikkurim*, he had to repeat the declaration that is found in today's Torah reading word by word after the *Kohen*, whether he could read or not, so as not to embarrass the illiterate; and the one that says that there should be no competition and no showing off allowed when it comes to burying the dead; and the one that says that when you go out on a date, you should be able to focus on the character of the person you are with, and not get caught up in a frantic and futile race to keep up with the Joneses.

These rules that we have studied today are more than two thousand years old, and yet I believe that they have much to teach us about how we should live today.

Let me finish with a personal story, the story of something that happened to me many years ago, that has stayed in my mind ever since. My first pulpit was in Swampscott, Massachusetts, which is on the North Shore of Boston. Swampscott, as some of you may know, was and is a very affluent community. And so many of the Jews who lived there, many of the Jews who were in my congregation, lived very well. Many of them had the best cars, and the best houses, and many other impressive luxuries.

The one exception was my next door neighbor. My next door neighbor was the president of the bank. His father and his grandfather and his great grandfather had all been presidents of the bank before him. And he drove a Ford!

I once asked him: "How come you drive a Ford?"

And I still remember his answer. He said to me: "Because I have had money long enough that I can afford to drive a Ford."

What I think my next door neighbor meant by that, was that he had had money long enough that he had no need to flaunt it, no need to prove it, no need to impress anyone with it, no need to keep up with the Joneses. My next door neighbor in Swampscott was not Jewish, but I believe that he was expressing truly Jewish values by what he said to me.

And so I quote him to you today. And I hope that all of us will learn from him: to live simply, to live wisely, and not to waste our energy and spend our strength keeping up with others. I hope that we will learn from him not to judge ourselves by whether we have more than our neighbors. I hope that we will learn from him today to "keep down" with our neighbors, instead of trying to "keep up" with them.

And who knows? It just might be – it could happen – that if our neighbors see us living modestly, that they will become envious of us, and they will try to live simply and modestly as we do.

And, if I may quote from the words of "My Fair Lady," if they did that – wouldn't that be "loverly"?

A Sermon About *"Autenticity"*

I WANT TO TELL YOU a wonderful story today, a story that I heard from Velvel Pasternak, the great scholar of Jewish music. There is only one catch. Velvel is a much better storyteller than I am, and he is much better at imitating dialects than I am. But let me try, and I hope that I can do justice to this story, because I believe that this story has much to teach us all.

Back in the 1960s, Velvel Pasternak, together with his colleague, Benedict Stampler of the Collectors Guild Recording Company, was invited to meet with the Bobover Rebbe at his home in Brooklyn.

The Rebbe called them in to ask them to record some of the music of the Bobover Chassidim. At first, Velvel was kind of surprised by this request, because it is the tradition of some Chassidic groups not to record and not to write out their *nigunim*, in order to make sure that they are not misused.

Velvel asked the Rebbe why he wanted to record this music, and the Rebbe told him. He said: My youngest son came home from *cheder* this week, and sang for me the melody that he had learned in school. The Rebbe asked his son if he knew where the melody came from, and the boy said he had no idea. So the Rebbe told his child that this melody that he had learned in school had been written by his grandfather. That was when the Rebbe decided that it was time to transcribe and record these melodies, because, if even his own son did not know where they came from, how could he expect his Chassidim and their children to know?

And so the Rebbe asked Velvel if he would be willing to undertake the project of recording these songs so that they would not be lost.

The two of them accepted the request. And then the Rebbe told him that the details of producing and marketing the records would be left to him. But, for the sake of Bobov, and for the sake of musical accuracy, they had to agree to work closely with his relative, Rabbi Laizer Halberstam, who was an expert on the music of Bobov. The Rebbe said that Reb Laizer would not only be the musical advisor, but he would be the soloist on the recording.

Several days later, they met with Reb Laizer and, during the course of several hours, they decided which of the songs would be recorded. No Bobover *nigunim* existed in print at that time, and so Velvel was appointed to transcribe them. Reb Laizer sang them into a tape recorder, and Velvel wrote them down from there. But before he began, Reb Laizer set down one condition. He told Velvel that these *nigunim* had to be sung in "*de autentic vay.*"

At first, Velvel did not know what Reb Laizer meant when he said that these songs had to be sung in "*de autentic vay.*" But he soon caught on. What Reb Laizer meant was that these songs could not be sung in *Sephardit*, which is the way Hebrew is pronounced in Israel, and they could not be sung in *Litvish*, which is the way Hebrew is pronounced by Lithuanian Jews. They had to be pronounced the way they were pronounced by the Bobover Chassidim, who came from Poland.

A few weeks later, Rabbi Halberstam came to Velvel's house, with a tape recording of fourteen songs, and Velvel began transcribing them. Once they were written down, he had to solve the problem of how to write the Hebrew lyrics beneath the melody line.

Why was that a problem?

Because Hebrew is read from right to left and music notes on staff lines are sung or played from left to right. So, if you write Hebrew letters under the notes, not only does the Hebrew appear to be backwards, but the syllables within the words move backwards. Somehow Velvel was able to figure that problem out. He simply put the treble clef on the right side of the staff, and wrote the notes from right to left.

That was the easy part. The hard part came next. How do you transliterate the Hebrew words according to the Bobover dialect?

If you were transliterating the first line of the Kiddush according to the Sephardic pronunciation, you would write: *Baruch atta*. If you were translating the first line of the Kiddush according to the Lithuanian pronunciation, you would write: *Boruch atto*. But if you were to transliterate the first line of the Kiddush according to the Bobover dialect, you would have to write: *Booriych a-too*.

Velvel looked at the first line he had transliterated, and said to himself; "Impossible!" So he went to the telephone and called up Reb Laizer. When Reb Laizer answered, he said to him:

"Rebbe, I know that you want to be authentic, but you can't possibly expect us to sing these songs with this pronunciation. It will destroy the sales potential of the record."

"*Und* how do you know *dat*?" Reb Laizer asked.

"Because most of the sales will be to non-Chassidim, who will buy them because they are interested in music as part of Jewish culture, and they won't understand this kind of Hebrew," Velvel said.

"*Und vat* makes you *tink dat* real *Chassidim vill* not buy *dis* record?" said Reb Laizer.

To which Velvel answered: "Look, Rebbe. I have been to lots of Hassidic homes, and many of them don't even have phonographs."

To which Reb Laizer said: "You are wrong, absolutely wrong! Besides, this is Bobov, and it must be *autentic*. Don't vorry. Just do it!"

Velvel hung up the phone and returned to the transliterations. When he looked at them, he was ready to throw up his hands in frustration. He called Reb Laizer again, and again he got the same answer from him: "This is Bobov, and it has to be *autentic*. Don't *vorry*. Just do it!"

The transliterations were finally finished, and it was now time to form a choir and hire musicians for the recording. Having had some rather difficult experiences in the past with Chassidic singers, Velvel decided to hire professionals. He decides to use sixteen cantors as a chorus. He figured that these cantors, who had strong Jewish backgrounds and who knew music, would be able to sing these Chassidic melodies, even with their unusual sounding lyrics. It was understood that these cantors would be paid minimum wages. The cantors all agreed that their primary reward would be the fellowship and joy that comes from singing together, and the privilege of helping to preserve a part of the Jewish musical heritage that was in danger of being lost.

They planned on two rehearsals before the recording, one with just the singers, and one with the instrumental ensemble. The first rehearsal was held in a rented studio on 57th Street in Manhattan. Reb Laizer arrived, and soon afterwards the sixteen members of the choir arrived. They were all introduced to him and to each other.

Velvel distributed the sheet music, and by chance the song "Simon Tov" happened to be the one on top. The song was well known to the singers because it is sung at bar mitzvahs and at weddings and at other *simchas* all around the Jewish community.

But when the singers saw the words that they thought they knew in the Bobover dialect, they nearly flipped. The words now were: "*Siman toiv ee mazel toiv yihai loonee ee lichol yisruael, oo-mayn.*"

Velvel was braced for some reaction, but he was taken aback by the first question:

"Hey, Velvel, what language is this?"

After a brief silence, Velvel replied: "Guys. This recording is going to be made according to the pronunciation of the Bobover Chassidim. I have been through this with Reb Laizer, and it is his strong conviction that this material must be preserved in the most authentic manner, and that means with this pronunciation."

The members of the chorale nodded their heads in understanding. Velvel gave the downbeat and they were on the way. The opening words "*siman toiv*" offered no problems. The next words: "*ee mazel toiv*" were okay too. But as soon as they got to the words: "*yihai looney,*" several members began to giggle.

"What's the problem?" Velvel asked, as if he didn't know.

"'*Yihai looney*' sounds crazy," said one of the members of the group.

"C'mon now, fellows," Velvel said. "Let's try it again."

Once again the group started and once again they got as far as the third phrase. "*Yihai looney*" brought the singing to a stop. They tried it over and over again, but the laughter got the best of them each time. Velvel put down his baton, and walked over to Reb Laizer.

"You see I was right," he said. "If these professional cantors can't get through this song without giggling, what will the rest of the Jewish world do?"

"Don't *vorry*," Reb Laizer said.

Velvel returned to the conductor's stand and said: "Gentlemen, let's try it again." But as will happen, when laughter begins, it often feeds on itself. "*Yihai looney*" stopped them every time.

"Velvel," said one of the singers, "Let us take care of it."

The sixteen cantors put down their music and walked over to Reb Laizer. He was a large, imposing man, meticulously dressed in a capote and an oversized black hat. As the cantors approached, he folded his arms across his chest. Everyone seemed to be talking at once.

"Rabbi, it sounds funny to say '*yihai looney*.' We know the words to this song, and we can sing them with normal pronunciation, but the way we have to sing this song is impossible."

Reb Laizer, with a marvelous twinkle in his eye, waited until the talking died down, and then said gently to the cantors: "Has everybody said *vat* they want to say? Has everybody finished *vit de* suggestions?"

The sixteen cantors all nodded.

"Now I *vant* to tell you and your *fency* conductor *mit da* baton a story. You see, when a *choosid* sees *dat* he can't convince people in the normal way, he tells *dem* a story. *Derefore*, I *vill* tell you a story."

The cantors moved a little closer to listen to Reb Laizer and his story. Velvel says that after all these years, he still cannot believe that the story that Reb Laizer told there that night in the recording studio was created there. He must have had it tucked away in some story bag in his head to be brought out when he needed it to explain the idea of authenticity. "To my mind," says Velvel, "I have never heard a better story with which to explain the importance of being true to yourself."

Reb Laizer began:

"A group of *tensers* from the Ivory Coast of Africa and their cultural minister approached the cultural minister of Israel and said:

"*Ve vood* like to have intercultural relations between our two countries. Dere*fore, ve vill send* you our *tensers* to perform in Israel, and you in turn will send your *tensers* to perform in the Ivory Coast."

"*Dat vood* be *vunderful,*" said the cultural minister of Israel. "It *vill* surely help our intercultural relations."

By the way, does everyone here know what '*tensers*' are?

'*Tensers*' are dancers in the Bobover pronunciation.

Back to the story.

"But before we come to Israel," said the Ivory Coast minister, "we must make you aware of one small problem."

"Problem?" said the Israeli minister. "*Vat* problem?"

"You see, in the Ivory Coast our *tensers* perform only bare-chested."

"Only bare-chested?" said the Israeli minister, "*Vat doz dat* mean?"

The Ivory Coast minister raised his hands to his neck and then brought them down slowly to his waist. "From up here to down here – nothing."

"You mean open, exposed, *nakid*?" said the Israeli minister of Cultural Affairs. "You know *vat vill* happen to me if you bring bare-chested *tensers* to Israel? The Chief Rabbi of Jerusalem *vill* put me over a cliff, and everyone *vill* trow stones at me. *Den*, the Chief Rabbi of Tel Aviv *vill* hang me from a light pole, and everyone who passes by *vill* kick me. *Vy* can't you bring me normal *tensers* so *dat ve* can keep our intercultural relations?"

Suddenly, the minister from Israel smiled. "Sha, sha," he said. "No problem. You bring your *tensers* to Israel. *Ven* you land at Lod Airport, *ve vill* have a *velcoming* committee who *vill* present your *tensers* with some *shmattes*. You *vill* put *dese shmattes* on, and cover up. (As he said this, Reb Laizer pointed to his chest and made a broad expansive circle with his hands.)

"Cover up? Cover up?" said the minister from the Ivory Coast in disbelief. "If *ve* cover up, *ve vill* no longer be the *tensers* from the Ivory Coast. Maybe *tensers* from some other part of Africa. But the *tensers* from the Ivory Coast can only *tense* open, exposed, naked and bare-chested."

Reb Laizer smiled at the conclusion of his story and then he drove his point home.

"*De* same is *mit* you and *mit* your *fency* conductor *mit de* baton," he said. "You are all embarrassed *ven* you sing '*yihai looney.*' It sounds too open, too exposed, too *nakid*, too *berchested. Derefore*, you *vud* like to take a little Lithuanian *shmatte* to cover it up so that the words should become '*yihey lonu.*' *Derefore*, I *vill* tell you simply *dat* if you cover up *de* pronunciation, *Siman toiv vill* no longer be a song of the Bobover Chassidim. Our music must be *autentic*! It must be open, exposed, *nakid*, and *berchested, vitout* any shame. And so now I ask you and your *fency* conductor to go back to your seats and sing '*yihai looney*' and all the other *berchested* words, and *dats dat*!"

The sixteen cantors and their fancy conductor walked back to their seats. And one of the cantors said:

"Velvel, if that man, with that beard, that *kappotah*, and that black hat could tell us that story in order to convince us of the value of authenticity, then we are going to sing it for him the way he wants us to."

And that is what they did. And guess what? The recording was a hit, and it sold in all circles of music lovers, and not just among Bobover Chassidim. Because people respect authenticity. This recording, with its dialect, rang true and felt authentic, and therefore everyone loved it.

And Velvel says that for years afterwards, he would meet some of these cantors at conventions of the Cantors Assembly. And whenever they met, they would great each other with the words: '*Siman toiv ee mazel toiv yihai looney ee lichol yisruael, oo-mayn.*' Those words served them as a memento of an incredible evening in which they helped to preserve a special part of the Chassidic heritage.

Why do I tell you this story today? Because I think that it has more to teach us than just that we should preserve the correct pronunciation of Hebrew words. I think that the point of the story is that we should value and respect authenticity, wherever and whenever we find it. For those who respect themselves, are respected by others and those who are uneasy with themselves, are looked upon with unease by others!

I think that that is the point of one of the great lines that appears in today's Torah reading. The Torah says: *vira'u kol amei ha'aretz ki shem Hashem nikra alecha, v'yiru mimecha* – "When all the nations of the world shall see that the name of the Lord is proclaimed over you, they shall revere you." I think that what that verse means is that if you walk about with a sense of who you are, with an awareness of who God and History have made you, then the nations of the world will respect you. But if you walk around in fear and trembling, if you deny who you are and where you come from, and what you stand for – then the nations of the world will suspect you, and will not treat you with respect.

Many years ago, the late, great Jewish writer, Ludwig Lewisohn, expressed this truth in this colorful way. He said: "The Jew who boards the subway, carrying his Yiddish newspaper and wearing his black hat and his long, black suit is a better American than the Jew who changes his name, and has a Christmas tree that is bigger than that of his neighbors, and who lives his life, not as a proud and self-respecting Jew, but as an 'imitating Christian.'" "Because the former person believes and demonstrates that America is a free country, one in which each group can be what it wants to be, and the latter lives in fear and thinks that he has to copy the ways of others in order to be accepted."

And so, this is a sermon in favor of *autenticity*. Let the story of the *tensers* who came from the Ivory Coast to *tense* in Israel and the story of Reb Laizer, who insisted that a Bobover song has to be sung the way that the Bobovers sing it – let these two stories speak to our hearts, and let them teach us to be ourselves and not to try to be imitations of what others believe or do, and not to be imitations of whatever is in fashion in the world around us. Instead, let us be ourselves, for if we are, then the name of the Lord will be called upon us, and the nations of the earth will revere us.

So may it be. And to this, in honor of the Bobover, let us all say: *Oomayn.*

The Lessons You Have Taught Me

BEFORE I BEGIN, let me just say that I hope that you believe everything that was said about me today and that I hope that I don't, because if I do, I will be really unfit to live with.

I am sure that you have heard this before, but do you know the difference between a eulogy and a testimonial? At a eulogy, there is nobody who believes everything that is being said. At a testimonial there is one person who does.

Let me just say three brief thank yous:

First, thank you to my classmate, Rabbi Herring, for your kind words and your generous praise.

Second, thank you to the officers and the board of this congregation for this lovely gift, which I will treasure.

And third, thank you to all of you for this wonderful year that we have spent together which I will treasure even more.

There is a passage in the Talmud that all the rabbis who are here today know very well, but which I must say that I never really understood until this year.

The Talmud quotes Rabbi Yehuda Hanasi who said: *Harbei lamad'ti mirabotai, u'mey'chaveyrai – yoter, u'meytalmidai yoter mikulan.* "I have learned much from my teachers, more from my companions, and most from my students."

When I learned that passage, I said to myself: what sense does that make? We who went to the Seminary had the greatest scholars in the world as our teachers. We had Saul Lieberman, who was the world's greatest expert on Greeks in Jewish Palestine as our Talmud teacher. We had H.L. Ginsberg, who was the world's greatest expert on Ugaritic as our Bible teacher. We had Heschel and Kaplan who were the masters of Modern Jewish thought. We had Max Arzt, who was one of the committee that translated the Bible from Hebrew into English. And the people in our synagogues were going to teach us??? I must tell you that when I graduated, that idea seemed really far-fetched to me.

But now I know better. My teachers may have been masters at how to translate the Torah from Hebrew into English, but the people in this congregation have taught me a number of lessons in how to translate the Torah into life. And that is why I have loved every minute of my stay here. And that is why I will take away from here many important lessons in how to live that I have learned from you.

Let me tell you just four of the lessons that you have taught me.

The first lesson you have taught me is that with will power and with determination, a human being can transcend his or her body.

I learned that lesson from the number of people in this room who come to shul every single Shabbos even though they can no longer walk very well. I watch them come in here . . . some of them arrive every week at the very beginning of the service . . . they come in slowly, one step at a time, and then I watch them park their walkers here in the front of the shul, and find their way to their seats. And I watch the caretakers who bring them in and then sit outside and wait for the service to end.

I must tell you that to me, this "parking lot" of walkers down here is a holy place, because it represents the courage and the determination with which these people come to shul every week. I have a rule which I try to keep . . . which is never to pass a person who is coming in with the help of a walker. It is just not right to do. To brush by somebody who can't walk as fast as you can is committing the sin that the Sages call *Lo'eg Larash*, which means: embarrassing someone who can't do what you can do. It is not right to embarrass a person by passing him by. I confess that I sometimes violate this rule, because there is one person here who walks so slowly that I am afraid that if I walk behind him, by the time I get inside, the services will be nearly over, but as a rule I try to walk with or walk behind anyone who comes in here with a walker, and not just pass him by.

But let me say that one of the lessons that these people have taught me, and one of the reasons why I have so much respect for this congregation, is that those who climb up onto the *bimah* every week for an *Aliyah* or in order to show people how and when to open the ark, and those who come in here every single week with the help of caretakers, or with the help of walkers, or with the help of canes – THESE PEOPLE ARE MY HEROES – they really are, for they have taught me that the spirit can be stronger than the body. God bless each one of you for teaching me this lesson.

The second lesson that you have taught me is kindness and compassion. I remember how many of you went to Rabbi Gerald Weiss's funeral, and I remember how many of you came here for the *shloshim* service that we held in his memory. More people from this *shul* came to his funeral than came from the synagogue that he served for ten years! And when I asked one of you whom I saw there at the funeral: Why did you come today? He said to me: Because I was not sure that anyone else would be here, and so I came just in case nobody else did.

That is the kind of kindness and compassion that you have taught me many times during this last year . . . and for this I am grateful.

And let me mention one more act of kindness for which I am grateful. On occasion – I won't say how many times, but on occasion – on very rare occasions – I have spoken a little bit too long. And when I did, there was tremendous pressure on Cantor Sapir to finish on time, for he batted last. And yet – he has not murdered me. At least not yet. If he did, no jury would convict him, and so, for this act of kindness I am very grateful to Cantor Sapir.

The third thing that you have taught me is that to be Jewish means to care, not only for yourself, and not only for your family, and not only for your local community. To be Jewish means to care about the welfare of the whole Jewish people, wherever they may be. You taught me that a few months ago, when things were bad in Israel, when people were being run over by terrorists who had cars or trucks, and when people were being knifed at bus stops, and two people in this congregation – Dr. Jerome and Barbara Cohen responded to those acts of violence by sending an ambulance to Israel. Do you remember that day when we went outside and dedicated that ambulance? I do. It was one of the best days that we have ever had in this *shul*, and I came away from that experience feeling so proud to be a small part of this great congregation.

And there is another lesson that you have taught me.

And that is that to be Jewish means to revere books and to understand that education, like youth, is too good a thing to be wasted on young people. You taught me that studying books is at the heart of our existence. You taught me that lesson twice this year.

The first time was when the army of ISIS conquered the city of Aleppo in Syria. Do you remember that day? Aleppo is one of the oldest cities in the world, and it is a city that contained priceless records that go back for centuries. It is a city that contained priceless manuscripts. And do you remember what they did? The first thing that the terrorists did when they took over that city was to break into that library and burn the books and destroy the manuscripts that were there.

And do you remember what we did that day?

I came to *shul* that day feeling disgusted and sick at heart because of what I had heard on the news. I remembered what the poet, Heine, said a century and more ago: People who start out burning books will end up burning people. I arrived here in a very sad mood.

And do you know what I found when I got here? There were a hundred people or more, standing outside in the parking lot, preparing to dance a new *Sefer* Torah into the ark. And when I saw that, I realized that this was our answer to ISIS. If they burn books – we will dedicate books. If they desecrate books, we will honor books. If they profane books – we will sanctify books. And so I came away from synagogue that day with joy in my heart. And I thank you for what you did that day.

And there was one more day when you made me very proud. That was the day when Rabbi Harold Kushner came to town, and Mr. and Mrs. Jack Bushinsky honored us by donating the new Etz Chaim edition of the Torah. Harold said to me that day: I have never seen such a crowd in *shul* as you have here – are they really all members? Or did you hire actors just to impress me?

That was the day when you taught me what respect for Jewish learning means, and I am very grateful to you for that.

And there is one more thing that I must say about the role of education in this place. I have been in *shuls* that are richer than this one is. I have been in *shuls* whose buildings are bigger and fancier than this one is. But I have never before been in a synagogue that has a class or a program or an activity going on EVERY SINGLE DAY OF THE WEEK. That does not happen anywhere else that I know of, and so, for teaching me that this is possible, which I would never have believed until I came here and saw it with my own eyes – for this, I thank you and I thank Larry Feinberg who has made it happen.

And so, for teaching me these four lessons:

Number One: that the strength of the spirit can triumph over the weakness of the body;

Number Two: that kindness and compassion are the way for Jews to live;

Number Three: that to be Jewish means to care about all Jews, wherever they may be;

And Four: that at a time when people overseas are burning books, it is our task to dedicate books and to study them;

For teaching me these four lessons, and many more, I will always be grateful to you, and I thank you very much.

I wish you well. I envy your new rabbi for the joy that will be his, and I wish him well.

And may God bless you and him with much happiness for many, many years to come.